TONGA

CHRISTIANITY

OTHER WILLIAM CAREY LIBRARY BOOKS*

Bradshaw, Malcolm R., CHURCH GROWTH THROUGH EVANGELISM-IN-DEPTH
Cox, Emmett D., THE CHURCH OF THE UNITED BRETHREN IN CHRIST IN SIERRA LEONE
Emery, Kinsler, Walker, Winter, EL SEMINARIO DE EXTENSION: UN MANUAL
Enyart, Paul C., FRIENDS IN CENTRAL AMERICA
Gaxiola, Manuel, LA SERPIENTE Y LA PALOMA
Hedlund, Roger, THE PROTESTANT MOVEMENT IN ITALY: ITS PROGRESS, PROBLEMS, AND PROSPECTS
Holland, Clifton L., THE RELIGIOUS DIMENSION IN SPANISH LOS ANGELES: A PROTESTANT CASE STUDY
McFall, Ernest A., APPROACHING THE NUER OF AFRICA THROUGH THE OLD TESTAMENT
McGavran, Donald A., editor, THE CHURCH GROWTH BULLETIN, VOL. I-V.
Mäläskä, Hilkka, THE CHALLENGE FOR EVANGELICAL MISSIONS TO EUROPE: A SCANDINAVIAN CASE STUDY
Mayers, Marvin K., NOTES ON CHRISTIAN OUTREACH IN A PHILIPPINE COMMUNITY
Mitchell, James Erskine, THE EMERGENCE OF A MEXICAN CHURCH: THE ASSOCIATE REFORMED PRESBYTERIAN CHURCH OF MEXICO
Randall, Max Ward, PROFILE FOR VICTORY: NEW PROPOSALS FOR MISSIONS IN ZAMBIA
Smith, Ebbie C., GOD'S MIRACLES: INDONESIAN CHURCH GROWTH
Subbamma, B. V., NEW PATTERNS FOR DISCIPLING HINDUS: THE NEXT STEP IN ANDHRA PRADESH, INDIA
Swanson, Allen J. TAIWAN: MAINLINE VERSUS INDEPENDENT CHURCH GROWTH, A STUDY IN CONTRASTS
Tippett, A. R., PEOPLES OF SOUTHWEST ETHIOPIA
Wagner, C. Peter, THE PROTESTANT MOVEMENT IN BOLIVIA
Winter, Ralph D., editor, THEOLOGICAL EDUCATION BY EXTENSION
Winter, Ralph D., THE TWENTY-FIVE UNBELIEVABLE YEARS, 1945-1969

*Greater detail and prices are listed in the back of this book.

TONGA
CHRISTIANITY

stan shewmaker

William Carey Library
South Pasadena, California

©Copyright 1970 by the William Carey Library

All rights reserved.
No part of this book may be used or reproduced in any manner whatsoever without written permission, except in the case of brief quotations embodied in critical articles and reviews.

International Standard Book Number: 0-87808-409-6
Library of Congress Catalog Number: 70-165519

Published by the William Carey Library
533 Hermosa Street
South Pasadena, Calif. 91030
Telephone 213-682-2047

PRINTED IN THE UNITED STATES OF AMERICA

Contents

FIGURES
MAPS
TABLES
FOREWORD
ACKNOWLEDGMENTS

Introduction *1*

PART ONE: THE LAND AND PEOPLE

   I. The Tonga Tribe and its Environment *7*
  II. The Tonga Tribe Social Structure *13*
 III. Tonga Religious Beliefs and Practices *22*
  IV. Acculturation: The Process of Culture Change *38*

PART TWO: THE HISTORY OF TONGA MISSIONS

   V. The Coming of the Churches of Christ *49*
  VI. Other Churches and Missions *61*

PART THREE: A DEPTH STUDY OF TONGA VILLAGES

 VII. Growth of Tonga Churches of Christ *77*
VIII. The Power Structure and the Church *92*
  IX. Obstructions to Church Growth *99*

PART FOUR: A NEW DIRECTION FOR THE CHURCH

- X. Changing Attitudes *119*
- XI. New Emphases for the Church: Theological *134*
- XII. New Emphases for the Church: Multiplying Congregations *150*
- XIII. New Emphases for the Church: Practical *156*
- XIV. Conclusion *165*

APPENDICES *169*
BIBLIOGRAPHY *183*

Figures

1 Composition of 26 Rural Churches of Christ *80*

2 Composition of 2 Mission-Station Churches of Christ *80*

3 Composition of 3 Urban Churches of Christ *80*

4 Composition of 31 Tonga Churches of Christ *81*

5 Agents of Conversion *86*

6 Means Used to Win Informants *86*

7 Mantanyani Village *97*

Maps

1 Zambia *6*

2 The Tonga Tribe and Its Environment *9*

3 Church of Christ Mission Stations *51*

4 Tonga Missions--Their Areas of Influence *66*

5 Local Churches--Churches of Christ *76*

6 Patterns of Rural-to-Urban Migration *154*

Maps

Tables

1 Local Congregations of the Brethren in Christ Mission, 1968 *65*

2 Five-Year Growth Figures of the Seventh-Day Adventist Church *71*

3 Local Congregations of the United Church of Zambia, Choma D.C.C., 1968 *72*

4 Meeting Places *83*

5 Tent Meetings, 1966 - 1967 *88*

6 Tonga Hymnals *157*

Foreword

What has sixty years of missions accomplished in a typical African land as far as establishment of the Church is concerned? This is a crucial question to any serious student of mission. All planning for the future depends on its answer. Christian mission must make sure that the feedback from its labors is correct and ample; otherwise, mistakes will be needlessly repeated, wrong directions will be contentedly followed, and brilliant opportunities to liberate millions lost.

This book is pertinent feedback, and an excellent answer to the crucial question. It portrays what the empirical Church *is* in one section of Zambia. It confines itself to the Tonga tribe, which it deals with in depth regarding social structure, religion, history of Christian labors, resulting Church, current problems, and future possibilities. The reader can here see exactly what the sixty years have produced by way of Church.

Is the Tonga a typical tribe in Zambia, and is Zambia a typical land in Africa? The answer is yes, with however, cordial acknowledgment that every tribe is different, every mission is different, and every African nation is different from every other. The story Mr. Shewmaker unfolds and the picture he paints of his constellation of congregations in the Tonga tribe is much more like other constellations in other lands than it is like--let us say--the Anglican Church in London, or the Methodist Church in California, or, for that matter, his own religious movement (Churches of Christ) comprised of about 2,500,000 baptized believers in the United States.

The Churches he depicts in the Tonga tribe are not like the great people movement Churches among the Yorubas, Ashantis, and Fantis; but they have marked similarity to numerous constellations of congregations which have arisen in most African nations through the school approach.

Anyone who would understand the expansion of Christianity in Africa should read Shewmaker. Qualify the Tongan picture as we must, it is a significant part of the African scene. It is time that discussions about Christian mission came down out of the clouds of what ought to be and rested credibly on the solid rock of what is. This book is not all the rock there is--Africa is far too complex, and Christian mission far too varied to be able to imagine that--but there is much rock of this sort. Here is a book worth reading.

DONALD McGAVRAN

Acknowledgments

I owe a tremendous debt of gratitude to Dr. Elizabeth Colson, an outstanding anthropologist and authority on Tonga social structure. Three of her well-written books, *Marriage and the Family Among the Plateau Tonga of Northern Rhodesia*, *The Social Organization of the Gwembe Tonga*, and *The Plateau Tonga of Northern Rhodesia: Social and Religious Studies*, have provided me with numerous insights into Tonga life which had never before occurred to me, even after having lived among the Tonga for almost twenty years.

I shall always be indebted to Dr. Donald A. McGavran, Dean of the School of World Mission and Institute of Church Growth at Fuller Theological Seminary, and to Dr. Alan R. Tippett, my advising professor, without whose patience and long-suffering I would have been unable to undertake and complete this study. Dr. Ralph D. Winter has taught me objectivity and Dr. J. Edwin Orr has inspired me to expect great things from God. I am grateful, too, for the financial aid received from the School of World Mission and from many interested churches and individuals who have generously contributed moral support and prayer, as well as money.

Such a survey would also have been impossible without my understanding wife, Jo Ann, whom God used through the long weeks and months to minister love and encouragement. I am grateful to Jeanne Bateman, a member of the San Fernando Church of Christ, for typing the manuscript. Her dedication to this task in the midst of a busy schedule will always be remembered with deep appreciation.

Dr. Prentice A. Meador, Assistant Professor of Speech at the University of California at Los Angeles, a close friend and colleague in the blessed "ministry of reconciliation," offered the constructive criticism which has made the book readable.

Introduction

Today's missionaries in sub-Saharan Africa are witnessing a growing receptivity to the Good News of Jesus Christ. Indications are that this willingness of the people to change will increase considerably over the next thirty years. Experts estimate that eighty million Africans will be remaking their life patterns before A.D. 2000. They will be listening to, and following, the advocates of either communism, Islam, materialism, Christianity, or syncretistic sects.

In view of such widespread responsiveness, it is imperative that missionaries realize more fully than ever before God's concern for the salvation of every lost soul. We must learn the essentials of the Gospel of Jesus Christ, and then preach the Good News expectantly. We must be concerned with numbers; God is. No longer should we remain content with proclamation which does not result in men and women being added to Christ's Church. Resources are far too meager for us to afford the luxury of just doing good "mission work," or of merely hurrying off to the field to "do something." The supreme task of Christ's messengers in the world today must not be lost in subsidiary activities. Our main objective must be *the multiplication of churches within the receptive pockets of mankind*.

The real division of Africa today lies along tribal rather than national lines. A few decades of superimposed colonialism have, in the main, failed to alter tight-knit tribal social structures, except where large-scale migration and detribalization have taken place.

Bearing in mind the vastness of Africa with its diversity of tribes, sub-tribes and languages, I was obliged to narrow the scope of the study somewhat.

Only the impact of Churches and Missions among the Tonga tribe were measured in detail. This may at first appear to be a rather limited treatment of the subject but an accurate picture of this one case of evangelism speaks volumes to those missionaries and national churchmen laboring in other Zambian tribes. I am confident that my detailed analysis of Missions (in particular the Churches of Christ missions which I know best) in this one tribe will make a significant contribution to missionary knowledge and methodology throughout Central Africa.

Basically, there were two reasons why an effort was made to ferret out the causes of non-growth and to bring to light the factors which *have* contributed to church planting. Firstly, the response of a tribe to the Gospel depicted in this study is not confined just to the Tonga tribe, but it is typical of the response which can be expected from most Central African tribes when approached in the same manner. The similarities within the tribal leadership, power structures, collectivism and traditional religious views combine to give this Tonga study a much wider application than merely one tribe in one African nation. Secondly, the "school approach" to evangelism, which is currently employed in Tongaland and which either has been or still is the main thrust of widely scattered Missions throughout Central Africa, needs reevaluation in view of the growing responsiveness to the Gospel. It has lost much of its effectiveness.

Five important purposes lie behind this church growth study. Of primary importance to us is a description of the social, historical and religious setting in which churches have been planted. Some knowledge of the culture and customs, patterns of leadership, historical background and tribal religious beliefs is tantamount to a more effective communication of the Gospel.

Secondly, brief historical sketches of Churches and Missions have been reconstructed, including early missionaries and as many of the prominent national church leaders as possible.

Thirdly, the methods and strategy of missionaries, both past and present have been examined as objectively as possible, to see if they have contributed to or detracted from rapid church planting and church growth.

Fourthly, an accurate picture of the Churches as they exist today has been presented using statistics gathered on the spot and subsequently rendered meaningful by means of charts and graphs.

The final purpose of this analysis is to suggest new approaches and better methods of not only proclaiming the Good News but of gathering the increase which God is pleased to grant into vital, self-propagating churches.

Most of the information presented in Chapters V through X was gathered in Tongaland during the three-month period between June and August, 1968. African church leaders were

Introduction

interviewed and encouraged to express their attitudes (whether favorable or unfavorable) toward their Churches, their mission stations, and mission policy.

I visited many of the local congregations in Tongaland, counted members, and classified the leadership. An attempt was also made to ascertain what the power structures were, and whether or not roles of leadership could be adapted and incorporated into the Church.

Tent meetings were surveyed and analyzed for effectiveness and follow-up. Mission-school converts were interviewed to find out how and when they were converted, and whether or not they were currently engaged in any active church.

To enable an objective, yet sympathetic, account of the actual state of the Churches among the Tonga to be written, national Christians were asked to express themselves as frankly as possible regarding withcraft, sorcery, magic, oracles, religious practitioners, *musamu* (medicine), and *mizimu* (ancestral spirits). They were also encouraged to evaluate their new life in Christ Jesus and the spiritual blessings they have enjoyed since becoming His followers.

Included also were interviews with non-Christian tribesmen in the hope that they would express some of their *real* objections to becoming Christians.

The fact that, having grown up in Tongaland, I speak Tonga fluently immensely aided the whole investigation. The language barrier for me did not exist. I present these findings with confidence that they represent the realities of the situation correctly.

PART ONE

The Land
and People

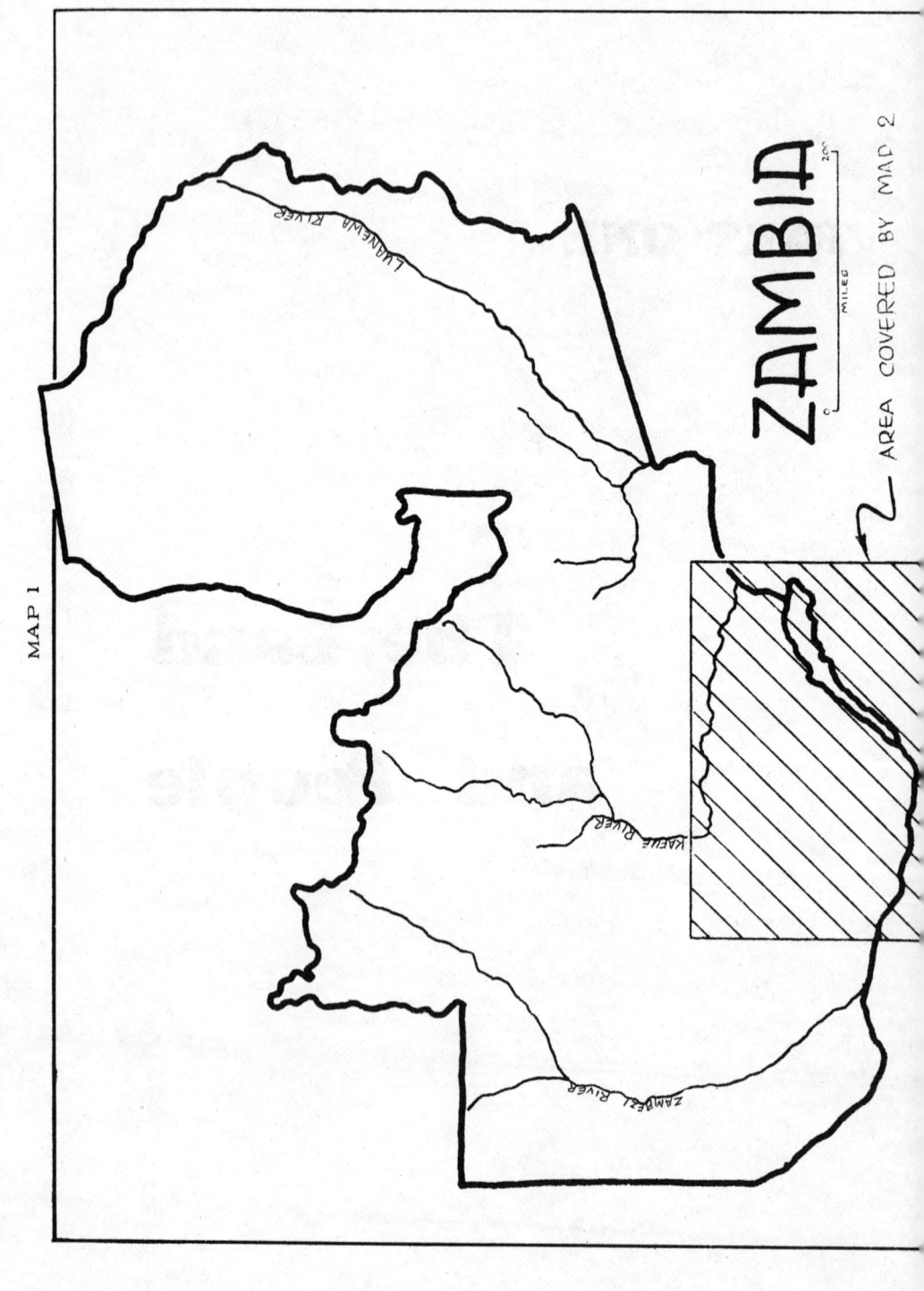

1

The Tonga Tribe and Its Environment

Most of the indigenous population of the southern province of Zambia (formerly Northern Rhodesia) accept the name Tonga. To facilitate administrative control the province comprises three political divisions: the Plateau Tonga of the Mazabuka district, the Valley Tonga of the Gwembe district, and the Toka-Leya of the Livingstone district. These districts are of dubious value. They are artificial so far as the people themselves are concerned, for they have no distinct linguistic, cultural, or political characteristics which would clearly set them apart and define boundaries between them. Furthermore, these divisions do not in any way provoke a sense of common identity or tribal loyalty.

Probably the most discernably different entity or homogeneous unit within the whole Tonga-speaking group is the Valley Tonga, or We, of the Gwembe district. These people, who have been isolated by geographical barriers almost five centuries, are regarded as inferior by the Plateau Tonga.

This study will deal with four main Tonga-speaking peoples: the Tonga (253,000), the Toka (11,000), the Leya (8,000) and the We (55,000). The Churches most carefully analyzed will be Tonga, Toka and Leya Churches.

HISTORY

Little is known about the origins and history of the Tonga prior to 1853. David Livingstone gives the earliest first-hand written accounts of the Tonga and of their encounters with the surrounding tribes, most notably the Kololo from the west (Livingstone 1857).

With no oral tradition about the origin of their tribe or legends concerning early migrations, the Tonga seem to have been part of a southward movement of Bantu peoples during the fifteenth and sixteenth centuries. Recent archaeological findings, however, prove that the Tonga settled in Zambia at least as early as A.D. 1200 (Hall 1965:11).

For some sixty years preceding 1893, Tonga country furnished a common raiding ground for the Kololo and Lozi from the west and the Matebele from across the Zambezi River to the south. Being almost exclusively pastoralists and tillers of the ground, the Tonga offered little military resistance. Flight seemed the only way of escape. In the process of this upheaval, Matebele herded thousands of cattle off to Kolololand and captured Tonga tribesmen, reducing them to slavery. Their raids, which ended with the defeat of the Matebele nation by the British in 1893, are still in the living memory of some of the old people, who recount their experiences in very dramatic fashion. The Kololo and Lozi raiders frequently overran the southwestern corner of the province, and consequently the Toka and Leya assimilated more of the culture of their conquerors (Jaspan 1953:13).

Livingstone found fifty-four human skulls mounted on stakes around "the village of Moyara" which is probably the modern-day village of Mujala. Presumably, these trophies were being collected by a number of Tonga chiefs who were competing against each other to see who could mount the most heads. Most of Moyara's skulls had belonged to sick and famished warriors the chief found returning from war with the Kololo, and at the time of Livingstone's visit to Moyara the Toka were very proud of their trophies and the fierceness of their chief (Livingstone 1857:530-531).

In 1855, while journeying through Tonga country, Livingstone also noticed "heaps of bones of cattle, which the Makololo had been obliged to slaughter, after performing a march with great herds captured from the Batoka." The country was "well adapted for the cultivation of native produce" and the lower plateau temperatures had "an exhilarating effect on my spirits" (Livingstone 1857:548-549).

Frequent invasions by enemy tribes forced the Tonga to change their settlements from large towns to small scattered villages. Uncertainty and terror dealt a damaging blow to the Toka, Leya, and southern Plateau Tonga. This destroyed their spirit of resistance, distinct tribal identity, and much of the tribal loyalty during these tempestuous years. The northern Plateau Tonga and Valley Tonga, however, were less affected by enemy invasions because of distance and geographical barriers.

Speculating about the origin of the Valley Tonga, or We, is pointless, according to Colson. She points out the conspicuous absence of tradition and myth among present-day Valley Tonga which might explain their origin (1960a:25-26). Livingstone only briefly alluded to the existence of the Valley Tonga ruled

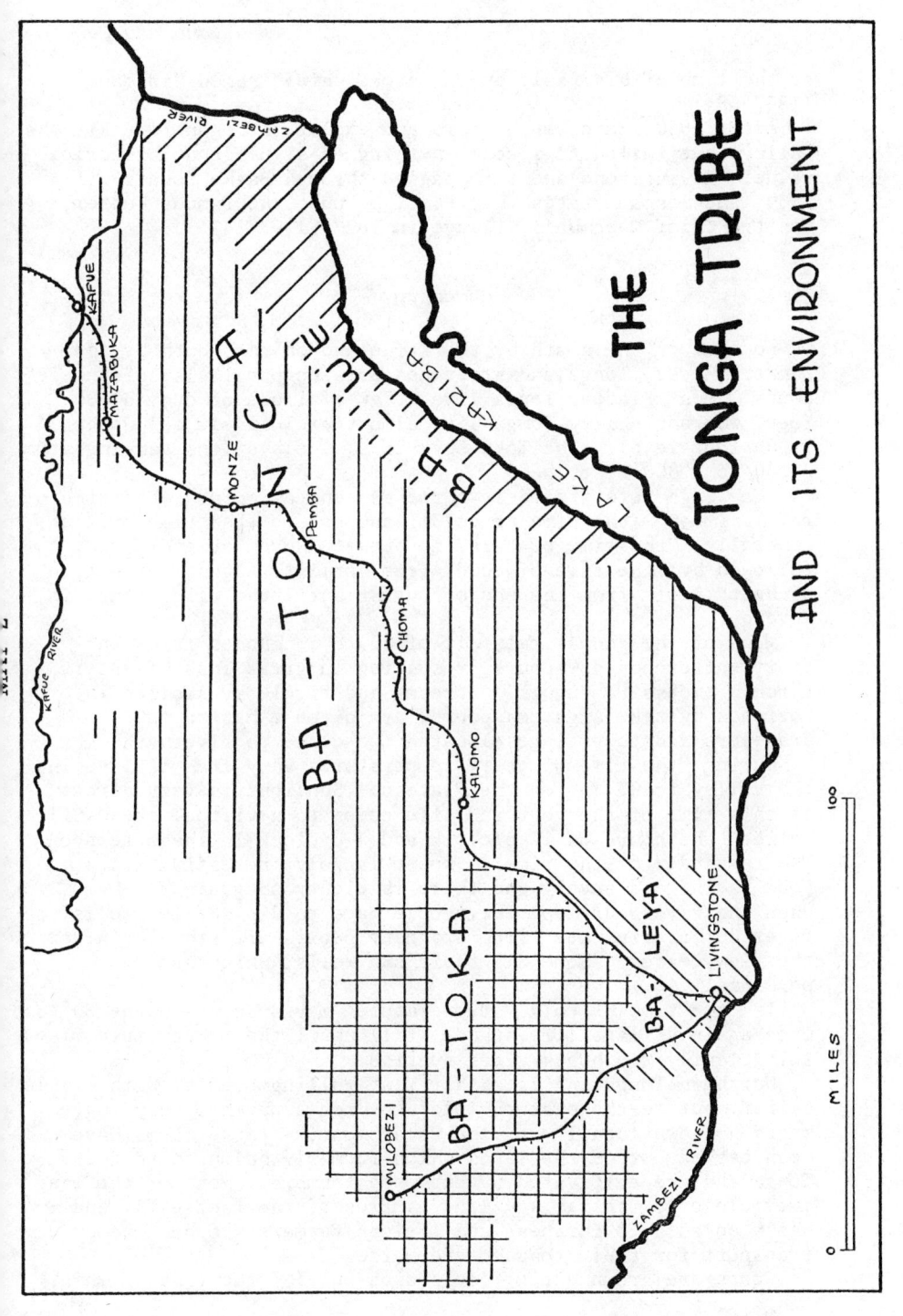

at the time of his visit by "a Batoka chief" named Sinamane (1857:554).

After 1860, European hunters and explorers began to visit the Valley, but failed to record anything of significant historical value. Livingstone and Kirk passed through Ba-We country in 1860, and Jaspan states that F. C. Selous, the famous hunter, visited Chief Mweemba's village in 1877 (1953:14).

GEOGRAPHY

Bounded on the north by the Kafue and on the south by the Zambezi River, Tongaland stretches between parallels 16° and 18° south. Most Plateau Tonga live at an altitude of over 3,000 feet, whereas Valley Tonga live almost exclusively below the 2,000 foot level. The Toka-Leya live at elevations varying from 2,000 to 3,000 feet.

The Tonga refer to their three seasons as *mainza* (the time of rain), *impeyo* (the time of cold), and *cilimo* (the time of heat). Generally, "the time of rain" is between November and March, followed by "the time of cold" from April to August; "the time of heat" lasts from the end of August until the rains start in November.

Much of the annual rainfall of 20 to 30 inches falls in short, afternoon downpours, resulting in great loss of water through excessive runoff. Streams and rivulets, swollen into torrents by the large downpours, are often a hazard to travelers and to villages located too close to riverbanks.

During "the time of heat" temperatures vary from 115° F. in the Valley to 95° F. on the Plateau. Sunlight is very direct at this time of the year and life comes to a virtual standstill between the hours of 12 o'clock and 3 o'clock in the afternoon. The remainder of the time is spent largely in festivities. Food is in good supply and there is plenty of grain for beer. When the rivers dry up, the people have to dig shallow wells in riverbeds or dip water from stagnant pools left standing after the flow ceases. Some dig their own wells, which are perennial.

In "the time of cold," temperatures may drop as low as 30°F. Once again village life stands still until the temperature rises sufficiently two hours after sunrise.

Northern Tongaland is rather flat rolling country with little relief, but to the east the plateau breaks up into very rugged terrain known locally as "the Escarpment." Large farms have been carved out of the lands which formerly belonged to the Tonga and are cultivated by European farmers. Most of the land area close to the railway line is free of the tsetse fly and has been sold to European and African farmers who need ready transport for their tobacco and maize.

Crops are grown during one season only: "the time of rain."

The Land and People

Planting normally begins in early November after the soil has become moist enough to plow. Cultivation is hard and demanding and there is little time for any other activity. The women do a large share of this necessary task while the men are earning cash on nearby farms or in towns.

We country has traditionally been confined to the lower Escarpment and Zambezi Plain, but the rising of Lake Kariba since 1960 has forced the evacuation and resettlement of 34,000 We on higher ground. Travel has, until recently, been extremely difficult in the rugged hills of the Escarpment and in the Valley. Having had the reputation for heat, malaria, and general discomfort it has repelled the stranger from settling within it (Colson 1960:4).

POPULATION

The total population of Tongaland was estimated at 168,000 in 1950 (Colson 1967:5), but W. V. Brelsford gives a more accurate and up-to-date figure of 271,961 (1965:151-152). His total includes 252,938 Plateau and Valley Tonga, 11,031 Toka and 7,992 Leya. According to 1956 estimates, the Valley had a population of 55,000 of which over 50 percent were subsequently resettled prior to the formation of Lake Kariba. This resettlement has had a tremendous sociological and psychological impact upon the life way of a people which had been virtually isolated for centuries.

The majority of the Tonga, Leya and Toka tribesmen live in the rural areas, formerly known as "native reserves," but the rural to urban exodus is gaining momentum as the demands for cash and consumer goods increase. Another factor in this migration is the increasing number of students who are finding it necessary to leave their villages in search of higher education. Considerable concentrations of Tonga tribesmen are moving to towns and cities along the line of rail. Towns like Choma, Monze, Mazabuka, Kafue, Kalomo and Livingstone have received a substantial number of emigrants during the last ten years.

The annual migration of Valley men to farms and towns where they seek seasonal employment has been characteristic of the We since the 1920's. Many of these men become restless and terminate their employment at the first sign of rain in late October. The urge to *lima* (plow) and *byala* (plant) is too much to resist. This concern about their crops is not without justification, for hunger conditions during the twentieth century have occurred in some sections of the Valley an average of once every three years.

The We were decimated by smallpox epidemics in 1893, 1925, 1926 and 1948. In 1918-1919 an influenza epidemic caused widespread deaths. Ever-present diseases such as bilharziasis, malaria, and dysentery contributed to slow population growth during the first half of the twentieth century. Infant mortality was particularly high until government health services began to filter belatedly into the valley in the 1950's and 1960's.

Leya country occupies 485 square miles and contains two groups of Leya people. In 1946, 1,300 people were under the chieftaincy of Chief Katapazi, and 2,500 people were subject to Chief Mukuni (Jaspan 1953:18). The average density was just under eight per square mile, compared with 58.2 per square mile in the Tonga areas (Colson 1967:6).

The next two chapters will deal with social structure and Tonga religious beliefs and practices. Serious students of missions will want to pay close attention to the whole complex of religious belief as it intricately intertwines with every aspect of the structure of the society itself. Without a solid understanding of the dynamic forces at work within the tribe, it would be impossible to utilize the most successful methods for bringing about the rapid multiplication of churches among the Tonga.

2

The Tonga Tribe Social Structure

There exists in African society a solidarity and collectivism which is difficult for the individualistic Western mind to comprehend and appreciate. Communal relationships in Africa do not depend upon the changes and chances of affection. Mutual responsibilities and obligations regulate the actions of each individual member of the clan or tribe. There is a strong underlying conviction that an individual who is cut off from the communal organism is a nothing. "This is the context in which an African learns to say, I am because I participate. To him the individual is always an abstraction; Man is a family" (Taylor 1963:93).

In an Africa which has been administered by various Western colonial powers during the nineteenth and twentieth centuries, and which is now faced with rising nationalism, there remains, in many cases, a strong tribal political structure within the indigenous social system.

POLITICAL STRUCTURES

Among the Tonga these structures are not as rigid or authoritarian as those found in some other tribes, but they nevertheless exist and are recognized as important by most Tonga.

The Clan *(Basikamukowa)*

Even the most progressive Tonga will admit to being a member of some clan. It is the most enduring unit of the society.

The clan has no corporate existence, but is usually dispersed over a wide area. Clan membership is derived through matrilineal descent. Tonga clans are exogamous, own no property, have no ritual centers or ritual leaders, and never have occasion to assemble as a group.

Although clans have lost some of their former functions in the new and changing way of life, no Tonga would deny their importance. From early childhood every Tonga is aware of his clan and believes that it is wrong to marry within it. In times of crisis, when no kinsmen are available, clan membership is of tremendous significance, for the clan member may call upon clansmen to perform kinship roles. When a tribesman moves to the city or some other strange locality in which he has no kinsmen, he can turn to his clansmen to fill kinship roles on ceremonial occasions and to help him become established in his new environment.

The Matrilineal Group *(Mukowa)*

The *mukowa* is a smaller body of tribesmen with a keen sense of rights and duties within its corporate kinship group. It is a much more cohesive unit than the clan because its members share a common matrilineal descent. Relationships between members of this political unit are much closer than those with outsiders even though group members may live in different villages and outsiders may live next door. The average size of matrilineal groups is decreasing in spite of the fact that most Tonga still stress the importance of having matrilineal kinsmen. This is largely because the *mukowa*, like the *basikamukowa* relationship, is being subjected to scrutiny and modification by more progressive Tonga who, in the interests of their own children, would like to shift to a system of familial inheritance (Colson 1967:23).

The Village *(Muunzi)*

Under colonial administration the minimum size of villages was limited to ten adult able-bodied men. Because villages with a definite hierarchy of tribal leadership were unknown among the Tonga, the administration never did really succeed in consolidating the Tonga into large villages under their headmen. Some villages are compact and may consist of as many as a hundred individuals; others are made up of small hamlets or homesteads which are within southing distance of the headman's hut, i.e., one-quarter to one-half mile away.

The cohesion of the *mukowa* is absent in the village. There is no communal ownership of property, no ritual which unites its members, and no common set of activities which distinguishes it from any other village or hamlet. In reacting to decades of slavery and colonial domination, the individual Tonga now wants

The Land and People

to be free to choose his place of residence. They say that this is characteristic of the free man or woman in contrast to the slave who had to live where his owner wished.

The headman has little real power over the rest of the villagers. When his orders are disregarded he can only enforce regard for his position by refusing to assist the offender in the future. In so doing he is following the customary Tonga method of dealing with the problem of reciprocal rights and obligations.

The Neighborhood (Katongo or Chisi)

The *katongo* is the largest indigenous local unit. It usually consists of four to ten villages inhabited by 200 to 800 people. Although these neighborhoods are not officially recognized by the administration, they are much more widely accepted by the people than are the chieftaincies which have been imposed upon them. The Tonga refer to the leader of the neighborhood as the *sikatongo* (owner of the area). He may be a dominant personality in the neighborhood, but more than likely he was the original settler or "clearer of the land." Leadership within the *katongo* will be dealt with in greater detail later in this chapter.

FAMILY AND HOUSEHOLD RELATIONSHIPS

The Family (Mukwaasi)

The smallest residential unit is the extended family unit which lives in a hut or series of huts in close proximity. Increasingly marriage is becoming an association between husband and wife instead of an alliance between kinship groups. This trend will undoubtedly escalate as animism breaks down and tribal loyalties are replaced by family interests and aspirations.

Although the Tonga are matrilineal in both descent and inheritance the family unit--husband, wife and dependents--works as a team for the welfare of the household. Colson notes that "in the new clash between the family unit based on marriage and the matrilineal kinship units based on descent, it is the family which is winning" (Colson 1967:63). There are a number of factors which are working together to bring about this very important change in Tonga social structure. The looseness of the clan relationship, the emphasis upon individual independence which has arrived with nationalism, and the mobility which has always been characteristic of the Tonga, are all contributing to this shift toward stronger family ties. The new conditions of life are intensifying this shift.

John V. Taylor, for many years a missionary to Africa, describes the family as "a delicately poised and interlacing organism in which each knows to whom he owes particular duties, from whom he can expect particular rights, and for whom he bears particular responsibilities" (1963:108).

Marriage is desired by every Tonga man and woman and forms the basis for much interesting conversation, even before puberty. Very few men ever pass the age of thirty without marrying, and one rarely sees a Tonga woman over twenty who has never been married. Exceptions to this rule are some of those who have advanced into secondary school and teacher training.

Few Tonga women leave the rural areas. Those who were once schoolgirls, however, do have some knowledge of life outside their neighborhoods. An increasing number of Tonga girls are enrolling in secondary schools and are beginning to assert their freedom of choice in selecting their future husbands. The incidence of pre-marital sex relations is very high at this stage and many are forced to withdraw from school.

Women are extremely important in traditional Tonga social structure for through them descent is traced and membership within the *mukowa* is established. The wives expect their husbands to be partners in life and to spend much of their time at home with their families. It is not unusual, therefore, to see the father and mother enjoying their children together in the evenings.

The proximity of the rural areas to the railroad enables many of the Tonga men to work along the "line of rail" and yet be at home with their families at night. Other Tonga men take their families to live with them in the laborers' accommodations on European-owned farms along the railroad. Due to the agricultural and pastoral background of the Tonga, both the European farmer and his Tonga farmhand know that the wife is much happier with a *muunda* (field) to care for. Often then, the farmer allocates each family a plot of ground on which the wife can cultivate her maize and peanuts.

Most of the men have no desire to leave their villages except as young men seeking education or bridewealth. The Tonga are contemptuous of men who have to make repeated trips to look for work. They believe that if a man is ambitious he will stay at home and farm.

Marriage is almost always the end of any distant and prolonged absence from the village. Some men are able to collect the necessary bridewealth by appealing to their soft-hearted matrilineal relatives for assistance.

Bridewealth "is not the purchase price of the woman but rather a compensation to her group (especially for the loss of her labor), and it has the advantage of creating a certain stability in marriage" (Nida 1954:103). Nida goes on to explain that bridewealth not only is a compensation but also legalizes the marriage and legitimizes the offspring.

Some husbands delay the final payment of bridewealth for several years, during which time the household is not fully sanctioned and the husband does not have full rights to his wife. During this period and, indeed, after the household is established, the dutiful wife will obey her kinsmen's demands whereas a strong-minded woman will remain with and obey her husband. If the young man delays too long in making his payments, he is sometimes reminded that the ancestral spirits of the wife's relatives may become angry and close her womb or send illness to her future children. This threat of possible sterility is usually sufficient to cause the husband to redouble his efforts to pay off the debt.

After the final payment of bridewealth is made, however, the husband is given full rights to his wife, which include the right to her labor and the right to control her movements. Along with these rights there are certain responsibilities which he must fulfill as her partner. He is responsible for her welfare; if she should become ill, he must locate a diviner and bear the cost of her treatments. He must provide her with a hut, a field, and certain household utensils. He must clothe her and her children.

The Household *(Ing'aanda)*

A household can be defined as that group of people which gathers about a common fire and usually consists of a single adult male and female and their offspring. It must not be confused with the family, however, because those gathered about the fire may also include some individuals who are related in some way only to the husband or wife of the household. The household does not feel the corporate responsibility for the actions of its members in the same way that the family does. It is a looser association.

Men establish their households only through women, and their status depends upon the continuation of their marriage. The man's chances of becoming head of the homestead, hamlet, or village depend to a large extent upon his ability to maintain control over his wife or wives. Although he is considered head of the household, he cannot transmit his position to his sons because in a matrilineal society his children are not members of his descent group but rather belong to his wife's line of descent. Therefore, ties are not as strong between father and sons as they are between husband and wife. It will be interesting to observe the changes in the lineal structure of Tonga society which will result as more progressive husbands seek greater freedom to bestow their inheritances upon their immediate families. These changes will undoubtedly enhance the importance of the household at the expense of the larger kinship units, particularly the matrilineal group.

Dr. Elizabeth Colson, who is the foremost Western authority on the Tonga, says that the creation of new areas of specialization in which people act independently of each other has diminished the importance of the household as a producing unit; but, at the same time, it is becoming more important in the emotional life of its members. She goes on to state that

> this may be partially related to the creation of striking differences in standards of living, and the standard of living applies to the household rather than to a kinship group or to a neighbourhood (1967:94).

Tonga society is therefore in a period of change and dislocation in which the locus of power is shifting from the wider kinship relationships to dominant men who are building strong households about them which become homesteads and hamlets. (See Chapter IV).

The husband's new position in the household can also be seen by noting the changes made in the house rituals. The house, in times past, was under the guardianship of the wife's ancestral spirits, to whom she made offerings at the door. But now, the house is placed under the protection of the husband's ancestral spirits. The wife's subordination can be observed in the fact that she now makes her offerings at the center of the house or near the bedposts and leaves the doorway offerings to her husband. Thus the husband also becomes ritual head of his household as well as the controller of its other affairs.

Polygyny is widely practiced throughout Tongaland, but is particularly characteristic of the Valley Tonga. In her interviews with wives in polygynous households, Colson found some who were violently opposed to the practice, but also those who favored it. Some of the wives found it convenient to have co-wives who could share the work loads; others found it more prestigious to be married to a husband who could afford more than one wife. On the other hand, bitterness was expressed by some of the co-wives whose husband was inclined to chuckle over his wives' quarrels and regard the jealousy and competition for his affections as healthy and not to be discouraged.

It should be noted that the more ambitious men are the ones most likely to be polygynous, because the extra wives mean greater labor force, and the larger labor force enables greater acreage to be cultivated. Chiefs, councillors, and headmen are also likely to be polygynists due to village conditions which one wife is unable to cope with. Since it is a matter of pride with them to feed every visitor, it would be virtually impossible for one wife to take care of all the necessary duties. (See Chapter IX for more on polygyny.)

Most women today do have the right to choose their own husbands or to refuse the men they dislike, but many agree to enter a polygynous union for fear of being debarred from marriage and the creation of a household.

Probably the most important goal in life for the Tonga woman is to find a household in which she can have children to extend her line of descent. This is in keeping with most of the so-called "primitive" world in which children are extremely desirable. In fact, one of the principal causes of divorce is supposed sterility. Most women, therefore, are anxious to prove their fertility (Nida 1954:110).

POWER AND LEADERSHIP STRUCTURES

The Tonga have never had a highly organized pattern of leadership. Throughout their history they have preferred to emphasize mobility and the right of the individual to plan his own life. They find any restraint upon their freedom very distasteful. This characteristic is being demonstrated today by the successful farmer, who is coming more and more to typify the Tonga ideal. Among the Valley Tonga, the successful fisherman fulfills the same ideal as does the farmer on the Plateau.

The development of the fishing industry along the shores of Lake Kariba has drastically changed the leadership structures of the Valley Tonga. Much of the decision-making is being shifted from the traditional headmen and the neighborhood assemblies to the ambitious and obviously successful fishermen, or fishing "cooperatives." One must not, however, be led to believe that the neighborhood assembly is being deprived of its function, because among the Valley Tonga it is still of tremendous political significance.

Valley Tonga Power Structures

Disputes among the We, or Valley Tonga, are generally settled by the neighborhood assembly, under the leadership of a headman or senior headman. Within each neighborhood the village headmen act as the official spokesmen for their respective communities. We headmen, like their Plateau Tonga counterparts, depend to a large extent for their authority upon the strength of their personalities. Although this authority appears to be slipping away from them into the hands of influential fishermen and other small-businessmen, the desire of the people to retain traditional leadership is much more pronounced in the more conservative communities of the Valley than in Plateau villages. A number of factors may contribute to this Valley conservatism, but probably the largest single factor is its isolation from industry and from the demands of a cash economy.

There are no towns or cities within the traditional confines of the Valley; consequently, a large percentage of the people have never been exposed to urban life with its new stresses and strains.

Although for almost half a century Valley Tonga men have left their villages in the Valley to search for temporary jobs

on farms along the railroad or in the cities of Wankie and
Bulawayo in Rhodesia, very few We women have ever left the
Valley. Their reticence to leave was very evident to me during
a visit to the Gwembe Valley in 1948. However, with the
building of Kariba Dam and the subsequent resettlement of
thousands of We, the women have adjusted to travel by truck or
lorry and now draw their water from the nearest government-dug
well.

The contacts which the men have had with a more progressive
way of life, and which the women have more recently experienced,
have had a profound effect upon traditional leadership patterns.
In some Valley neighborhoods, the *sikatongo* (owner of the area
or neighborhood) has considerable authority which he may derive
from the fact that he, or his immediate predecessor, was the
first to move into the area and convert if from bush to
neighborhood. It is doubtful whether this authority would
entitle him to call upon his people for labor or tribute since
it is almost entirely dependent upon his personal qualities.
The *sikatongo* fulfills a significant leadership role in the
communal rituals, and any encroachment upon this ritual office
is severely punished.

Another prominent figure in We society is the prophet, or
diviner. In one sense, he has more power than the *sikatongo*,
for he may accuse the *sikatongo* of failure to fulfill his
customary procedures. The diviner has no inherent authority,
but is rendered powerful only while he is possessed by the
basangu (rain spirits).

Plateau Tonga Power Structures

Leadership among the Plateau Tonga is largely in the hands of
the *mukowa* (matrilineal kingroup). This tight-knit social unit
acts as a group upon the most vital issues of life. Upon the
death of one of its members, it gathers and mourns at his
funeral; it then oversees and divides the inheritance of the
deceased among his surviving kinsmen and, finally, attends to
the purification rites of the spouse of the deceased.

The matrilineal group rarely exceeds 20 to 30 adult members
and is not localized but may be spread over a number of villages.
It is held responsible for the action of its members, and it is
a body which can demand and get compensation for injury. Last,
but by no means least, it provides and receives bridewealth.
"Rights and obligations therefore vest in the matrilineal group
as such and not in particular segments" (Colson 1967:17).
Matrilineal groups are bound together by ties which are purely
temporal and tied to the life span of particular individuals.

One can almost feel the security provided for the individual
member by the *mukowa* relationship, for, as one Tonga has
expressed it, "No man is born alone even if he is the only one
from his womb, for all have *mukowa* and they are as close as

those of one womb" (Colson 1967:17). Further investigation into the roles and functions of the matrilineal group ought to be made by church-planters to enable the true potential spiritual strength, cohesion, and vitality of a "neighborhood" church composed of a converted *mukowa* to be seen and evaluated. (See Chapter X.)

As was previously mentioned, most Plateau and Toka communities are more progressive than Valley neighborhoods because of their proximity to the railroad and the towns and cities which have grown up along the line of rail. In many of these Plateau neighborhoods the people have no single recognized leader and disclaim the right of anyone to usurp a position of authority. There are likely to be a number of leaders whose prestige depends upon and appeals to different bodies of followers within the neighborhood. One may be a schoolteacher, another a big farmer, and a third a small trader or tearoom operator. It is obvious to the observer that the position of the *sikatongo* is far more precarious on the Plateau than in the Valley. His position is weakened even further by the emphasis being placed upon the individual, as opposed to the wider social units, by the nationalist government. The people are exhorted to exercise their individual voting privileges in the election of representatives to the national parliament instead of supporting the chief, local headman, or *sikatongo*.

The small isolated homestead is becoming an increasingly common feature of the Tonga landscape as many of the pressures which held people together are relaxed. But the hamlet as an alliance of a number of homesteads probably has a long life ahead of it because it is practically impossible for a single homestead to continue its existence for any length of time without cooperating with other homesteads (Colson 1967:41).

In this chapter attention has been directed primarily toward a description of the traditional political structures of Tongaland, and toward a few of the external forces which have been brought to bear upon these structures: first, by the colonial administration, and secondly, by the nationalist government. It has been noted that in everyday Tonga life the clan and the matrilineal group are still important influences, but that the neighborhood and village relationships have already undergone considerable modification. The smaller units of society are assuming responsibility for their own decision-making and maintenance.

The homestead, the household, and the family are the Tonga ideals in the more progressive areas and, in my opinion, the areas which are now rather conservative will adopt similar patterns of leadership in their social structures within the next ten years. It is important that these social structures not be torn down in the process of Christianization. They should, instead, be incorporated into the churches, for they offer a good foundation for a Christian society.

3

Tonga Religious Beliefs and Practices

A large majority of the Tonga are adherents to traditional African religion. These beliefs (variously designated paganism, animism, or spiritism), which we shall refer to as *animism*, form the matrix from which African thought and action have sprung in the past and are the chief spiritual environment for well over one hundred million Africans (Hogg 1963:11).

In view of the fact that vast expanses of the world are peopled by animists, it behooves the church-planter to give serious consideration to their beliefs and practices. In Africa animists total more than the combined communities of Christianity and Islam. However, this proportion is rapidly decreasing as Christianity, secularism, communism, and Islam win converts and fill the vacuum left by crumbling traditional structures.

WHAT IS ANIMISM?

One of England's greatest anthropologists of the last century, Edward B. Tylor, defined "animism" as "the belief in spirit beings." He went on to add that, in its fullest development, animism "includes the belief in souls and in a future state, in controlling deities and subordinate spirits," and that these doctrines result in some kind of active worship (Tylor 1965:12). Tylor lived and wrote when the theories of evolution were coming into vogue during the last part of the nineteenth century, and his development of religion followed an evolutionary pattern. It was his belief that primitive man first discovered the presence of the soul when he attempted to distinguish the difference between a living and a dead body.

Eugene Nida and William Smalley, in their concise little book entitled *Introducing Animism*, state that

> the precise or technical definition of animism is a belief in spirits, including the spirits of the dead people as well as those that have no human origin (Nida and Smalley 1959:5).

This study will include more than Tylor's minimum definition of animism, and will briefly mention magic, divination, sorcery, and witchcraft. All of these practices form such an entity that to mention one without the other would present a distorted view of African traditional religion.

ANIMISTIC PHILOSOPHY

Placide Tempels, a long-term missionary-anthropologist among the Baluba tribe of the Congo, divided African philosophy into four categories: *Muntu* (human being), *Kintu* (thing), *Hantu* (place and time), and *Kuntu* (modality). According to Tempels, "all being, all essence, in whatever form it is conceived, can be subsumed under one of these categories. Nothing can be conceived outside them" (Jahn 1961:100).

Tempels succeeds in convincing the Westerner that there is far more complexity within the African philosophical context than most of us had ever dreamed existed. One of the most important concepts which Tempels develops is the presence of *vital force* which permeates every living thing. The dead are esteemed only to the extent to which they increase and perpetuate their vital force in their progeny (Tempels 1959:31).

Although there are great variations of belief, three articles may be said to be common to African animism: (1) the belief in a Supreme Being; (2) the belief in the survival of the human personality after death, or ancestor worship, and (3) the belief in an impersonal energy or dynamism, such as the Melanesian *mana* (Smith 1928b:191). This division into separate elements of philosophy and belief is artificial and is employed only for purposes of description and comparison. Actually each tribal religion and system of life is an autonomous living unity with many characteristics peculiar to it (Kraemer 1963:150). All social, religious, and economic matters of life are interrelated, and the tribesman fits into the overall plan as he executes the duties dictated by his tribal grouping.

Supreme Being

Wilhelm Schmidt said that the purest form of the concept of the Supreme Being, Creator, and Disposer of the Universe is to be found among "primitive" peoples. He is the causal force of all life and whenever a human being is conceived, the conception is exclusively and expressly attributed to an act of God (Tempels 1959:73).

Even though there is an almost universal belief among Africans regarding a Supreme Being, He does not enter into their daily life as a vital and effective force as does the belief in charms and ancestral spirits. Generally the Supreme Being is thought of as a Person, but the idea of what 'person' is not very clear in the minds of Africans (Smith 1936:45).

African myths indicate a common belief that God was once much closer to man but, for a variety of reasons, deserted man and withdrew to some distant place. One of these myths concerns a woman who raised her pestle so high while pounding grain that she struck God in heaven who, in anger because she refused to stop, got up and left. A second myth which is told to explain the distant Supreme Being says that people kept wiping their dirty hands on the sky, which was much lower in those days, so God left in disgust (Nida and Smalley 1959:15-16).

Some believe that the Supreme Being is capricious, subject to fits of temper and inconsistent in his dealings with man. He is thought of as the controller of great events, but uninterested in the small things which men do.

God is sometimes conceived of as the Law-giver and Judge, indicating some belief in a law of righteousness and a Source of morality. Laws may be made by men, but they are still God's laws. The punishment for violation of these laws may be meted out by men and may come from the spirits, but it really is God who is behind them. The wrong-doer then is breaking God's laws and for that reason the hand of God is against him. Many Africans are firm believers in God as Judge.

Great numbers of Africans believe that in the beginning God made man. He and man lived together on earth in perfect harmony but, because of man's wrong-doing or foolish behavior, a great separation has taken place. Persons who hold this belief (one which closely resembles the biblical account) should be given every opportunity to recognize that God has not withdrawn Himself; on the contrary, man has forsaken God and has followed the foolish imaginations and desires of his own mind (Romans 1:20-23).

Edwin W. Smith, the late renowned Africanist and missionary-anthropologist, notes that images of the Highest Being are not common in Africa; in fact there are almost no images of Him. When a man puts up a stone, or the stem of a tree, cutting the wood roughly into the form of a man, and says: "This is God," his words are not to be taken narrowly (Smith 1936:39).

Some Africans believe that since God is so distant and the Owner of all things anyway, there is no real need to pray to Him because He is too far away to be concerned and has no need for anything which they would be able to give Him. Therefore, instead of praying to God, they address their petitions and make their offerings to ancestral spirits or subordinate gods. These were once men who are still near enough to hear and have an intimate understanding of the problems of men.

Ancestor Worship

The second universal belief among Africans is the belief in the survival of the individual after death, and in the identity of the spirit of the deceased with the previously living man. The inevitability of death does not dissolve the continuity of personal existence (Harris and Parrinder 1960:30). Edwin Smith agrees with this concept of the unity between the living and the dead when he says that

> African society does not comprise the living only; the living and the dead compose a close interdependent community, and anything which disturbs the harmony between them is regarded as a crime (1928b:192).

Ancestor worship occupies a much greater proportion of the animist's attention than does the worship of the Supreme Being. Ancestral spirits are all about him and involved with him in the vital issues of life. The dead are alive, although they possess a diminished vital force (life energy). He believes that his deceased ancestors have a greater knowledge of life and of vital or natural force and serve the living by reinforcing their vital force.

According to African philosophy, the deceased are spiritual forces capable of influencing their living descendants. By increasing the life force of their descendants, it is believed that the ancestors thereby continue to live vicariously in the lives of their descendants. When a child is born to one of the living, thanks is offered to the ancestors, to whose helpful influence he owes the child.

Animists, like everyone else, have the desire to live forever, but since death is inevitable, they seek to prolong their existence in the lives of their descendants (Jahn 1961: 109-110). This necessitates a close interdependency between the living and the dead. The living desire the vital force and knowledge of the deceased, while the dead seek to perpetuate their "life" in the lives of the living. The position of the dead depends upon the condition and behavior of the living. The deceased are comfortable in the kingdom of the dead only to the extent that they are honored by their survivors. The dead man is therefore entirely dependent upon the consideration and social position of the living.

Another aspect of this philosophy is the emphasis upon fertility and reproduction. Man, in the animistic view, is constructed for reproduction and this is his supreme purpose for existence. To die without children to carry on the family line is the worst evil that could possibly befall a man. There is no greater curse than to wish a man to die childless.

The concept of fertility and all of its implications is ingrained into African minds at a very early age. I recall an incident which illustrates vividly the emphasis placed upon fertility and the fear of sterility which every youngster lives with until he is able to prove to the contrary. While on a hike some years ago, an African companion and I stopped to eat the picnic lunch which my mother had prepared for us. The lunch included some hard-boiled eggs, one of which I offered to my friend. He refused it, saying that the old people had warned him that sterility would result from eating eggs. He was only about eight or nine years of age but was already aware of some of the social pressures and taboos which kept the family, kin-group, and clan together, and insured its continuation. I also came to find out that young men were forbidden to eat fatty meat, sugar or candy lest these should cause sterility.

The worship of ancestors is rooted not in piety, but in fear. The spirits of angry ancestors are thought to be the cause of disease and death among animists and constant propitiation is necessary to preserve or restore normalcy within the family, village, or clan. In some tribes an ox or a cow is offered to the spirits with the words,

> We offer unto you, spirits of our departed relations, this beast, in order that you . . . may invite all your other spiritual relations to partake of this beast offered to you . . . satisfy yourselves and show kindness unto this patient, your relation, by giving him good health (Willoughby 1928:190).

In every case, the question is not "What?" has caused the illness, but "Who?" is responsible.

Dynamism or Mana

A third universal in animistic belief is the concept of dynamism or *mana*. This supernatural force may be likened to electricity which can be transmitted from one object to another. Its power is just as real as size, shape, or color (Nida and Smalley 1959:18).

R. H. Codrington, who in 1863 went to Melanesia as a missionary, discovered that the people of Melanesia had an abstract concept for all forms of supernatural power. This power was called *mana* and was described by Codrington as being not physical but supernatural, not fixed in anything but capable of being conveyed in almost anything. He noted that not only spirits and men could possess and impart it, but that inanimate objects also might possess it (Lessa and Vogt 1965: 255-256).

The Land and People

One experiences some reluctance and frustration when forced to use a Melanesian term for a similar concept which is one of the most important aspects of African life. Edwin Smith found great difficulty in discovering equivalent terms in African vocabularies for the concept of *mana*, but he said that "unless we presuppose a belief in *mana* it is impossible rightly to appreciate many important elements of African life" (1928b:192).

In Africa, as in Melanesia, religion consists largely in accumulating *mana* for oneself, or in getting it used for one's benefit. This explains why charms play such an important role in African daily life for they are vehicles of *mana*. Indeed, mascots and rabbit's feet continue to fulfill a similar need among more emancipated Westerners.

The vast majority of Africans believe that if a man becomes prosperous it is not because he has worked hard for his wealth, but because he has accumulated a large store of *mana*. When a man is captured by an enemy, he has lost his *mana* or has been overcome by someone who has a greater supply. Other evidences that a person has *mana* are such qualities as strength, prestige, reputation, skill, dynamic personality, and intelligence (Smith 1947:120).

Other Beliefs and Practices

As has already been pointed out, African philosophical and religious beliefs are complex and unified. Hendrik Kraemer, missionary-theologian of Indonesian fame, has said that

> tribal life . . . is permeated by a deep sense of being taken up into an all-embracing "order," affecting in undivided unity the world at large, tribal and social life, and the individual (1963:150-151).

Brief mention will be made of some of these other beliefs which are part of this "unity" of traditional religion and which vitally affect daily life.

1. *Magic*. Animists employ magic to manipulate more potent forces around them. It gives them a sense of security, hope, and optimism; for they are convinced that, given the right medicine man with the proper formulae, it will usually work. Bronislaw Malinowski emphasizes that

> the function of magic is to ritualize man's optimism, to enhance his faith in the victory over fear. Magic expresses the greater value for man of confidence over doubt, of steadfastness over vacillation, of optimism over pessimism (1954:90).

There are two general divisions within the practice of magic:

(1) white magic, which is used to procure good, and (2) black magic, which is used to cause harm to people or things.

2. *Divination*. This is the act or practice of foreseeing or foretelling future events or discovering hidden knowledge. Probably the most important type of information which the diviner seeks is the cause for such calamities as sickness, death, drought, and epidemics. Since most animists believe that there is a cause for every event, they find it impossible to accept sickness or death as a natural occurrence, but must determine *who* has caused it. This is where the diviner comes in. He is usually called in by the relatives of the victim to find out *who* is working magic against the ill person or, in case of death, *who* has eaten his soul or which spirit has been angered.

A few years ago, I had occasion to question a young African, in whom I had a great deal of confidence, concerning a serious illness from which he had just recovered. He told me that he had been admitted to a government hospital and had been treated for several weeks without any apparent success, so had decided to go to another hospital for treatment. But having given up hope of recovery in the second hospital, he decided to return to the village where he could receive the "attention of the old people." He disclosed this latter fact rather sheepishly for, being a Christian, he feared that I might ridicule or even scold him for having reverted to old practices. While in the village, the cause of his illness was diagnosed by a diviner, or witch doctor, and then the old people administered their tribal medicine. Although he looked extremely drawn and weak, he was convinced that the government medical doctors had been unable to find out *what* was making him ill, but that the "old people" determined *who* was responsible for his sickness. His subsequent recovery was sufficient evidence to convince him of the efficacy of traditional medicine.

Interpretative devices used by diviners are myriad. Some observe the behavior of a praying mantis, or the attitude of an antelope's horn around a fire, a termite's choice of sticks to feed upon, or the effect of benge poison which has been given to chickens. Other methods include: cards, numbers, casting of dice, tea leaves, lines in the hand, and livers of sacrifices (Nida and Smalley 1959:36-37).

3. *Sorcery and Witchcraft*. Geoggrey Parrinder, noted authority on African traditional religion, makes a distinction between sorcerers and witches. He says that a sorcerer is an individual who uses black magic against his neighbors or fellow villagers, whereas the witch may not be a person at all. A witch may often be a spirit who exerts a tremendous psychological effect upon his victims. The African dislikes and fears both the witch and the sorcerer and attempts to counteract

their evil influences by employing witch doctors, diviners, and their magical medicines. Parrinder says:

> There is no doubt that Africans fear and hate witches, and therefore take stern measures to curb their activities. Missions and governments often claim that their aim is to deliver the African from the fear of witchcraft. This is undoubtedly true. But it is also true that their efforts do not seem to bear much fruit in this sphere, that most educated Africans still believe profoundly in witchcraft, and that there are statements made on many sides that the fear of witchcraft is increasing. The coming of European ideas and customs has unsettled society in Africa, and the increasing insecurity adds to the force of the belief in witchcraft which is held responsible for unknown and incalculable dangers (1963:129).

If someone hears that he has been bewitched or cursed, he usually becomes ill and may die. The belief that he is doomed has such a strong psychological effect upon the victim that he becomes "scared to death" and refuses to eat or exercise. Unable to rid himself of the sickening fear of death, he dies (Nida and Smalley 1959:41). He believes that the only possible way to effect a recovery is for a witch doctor or diviner to use a magic more potent than that of the sorcerer. Witch doctors, then, are regarded as helpful in maintaining the physical and mental health of the community, and they do not find it necessary to work clandestinely.

4. *Unity of All Nature*. Essentially all nature is a unified whole. There is no distinction between spirits and men, animals and men, or between animate and inanimate existence. People may change into animals; and trees, stones or mountains may possess souls. Relationships between the ancestors who are deceased and with one's descendants of the future are so close that everything is essentially contemporaneous (Smoker 1961:25). The souls of the dead still exist and participate in man's life, protecting him from danger and keeping him faithful to the traditions (Nida and Smalley 1959:51).

The foregoing has been a short summary of the most important African beliefs and practices and it is hoped that this description will stimulate further sympathetic research by missionaries into the complex and unified religious structure of animism. Furthermore, it should provide a context in which a specific consideration of Tonga beliefs and practices will be rendered more meaningful.

THE TONGA CULT OF THE *MIZIMU* (ANCESTRAL SPIRITS)

Tonga life is permeated by the belief in *mizimu*. These spirits are involved in all the affairs of men. They regulate and determine the patterns of leadership and distribution of authority, and play a decisive role in the transmittal of property and bridewealth.

Religion is not compartmentalized among the Tonga, but is woven into the fabric of every aspect of the society. A Tonga eats, drinks, and sleeps his religious life. Prayers are said to all these *mizimu* and feasts are made in their honor. At these feasts, both the *mizimu* and the living take part. Many Africans hold this belief (Smith 1936:47).

Offerings are constantly being made to the *mizimu*. Sometimes these offerings may be so subtle as to pass the attention of the Westerner without being observed. Offerings may range from the deliberate spilling of crumbs from the hand during the meals around the common pot to the expectoration of the first mouthful before taking a drink of water. On innumerable occasions I have noticed Tonga women fill their buckets brimming full of water and then proceed to pour some of it on the ground before placing the buckets on their heads to carry to their homes. I am convinced that this is an offering.

Cecil R. Hopgood, for many years a missionary-linguist among the Tonga, has said that

> the mizimu . . . are constantly impinging on the life of the living; it is essential to keep on good terms with them, for they possess considerable power both for good and for ill. Sickness and misfortunes of every kind are commonly attributed to the influence of an offended spirit, and in times of trouble it is frequently necessary to make offerings to appease these *mizimu* (1950:61-62).

He has found, however, that even though they play such a vital part in human life, they are thought of as inferior to God in their power and authority. They act as mediators between their human kinsmen and God, who is thought to have withdrawn Himself to a great distance.

There are many kinds of ancestral spirits or *mizimu*, but Colson divides them into five general classifications.
1. *The mizimu of the matrilineal group.* Each matrilineal group (*mukowa*) has a united body of spirits which belong to the group and affect, to a large extent, the solidarity of the group.
2. *The guardian mizimu.* These are the spirits which infants receive shortly after birth and are specially associated with the name of the child. They provide guardianship for him throughout life and are thought to give him his personality.

The Land and People

3. *The house mizimu.* Every household must have its particular spirit which must be installed by the adults of the household and constantly appeased at the doorway by the husband.
4. *Inherited mizimu.* As a part of the funeral rites, the *mukowa* decides who is to receive the *muzimu* (singular of *mizimu*) of the dead person. To whatever persons these spirits are assigned, they are regarded as inherited *mizimu*.
5. *Own mizimu.* These are *mizimu* which come into being only after people die. No living person has his own *muzimu* (Colson 1965:439).

The ancestral spirits of the matrilineal line may affect any number of their group but have no power over persons of another clan or kingroup. This particular body of spirits is, with the exception of the *mizimu* of the father and father's father, thought to be rather temperamental and capricious. With little provocation they may become angry and without the protection and persuasion of the spirits of the father and father's father they might kill many people.

The Valley Tonga say that the duty of the father's spirit is to look after you and plead with the lineage spirits to spare you from harm. Any adult person may appeal on his own behalf to the spirits of the matrilineal group. Among the Tonga there are no ancestral shrines or localized foci for the cult, but the ancestors follow each person in his travels (Colson 1967:19).

Guardian spirits have special significance in each person's life. When assigned a name, the individual assumes certain social responsibilities and comes under the guardianship of the spirit. Until the child receives a name several months after birth, he has no guardian *muzimu*. The child's first name is given by the father or father's relatives and is usually a name which belonged to a former member of his line. The second name is given by the mother's relatives and is the name of a former member of her line. The significance of the guardian *mizimu* as a cohesive agent can readily be seen in that both the father's lineage and the mother's lineage are joined in the child, all under the surveillance of the *mizimu*.

When the Tonga build a house or otherwise establish a household, the adult members install the house *mizimu* to guard and provide a certain measure of security for all members of the household. Formerly, the most important spirit was that of the mother's line, but the father is coming more and more to fulfill the role of household priest. He makes offerings to the *mizimu* at the doorway of his house while his wife makes her offerings at the center post of the hut or bedstead. This indicates a subordination of the influence of the wife's matrilineal line and the dominant role of the husband within Tonga households. It becomes evident that the message of Jesus Christ must be presented to these household priests and that their acceptance of the Gospel will have tremendous consequences for the Church in the winning of households.

Every funeral involves the choosing of an inheritor for the dead man's *muzimu*. Ideally this inheritor must be an adult member of a household so that he will be able to make offerings. A man's inheritor should first be his own brother, then the oldest son of his oldest sister. A woman's inheritor should be first her own sister, then her oldest daughter's oldest daughter (Colson 1960b:124-125). The surviving members of the lineage choose the inheritor. This inheritance carries with it prestige, authority, and social responsibility; the *mizimu* expect to be remembered with offerings so that "life" will continue as it was while they were alive.

It is only after death that one's own *muzimu* comes into existence. When a person dies, his *muzimu* is eligible for inheritance by someone within his lineage. But a person is assured of becoming a *muzimu* within the matrilineal group of spirits only if he has made offerings to the *mizimu* during his lifetime.

If a child dies, his *muzimu* is not considered significant enough to be inherited and his spirit becomes merely a disembodied ghost (*ceelo*). From this it is obvious that the establishment of a household is very important to the Tonga who is not a Christian. For him to be honored and appeased after his life on earth, it is an inexorable requirement that he offer beer to the *mizimu*, and to offer beer he must be an adult member of a household. The whole system of prestige, offerings, inheritance, appeasement, and adulthood fits together to produce quite a solidarity and security within the traditional social and religious structure.

The cult of the *mizimu* is the strongest religious force among the Tonga, for it is present in, and regulates the behavior of, almost every activity that a person engages in. The Gospel has made a great impact upon the lives of many Tonga, but it is my opinion that the deep-seated faith in the power and role of the *mizimu* is still present in the lives of even the most progressive Tonga. This may be because this particular accumulation of beliefs has not been regarded by advocates of change as a totality, or as a system with many interacting points.

There has been a very noticeable tendency among those of us who are missionaries to cut out or displace certain practices within the cult, without recognizing that the appeasement, offerings, and continuity of the *mukowa* was really a functioning whole. Radical displacement of the cult could destroy the Tonga social structure, stifle church growth, and arouse strong resentments. It would seem far more reasonable for missionaries to recognize the function of the cult, and provide *functional substitutes*. For example, a positive gospel message embodying strong doctrines of "God's *mukowa*" (the Church), of the power and dynamic of the Holy Spirit as He is revealed in the Bible,

The Land and People   33

and of Jesus, the Mediator who is both God and man, are some
elements which make up a relevant message and which would appeal
to these people. (See Chapter X.)

TONGA IDEAS OF *LEZA* (GOD)

Tonga ideas of God are developed more fully than those of
many other African tribes. Dr. Edwin Smith, who has collected
African ideas of God from all over the continent has come to
the conclusion that there are very few, if any, African peoples
who have no belief in God. Pioneer missionaries agree with
Smith because they have left records of their initial encounters
with Africans who had such ideas.

This credence which the Tonga have concerning *Leza*, as they
refer to God, is a point of contact for the Gospel. The message
of a missionary or national preacher who teaches about God as
He is revealed in Jesus Christ falls upon receptive hearts.

Hopgood, in his study of Tonga conceptions of God, says that
"*Leza* as a father watching over the interests of his human
children seems, quite apart from Christian influence that is
making itself felt today, to be fairly common amongst the Tonga"
(1950:65). And I can personally testify to the fact that *Leza*
is spoken of constantly by the people in their daily round of
life, though generally His name is used as a threat or to lend
authority to an oath. God is "thought of as directly connected
with every experience and event, whether great or small, of
everyday human life" (Hopgood 1950:63).

The Tonga have many other names for *Leza* which describe His
activities and relationship to men in nature. He is referred
to as *Cilenga*   (Creator),
   Munamazuba (Ancient of Days),
   Syatwaakwe (Owner of His things),
   Mutalabala (Limitless One),
   Namampinde (Changer of the Seasons),
   Ciyobolola (Preserver),
   Civuna   (Deliverer), and
   Keemba   (Angry One).

The generally accepted ideas of God which are common among the
Tonga frequently compare with the Old Testament Hebrew
conception of an All-powerful and Transcendent Being. He is
thought of as eternal, in contrast with mortal man, whose days
are few (Hopgood 1950:73).

The Christian view of the Eternal God who is a loving Father
has been accepted by many Tonga, but those who are still
animistic do not think of God as being near or concerned about
the welfare of His children. He is called upon only when the
mizimu have failed to provide the desired results. Sometimes
when divination after divination has been unsuccessful, the
people will conclude that God must be responsible for the

sickness or death. In one account an offering made to *Leza* by the head of the family was accompanied with this prayer:

> *Leza*, I make this prayer. If it is you who has made our brother ill, let him be, so that your servant may go about by himself. Was it not you who made him and said he was to have the power of walking and to put his faith in you? *Mutalabala*, the Ever-living One, we make this prayer to you, you are the Great Chief (Smith 1936:73-74)!

Again, He is often entreated after the diviner's medicine and the prayers to the *mizimu* have failed to grant a woman's request for a child. God is sought only as a last resort because of His apparent remoteness and inability to understand the problems of man. How pertinent must be the preaching of Jesus who

> likewise partook of the same nature, that through death he might destroy him who has the power of death, that is, the devil, and deliver all those who through fear of death were subject to lifelong bondage (Hebrews 2:14, 15).

Their hearts cry out for a mediator who can "feel with them" in their daily lives but who also can approach the Supreme Being.

THE TONGA CONCEPT OF *MUSAMU* (MEDICINE)

Running parallel to the cult of the *mizimu* and the ideas of a Supreme God is a third element in Tonga religious thought. This is the concept of *musamu*, or medicine. It is very closely akin in its characteristics to the Melanesian force called *mana*, which is also referred to as dynamism by some writers. One authority on Tonga religion has written:

> For the Tonga 'medicine,' *musamu* is anything that has valuable properties or achieves certain ends, whether it be a remedy for a disease, polish to clean one's shoes, or a charm supposed to ensure success in hunting, the discomfiture of one's enemies in battle, or some other such end. In this idea of *musamu* one has perhaps traces of a 'magical' conception of life that should be placed alongside the belief in Leza and in the *mizimu* as a third strand in Tonga religious thought (Hopgood 1950:71).

My Tonga friends are more open in their discussion of *musamu* than they were when questioned about their ancestral spirits. They frequently attribute superior physical strength to the presence of *musamu*. When the mission-school football team lost a game, the players would say that their opponents were older and had *musamu*. They were sometimes apprehensive about tangling with an opposing player who reputedly possessed "the power to break one's leg." In a boxing match, if one of the combatants is knocked down or rendered unconscious, the only way for the victim to recover is for the victor to wash his hands and allow the loser to drink the water. The prosperity of a farmer is ascribed to *musamu*. He cannot by hard work and frugal living possibly become well-off without generous portions of *musamu*. Nothing is left without a cause or explanation. If no other cause can be found, it must be due to that mysterious supernatural energy, *musamu*.

RITUALS

A growing number of younger Tonga are beginning to disregard the efficacy of rituals. These progressives refuse to participate in what they term "pagan rituals." Those who do attend the neighborhood gatherings are probably more attracted to the beer which flows so freely at such assemblies than they are to the actual ritual itself. An exception to this generalization is the funeral ritual which is still taken seriously by most Tonga. I will briefly mention only three of the rituals which are generally observed throughout Tongaland.

The Rain Ritual

Shortly before the rains begin to come in earnest in November, beer is prepared for what is known as the *luinde* (rain ritual). The ceremony is convened by the *sikatongo* (neighborhood ritual leader) and the inhabitants of each village spend the evening dancing from house to house. Rain-songs are sung and the *basangu* (rain spirits) are implored to send rain. This continues throughout the night. The next day the village dancers move the scene of their dancing to the local rain-shrine where the dancing around the rain-shrine is repeated each day until the rain comes.

The Puberty Ritual

Among animistic societies "puberty marks a time of great transition, when the mysteries of sex frequently inspire belief in supernatural power" (Nida 1954:165). The neighborhood gathers to offer sacrifices to the *mizimu* of their line. Many cattle are killed and it is a time of rejoicing and thanksgiving.

The Funeral Ritual

This is by far the most far-reaching ceremony. Death is taken seriously, and a man or woman makes every effort to return to his homestead or neighborhood before death. An old person who has spent a number of years in the city will always try to find a way back to his *muunzi* (village) when he senses death approaching.

The whole neighborhood is expected to attend the mourning ceremonies. This once again demonstrates the essentiality of neighborhood solidarity. I have known Tonga men to leave their jobs and walk over one hundred miles in order to "go and weep." The whole *mukowa* must be present. Within the space of three months a Tonga worker may request leave two or three times to "go and weep" in his neighborhood for his "mother." In actuality, his "mother" may be any older woman in his matrilineal group, and is not limited to his real mother. At the funeral ritual, the deceased person is usually given his own *muzimu* and beer offerings are made during the assigning of the new *muzimu* to its place among the other *mizimu*.

SORCERY AMONG THE TONGA

Sorcery to the Tonga is always evil and detrimental to the society. The *mulozi* (sorcerer) is, in effect, the number one enemy of the society and his evil power must be offset by greater power. This is where the witch doctor comes in. He practices openly to negate or overpower the medicines of the *mulozi*. The witch doctor is the public benefactor while the sorcerer is the public enemy. There must be no confusion between the two because they work against one another.

Bulozi (sorcery) is considered the most degraded and heinous of crimes among the Tonga. According to Edwin Smith, the

> . . . three greatest crimes in the eyes of Africans are having sex relations inside the family or clan, the putting of near relatives to death, and the use of evil and unnatural powers--that is to say, *bulozhi* (sorcery) (1936:65-66).

The *mulozi* goes against the accepted laws of nature, reproduction, continuation of the lineage and everything else considered essential to the life of the clan or kingroup. He must be recognized and rooted out of society at all costs.

The threat of sorcery is a very effective equalizer of society. I have known several cases where progressive Tonga men have deliberately refrained from "rocking the boat" when they returned to their villages lest they fall victim to "evil medicines" or witchcraft. They have a very real fear of the sorceries of their envious neighbors.

When I asked a competent bricklayer if he would build himself a comfortable brick home when he returned to his village, he replied that the people would be jealous and employ sorcery against him if he did. He would, therefore, live out the rest of his days in a pole-and-mud hut even though he was ambitious and desired to live in more comfortable quarters. Tonga men have on a number of occasions told me that "my people are very jealous and will use medicines to kill me if I attempt to be too progressive."

A worker may use sorcery against a more highly paid employee so that he can take his place when he sickens or dies. The victim may suspect that he is being bewitched and go to the witch doctor or diviner to find out who is responsible.

A few years ago a man confided to me that the reason for his frequent illness was that his "brother" (clan member) was trying to bewitch him so that he could have his job. Being totally unaware of the gravity of the situation, I tried to assure the man that I knew his brother would not resort to sorcery. But the man was not to be convinced in the least and within a few days he had all the proof he needed that his brother was trying to poison him. He recounted how the evening before he had gone to work at 5 o'clock in the afternoon, but before leaving his house, he shook out his blankets and made up his bed so that it would be ready when he returned home in the dark. During the night his back began to hurt and he became restless. After tossing and turning for some time, he decided to light the lamp and see what was causing the pain. After carefully inspecting the blankets he discovered two pieces of straw each about an inch long lying in his bed. He was convinced that these straws had intentionally been put in his bed by a sorcerer with evil intent. He explained to me that this was the reason why he had been sick with pains in his back for so many days.

Sorcery is a potent social control and the threat of it is often all that is required to promote generosity by a wealthy member toward his kinsmen.

4

Acculturation: The Process of Culture Change

There has been a marked increase in the tempo of culture change in Zambia since it became an independent nation October 24, 1964. Even the Tonga, who constitute the largest of Zambia's seventy-two tribes and who have traditionally been pastoralists and content to remain for the most part in their own villages, are beginning to experience the new pressures of modernization. As the Zambian nationalist government seeks to raise the standard of living of all its peoples, the resulting development is extending into even the remotest areas of Tongaland.

More money has become available since independence for the expansion of national projects such as hydroelectric systems, schools, hospitals, and roads. Prior to the dissolution of the ill-fated Central African Federation of Northern Rhodesia, Southern Rhodesia and Nyasaland, much of the wealth of Zambia (then Northern Rhodesia) had been used to maintain the financial solvency of both Nyasaland and Southern Rhodesia. For decades the British South Africa Company had collected substantial royalties from Zambian copper and other minerals.

Expatriate industry has opened up much of the mineral wealth of Zambia, and to a certain extent it is still found to be necessary to employ skilled expatriates to carry on vital services. Unfortunately, many of these foreigners do not have any real stake in the country and feel no particular loyalty to the nation itself. As a result, President Kenneth Kaunda in his famous speech on "Economic Independence" delivered before the National Council of the United National Independence Party (UNIP) at Mulungushi on April 19, 1968, made it quite clear that

The Land and People   39

in the future businessmen would be required to invest more of their profits in the nation rather than making their fortune and then departing with it to some place outside the country.

The availability of more cash has enabled the Zambian government to initiate bold programs in education and medical facilities. Per capita income has risen to an all-time high. With this new infusion of ready cash into an economy which has functioned on a subsistence level for centuries, a number of cultural changes are becoming apparent in Tonga society.

RURAL TO URBAN MIGRATION

Prior to the 1960's the Tonga were not known for their mobility or rural-to-urban migration. Generally those who left their villages did so only to seek adventure and to demonstrate their independence, to obtain bridewealth, to earn enough cash for poll tax, or to solve some other financial crisis which needed immediate attention. Tongas who left home could be expected back after only a short stay among the *makuwa* (white men). The exceptions to this rule were those who had been fortunate enough to get a higher education and consequently would seek better jobs among larger opportunities for employment in the towns.

Valley Tonga men, however, have been much more migratory than their cattle-owning neighbors on the Plateau. Colson estimates that in 1956 over 41.5 percent of the taxable males were out of the Valley at one time (1960b:32). The We men generally crossed the Zambezi into Rhodesia to find employment in the coal mines at Wankie or in the industrial city of Bulawayo. (However, since 1965, when unilateral independence was declared by Rhodesia, these Zambian men have not been allowed to cross over into Rhodesia. Work has had to be found, and to some extent unemployment problems have been alleviated by the development of the fishing industry around the northern shores of Lake Kariba, where many of the Valley people now live.) Colson also notes that in spite of the long-term absences of some husbands marriages are usually maintained. Ties are very strong and the Valley people pride themselves on their closeness.

The Plateau Tonga shifted from subsistence to cash crops between 1925 and 1930 (Colson 1967:66). This tended to hold the tribe together. Many of the young men went to the towns to gain prestige, but returned soon afterwards to farm and sell their produce. Very few Tonga sought work on the Copperbelt.

By 1963, however, with more and more jobs opening up throughout Zambia, the migratory trend had turned away from the villages, to the towns and cities. Barrie Reynolds found that

> most [villagers] find town life much more attractive, and return home only during their leave. The presents they

bring ensure them a welcome, but often they do little to
help and are merely an added burden until their leave is up
or, tired of dull country fare, they escape again to the
bright lights of the towns (1963b:14).

In 1968 I found the situation had changed considerably from
what Colson had noted in the 1950's. Many of the villages in
the Leya area of Chiefs Musokotwane and Nyawa were almost
entirely divested of their youth. During the school term this
can easily be explained by the fact that they are away in
schools; but even during the holidays a large percentage of the
young people prefer to visit relatives in town.

With the realization of independence, young people are
moving out of the old traditions of their fathers to the bright
lights of the cities. More jobs are available, but still not
nearly enough to cope with the influx of young men and women in
search of good paying positions.

Churches among some sections of the Tonga suffer from the
lack of adequate leadership mainly because adult Christian men
have moved to the line of rail to find employment. Often they
take their wives with them.

Although the Tonga have never been noted for migration, this
certainly is a factor with which the Church will need to grapple
in the near future. The question arises, "Where should churches
be planted first--in the villages or in the towns?" Ideally the
Church needs to be strong in the rural areas so that strong
Christians will move to the cities, but a vital and dynamic
urban Church is also needed to receive these socially dislocated
village Christians. (See Chapter XI.)

THE EFFECT OF EDUCATION

One of the greatest single factors affecting the process of
culture change among the Tonga is education. As late as 1960,
an eighth-grade primary education was thought to be ample by
up-and-coming young Tonga. Some were fortunate enough to
receive a secondary education; still fewer went on to university.
In a few short years, however, the crash programs initiated by
the Zambian government have made it possible for most Tonga
young people to get not only an eighth-grade education but also
two years on the secondary level. Several Missions have moved
from their early emphasis on primary education to providing
secondary schools for "their" young people. The government is
still encouraging Missions to build, staff and maintain
secondary schools. Some Missions are following the government
lead and at present are operating or are in the process of
building secondary schools.

Education, particularly on the secondary level, is having a
profound effect upon the social attitudes of the Tongas. Older

people are lamenting the fact that they no longer have control over their children. Whereas the parents or kinship group formerly made the decision regarding who should be marriage partners, the young students now do not feel it necessary to abide by the dictates of their parents.

One Christian parent, who is raising a large family of ten, told me that his older children sometimes question his requests. "In the old days, my word was law. When I was a boy, or even now, I tie my tongue when speaking to an older person." He went on to add that he was getting old, but did not know for sure whether his older children would help send the younger ones through school. Such disrespect would not have been tolerated a few years ago.

An Anglican priest-in-charge of a large mission station remarked to me that young educated boys and girls now do what they wish regarding marriage. They make their own marriage arrangements and often the parents are not even consulted. The priest, who is a Tonga father of ten children, mentioned another difficulty which his Church is faced with:

> The practice of *kutiizya* (premarital intercourse) has become a very great problem among the young people of our Church. They no longer ask their parents whether it is alright to marry someone. A young man merely *kumiisya* (impregnates) the girl and the parents cannot stop the marriage. This is destroying our old *zilengwa* (customs).

The Christian vice-principal of a large 800-student government secondary school made a similar statement when he said that young Tonga boys and girls are being thrust together into close social relationships with which they are unable to cope. He indicated displeasure and concern about the rapid breakdown in tribal marriage customs and discipline. Colson was aware of this trend almost two decades ago when she noted that "the impact of change and wider knowledge has brought about a general questioning of old standards" (1967:12).

The growing rift between the old traditional tribal life and the new Westernized national life was quite apparent in 1968. The spirit of reaction, restlessness, and rebellion, and an air of superiority among educated youth was set in array against the conservatism of the older uneducated people. Oldsters are pessimistic about the "world situation" (which generally means the tribal situation) when they no longer receive the prestige which they have grown to expect. This gulf is being widened by the inter-tribal associations which occur in the secondary schools. The village standards of housing, hygiene, and protocol fail to meet the needs and desires of the rising progressive who is daily being exposed to Western ideas of democracy, free speech, and modern science. Regarding the relief and avoidance wants of innovators like these young Tonga progressives, H. G. Barnett has pointed out that

> many times they want a change of existing conditions because they experience physical or mental discomfort with those conditions. The motivation of such individuals is therefore to escape customary means, ends, and conditions by creating an alternative that is more congenial to their personal ideals or endowments (1953:156).

Secondary school graduates find the unhygienic conditions of their village almost intolerable. They may begin to insist upon drinking boiled water and eating cleaner food, which in itself constitutes a problem between the young and the old because it has always been held that sickness was not caused by germs or viruses but by *luwo lubi* (bad air) or by someone who has bewitched the victim. Sickness is caused by some *one* and is not due to some *thing*.

Probably the intolerability of village conditions is second only to the lure of more money and better jobs as a contributory factor in the migration of Tonga youth to the cities and the line of rail.

THE BREAKDOWN OF VILLAGES

The average size of Tonga villages is decreasing not only because of the rural-to-urban migration but also because of the raising of restrictions previously imposed by the colonial administration. Under British rule, rural Africans were required to congregate in villages of not less than ten taxable males to facilitate the collection of the annual poll tax and the implementation of other government decrees. Independence has allowed villagers more freedom to live where they please. Since the Tonga have always been inclined to resent dictatorial chiefs and headmen anyway, this new-found freedom has resulted in the scattering of village populations.

One informant, when asked why some individuals or individual households moved from village to village or to a separate dwelling altogether, responded with the following reasons:
1. To avoid the incessant quarreling which takes place when "one's chickens begin to hatch their eggs in someone else's hut."
2. To increase one's own personal wealth.
3. The individual dweller is a misfit who cannot get along with village population as a whole.

My own observation during 1968 was that the desire to increase one's personal wealth is the most dominant factor in this breakdown. Farmers are finding ready markets for their maize and peanuts, and to meet this demand for more and more produce, individual farmers need larger fields; to have the necessary space, the must spread out.

Another informant responded simply that more and more people are living where they want to since "this is now Zambia and we have our own government. No one can tell us where we must live now."

An old Christian headman who lives in Chief Musokotwane's chieftaincy recalls when there were very few villages in his area but "they were very big villages." In one area which I surveyed rather extensively in the chieftaincies of Nyawa and Musokotwane, there were forty-five villages within a radius of ten miles from the village of Mujalanyana. This is a very high density and is not typical of much of Tongaland, but many of these villages are small break-away groups from larger villages. The average number of men, women and children in each of these forty-five villages was 69.8 (Government Census 1963).

This breakdown of large villages is taking place constantly; villages which were large and compact two years ago now exist as scattered groups of from two to six huts but still call themselves by the original name of the village.

THE RISE OF MATERIALISM

The desire for material wealth and the acquisition of things is nowhere so distinctly observed as in the towns. Earning the necessary cash to purchase cars, radios, record players, furniture, and liquor preoccupies the thoughts and actions of most city dwellers. Accompanying this rapidly rising standard of living and the tide of materialism is the sharp increase of promiscuity and drunkenness.

Like many other African tribes, the Tonga are going through a period of rapid transition from old to new life ways, and many of the city dwellers have already made their transition to materialism. The society is fluid at present and the Church is confronted with a tremendous challenge. It is much harder to convert a materialist or a secularist than it is to win an animist.

A Tonga preacher was plainly discouraged by the fact that he had witnessed his congregation dwindle from 112 members five years ago to the 25 at the time of my visit. Why?

> They like the things of the world better than the words of God. The men are busy earning money or drinking beer; the women do not drink but they are always anxious to make drums of beer to sell to the men. In the old days, the women had to receive their money from their husbands; now, many earn their own money by selling beer.

A second minister substantiated this conclusion but was not as pessimistic about the influence of materialism. He believed that the failure to win people to Christ was not so much their preoccupation with materialism as it was the apparent inability of God's servants to back their words up with action. He put it this way:

> We as God's servants have been weaker than the servants of Satan; we have failed to show people our actions. It is easy to move the lips but difficult to do the works. We must be strong and win these lost people to Christ.

Among the Tonga I observed a definite increase in beer-drinking and drunkenness. As wages have gone up, so has the incidence of drunkenness.

THE CHANGING MARRIAGE PATTERNS

Dating back to the nineteenth century, when Tongaland was the raiding ground of warlike tribes from the south and west, the Tonga have been easygoing and have not shown much resentment toward other tribesmen who have settled in their tribal lands. Ngoni, Lozi, Bemba and Vale men have taken wives and settled down among the Tonga, but not until the past four years has there been any widespread intertribal marriage or intermingling of tribes.

Zambian nationalism and the mobility of government employees has paved the way for different attitudes toward marriage and social relationships. More progressive Tongas are taking up the cause of nationalism and raising its clarion cry of "One Zambia, one nation." The older, less educated element fears what the future may bring. Their social patterns are beginning to crumble about them. The cohesion of the tribe is threatened by intertribal marriage. No longer does one man know where another stands or what role each individual is to play in the whole. An older informant said sadly,

> This country is different now. There is a different *luwo* [spirit]; I do not know why it is here or where it has come from. Where have we made a mistake?

Marriage arrangements are often made at secondary school where all the students are required to speak English and where tribal differences and social restraints are diminished during the passion of the moment. No doubt intertribal marriages do take place occasionally, but I failed to find one which had taken place in a village. The intermingling generally occurs in towns or in small urban communities.

THE CHANGING SOCIAL ATTITUDES

The "little things" which "mean so much" in the lives of people, and which make life more pleasant and stable, are feeling the pressure of culture change. Relationships which have been maintained for centuries by status and prestige are experiencing stress. The old are frustrated by their "disrespectful" youth and the young people are embarrassed and angered by what they consider unnecessary rules and "old customs." One of two older informants volunteered the following:

Today the young people say to us, their elders, "These things [obviously their elders] are foolish because they are still afraid of the Europeans." It is not fear, it is only because we were taught to respect all men no matter how small he was. When an older man sends me on an errand I must and will carry out the errand out of respect. I would not think of doing otherwise. But today, our own children say to us, "Why are you sending me on an errand? Are you my father?" The *luwo* [spirit] today is very bad and we do not like it.

The second, who was listening to the first, offered this account:

I went to a village not far from here one day and was well received by the elders of the village. They brought me some food to eat and a chair to sit on. I received both respectfully and we were getting along fine. A young man walked up wearing a suit and tie. He said to me, "Old man, give me that chair." I gave him the chair I was sitting on. Someone asked me why I had given the young man my chair but before I could answer, the young man explained that he was wearing a nice suit and would spoil it if he had to sit on the ground. I left that village quickly without waiting to eat any more food. This is how the young people are today. Their *luwo* [spirit] is bad!

POLITICAL CHANGES

The Tonga had their first opportunity to elect a representative government in 1963, and they voted almost solidly for the African National Congress (ANC) (Hall 1966:227). The ANC leader, Harry Nkumbula, was an Ila from the Southern Province and most Tonga considered him one of them. Their loyalty was built along tribal lines. Since 1963, however, remarkable changes have taken place. With the increasing rural-to-urban traffic and the shifting of government employees from other tribes into Tongaland, there has been a noticeable breakdown in the ANC stronghold. Blind loyalty to one political party has been replaced by an open, more democratic attitude toward representative government. Progressives hold the position that it is no longer so much a matter of which tribe or party a political candidate belongs to as how productive he is in terms of social reform.

The gulf which has grown between the young and the old in Tonga society can also be observed in the political realm. Young Tongas tend to join the ruling United National Independence Party (UNIP) while the older people still staunchly support the ANC. Members of the ANC consider their party the original party, or the "father of all parties," in Zambia. They are loyal to Harry Nkumbula because "he started us on the road to ruling ourselves," but I believe the tribal connection is the most significant factor in this loyalty. The young, on the other hand, see UNIP as standing for progress, development, and leadership. Politics are altering the face of Tonga society rapidly.

These are some of the forces and pressures which are bringing about rapid change among the Tonga. The Church must respond to the challenge of "being where the action is" in order to provide stability and meaning for thousands of people who are in the process of making a big transition.

Urban churches must be the spiritual home for the socially dislocated who are trying to adapt as quickly as possible to a new way of life. The anonymity of city life causes strong Christians to become weak and weak Christians to revert simply because there is no one to restrain, no one to encourage, no one with whom to have real fellowship.

PART TWO

The History of Tonga Missions

5

The Coming of the Churches of Christ

EARLY BEGINNINGS AND PROMINENT PIONEERS

The first converts to become members of the Churches of Christ in Tongaland were, unlike most missions in Zambia, won by African preachers. The entire evangelistic program of the Church was carried on by nationals for thirteen years before the arrival of an American missionary in 1923.

The first church was planted by Peter Masiya at the village of Mukuni near Livingstone in 1910. Masiya was an Nsenga tribesman from Nyasaland (now Malawi) who had been converted to Christianity in 1909 while employed as a laborer in John Sherriff's stoneyard in Bulawayo, Rhodesia. Sherriff, a stone mason by trade and a native New Zealander, had come to Rhodesia in the 1890's and opened up a stoneyard after failing as a prospector. His business prospered and by 1922 he was able to give his full time to mission work. He converted his business partner at Bulawayo, and others whom he contacted (Hobby 1945).

Following approximately one year of intensive Bible training and study while at the same time fulfilling his duties at the stoneyard, Masiya was sent by Sherriff to preach north of the Zambezi River in what was then Northern Rhodesia. Masiya preached mainly in Mukuni and Mujala villages and succeeded in planting substantial churches in both villages. He was unpaid and itinerated widely. He could not speak Tonga fluently, but his burning zeal and dedication to his Lord bridged many of the communication barriers. Arriving in Tongaland shortly after a raid by Lozi and Ndebele warriors, he found the villagers receptive to his message. After decades of strife and uncertainty they were willing to accept a message of peace and hope.

So successful were the evangelistic efforts of Peter Masiya that when W. N. Short, the first foreign missionary, arrived in 1923, two small but strong churches already existed at Mukuni and Mujala with a total membership of 200 communicants. W. N. Short established Sinde Mission on a thousand-acre farm shortly after moving to Northern Rhodesia in 1923, but Masiya did not live to witness the development of the mission station. Although his life came to an end in 1923, his dreams have lived on in the lives of his converts, whom he had so diligently trained to preach. Among his converts were Kambole Mpatamatenga and his wife, Mafuta Simbeza, and Mujalanyana. All were baptized the same day in 1918 and, with the exception of Mujalanyana, have been strong and faithful leaders in the church ever since.

Kambole Mpatamatenga (upon whose firsthand accounts much of this chapter is based) had been a cook for a government medical doctor in Livingstone for many years, but after his conversion became an interpreter for W. N. Short. After working with Short for three years, Mpatamatenga was appointed schoolteacher of the first primary school started by Churches of Christ at Siamundele village. He taught for six years before beginning his self-supported preaching ministry along the Ngwezi River. In 1968 at the approximate age of 75 years, Mpatamatenga still supported himself by cultivating the largest maize crop in his area. An amazing man of God with only six grades of formal education to his credit, he is the author of two manuscripts (one of which has been published) and carries on his daily Bible study in three languages.

Three years after Sinde Mission among the Toka had been established, the decision was made to open a second mission station in Chief Simwatachela's chieftaincy at Kabanga. An application was made to the government administration and permission was granted in 1927 for J. D. Merritt and Ray Lawyer to establish the work at Kabanga. All travel and communication were by foot or ox-cart; consequently the work of construction proceeded slowly. Staff was scarce and the missionaries overworked. To complicate matters further, tragedy struck when Lawyer tripped and fell on a hunting spear and died before his wounds could receive adequate medical attention.

Namwianga Mission among the Plateau Tonga was established in 1932 by W. L. Brown, who had begun his missionary service at Kabanga three years earlier. In later years this was to become the largest station, where most of the missionaries were based and a major share of the funds were used to construct school buildings and missionary dwellings. Although Churches of Christ uphold the local autonomy of churches and maintain no headquarters, due to circumstances which were not easy to control, the Africans gradually came to recognize Namwianga as "headquarters" simply because of the concentration of money and missionaries at that location.

MAP 3

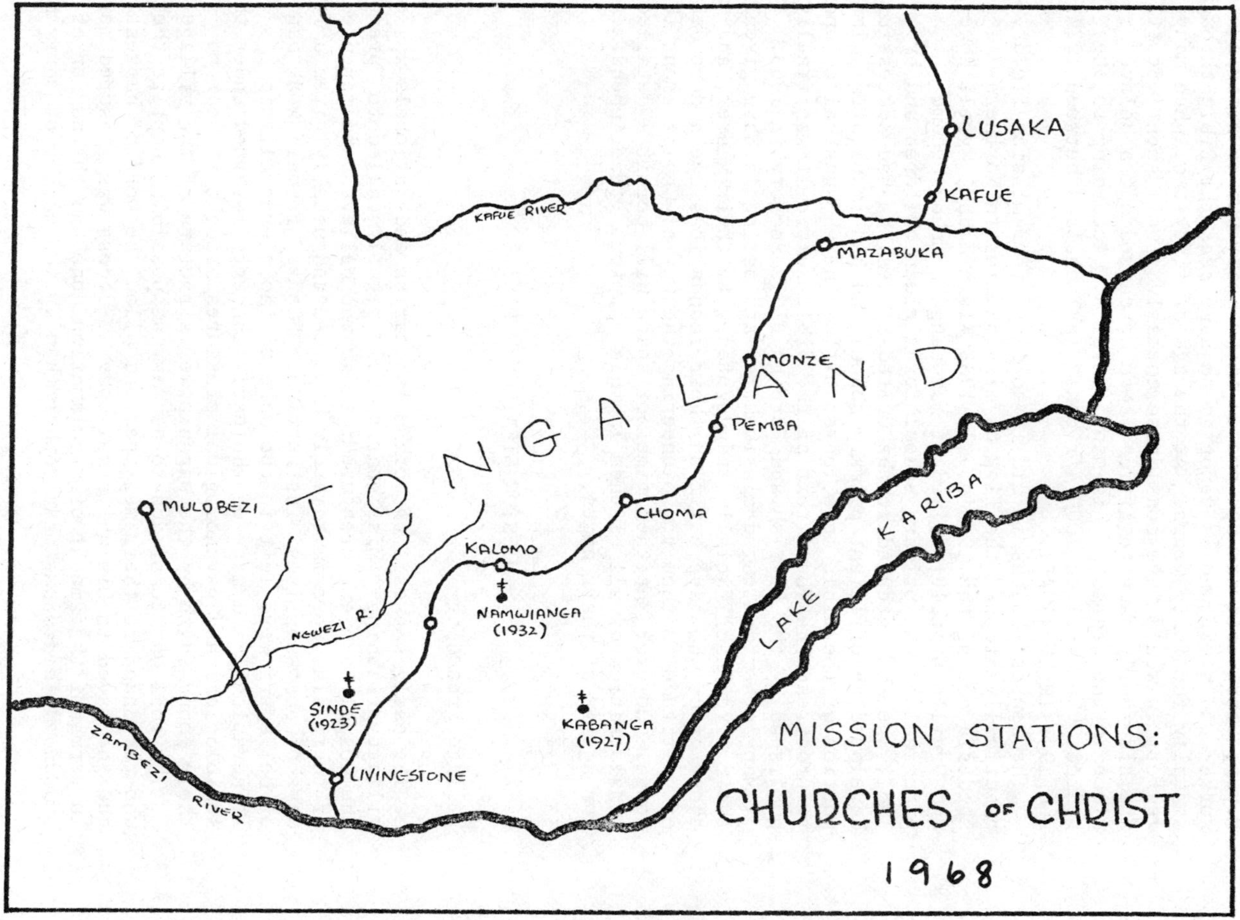
LUSAKA
KAFUE
MAZABUKA
KAFUE RIVER
MONZE
TONGALAND
PEMBA
CHOMA
KALOMO
MULOBEZI
NAMWIANGA
(1932)
NGWEZI R.
LAKE KARIBA
SINDE
(1923)
KABANGA
(1927)
LIVINGSTONE
ZAMBEZI RIVER
MISSION STATIONS:
CHURCHES OF CHRIST
1968

In 1927 George Scott came to labor among the Tonga. It was not long before Scott had developed a close relationship with the nationals and his extensive itineration has never been forgotten. An old Tonga Christian recalled with much pleasure that "there was not a village in this area [along the Ngwezi River] that Scott did not preach in." Scott was a prodigious worker and a man who is reported to have read the Bible through annually for forty years. At the age of fifty-two, when many lesser men would have considered themselves well spent, Scott and his family came to Africa where he carved out a beloved place in the hearts of his many converts. According to one source, "he baptized 1000 Africans" in Tongaland between 1927 and 1941 (Hobby 1945).

The Depression, as it did in so many other mission fields, practically stopped the flow of missionaries to Northern Rhodesia during the 1930's. In 1938 Alvin Hobby, Myrtle Rowe, and Orville Brittle arrived at Namwianga. Hobby became principal of the primary school for African children and by 1961, when he returned to the United States, he had successfully developed an efficient primary school and had translated a large portion of the Bible into Tonga. It was he who was called upon to proofread the Tonga text of the Bible before it was finally published by the British and Foreign Bible Society in 1963.

Many other dedicated missionaries and nationals have given their lives sacrificially and devotedly to their Master, and those of us who have built on their foundations owe a deep debt of gratitude to them for pioneering the way of Christ among the Tonga. However, neither time nor space will permit a detailed consideration of all of them in this chapter. (See Appendix A for a list of their names.)

MISSION STRATEGY: PAST

Village Preaching

The early emphasis of both missionaries and nationals was on village preaching. Missionaries felt rightly called to "preach the Gospel to every creature"; those who believed and repented of their sins were immediately baptized and usually given a few days of post-baptismal instruction. Scores of small weak bands of believers were left in the wake of their evangelistic itinerations, and many of the early converts reverted under the sociological and psychological pressures brought to bear on their young faith by the pagan power structure of the village.

The goal was to preach to as many as possible, baptize those who responded to their message, and allow the Lord of harvest to add the saved to His universal body. Success was measured more in terms of the amount of proclamation done and the number of *individual decisions* made rather than by the number of *churches planted.* Consequently, several hundred individuals were baptized in a few years but very few of these new converts found themselves in an independent and growing New Testament fellowship. Little stress appears to have been put upon vital, corporate church life. Each individual Christian was an island, and once the missionary left his village the tidal waves of ridicule and ostracism overwhelmed him. Although numerous accounts tell of individual decisions made in many villages, there is no record of a complete social unit either having been sought or having become Christian at the same time such as we read of in Acts. The missionaries had little idea--perhaps no idea--of the social structure. At that stage they could not have known of it.

Practically all of the pre-World War II missionaries itinerated widely and were well known for their preaching tours throughout the rural areas of southern Tongaland. This is truly commendable in view of the means of travel which were available to them in those days. George Scott was reported to have gone just about everywhere with his Model T Ford and a roll of wire for repairs. For almost two decades after the arrival of the first missionary in 1923, village preaching and teaching continued to be the main emphasis.

Interpreters were used almost exclusively by these early missionaries because, with all that so desperately needed to be done, there seemed to be little time for language study. Besides, mastery of the Tonga language was not considered a prerequisite to effective communication.

A fluent interpreter was "more to be desired than fine gold" and was generally believed to be an adequate means of conveying the gospel message. In spite of the fact that some of the missionaries came to realize the basic weakness in the system (as evidenced by such remarks as, "The interpreter and I both presented good lessons today, but they were not the same sermon."), these interpreters continued to be used. It is even said that on one occasion a missionary actually fell asleep while the interpreter was translating his last thought!

Instead of interpreters being used for a short interim period during which time the missionary was gaining a working knowledge of the language, they became perpetual crutches upon which the missionary continued to support his message and ministry. Because of so many other pressing responsibilities which consumed his time, he soon discovered that it was far less demanding to use the crutch than to learn the language.

The following three reasons have been most often given for not learning the language. All three have to do with the lack of time:
1. We are too old to assume the task of learning a new language.
2. We can give only a few years to mission work; therefore, these years should be used to preach and teach as much as

possible.
3. It is senseless to spend up to two years learning Tonga when all the Africans will be speaking English in a few years anyway.

Whatever the reasons given for not acquiring a good working knowledge of the language, the facts show that *only one* of the pre-World War II missionaries learned and used Tonga consistently in his preaching and day-to-day contacts. The post-World War II picture is not much better. *Only three* missionaries in this period have used the vernacular language in their daily interaction with the nationals! This has been one of the most serious weaknesses of past mission strategy.

Eugene Nida has stated the case against the use of interpreters very well when he writes in his book, *Learning a Foreign Language*:

> If interpreters are not good, they are doubly bad, for they interrupt the flow of the message and fail to reveal its contents. If interpreters are good, then they can more profitably be trained to do the speaking themselves, following the instructions and suggestions of the missionary. Only those who have been forced to use interpreters can understand the fatal effects of such a procedure upon the message, for it is not so much the words uttered by the preacher as the fire burning within his soul which actually kindles conviction in others. For the most part, interpreters cannot communicate this characteristic of the personality (1957:3).

Mission Schools

The missionaries began to reconsider the effectiveness of village preaching in the late 1930's. The tours yielded fewer responses, the initial novelty had worn off, and there was an extremely high percentage of reversion among their converts. A note of discouragement is evident in the writing of one missionary:

> The work of the evangelist is hard, whether he is a native or a white missionary, and the problems are many. Perhaps the greatest discouragement is seeing so many be baptized and then backslide. In this work we are working as it were in Satan's own backyard, and it takes all the patience and faith one can command.

A theological basis was used to support the gradual shift from preaching to teaching. From Jesus' statement in Matthew 28:18-20, it was argued that teaching was "one of the most important phases of a missionary's work. Logically, perhaps it must precede the work of preaching." Slowly but surely, schools began to be used as the main tool of evangelism because it was felt that if students could be exposed to the Bible every day, "God's word would not return unto Him void," and much stronger Christians would result.

Requests for village schools poured in from headmen and villagers, and there were more opportunities than money to provide schools in the villages. But as time and funds permitted, schools were bult and supervision assumed by the missionaries. Secular studies were taught along with the daily class in Bible "to bring the African out of darkness and raise his level of enlightenment."

Along with the expansion of the schools system came the need for more teachers. Missionaries believed that "untold good could be done" if Christian teachers could be placed in every classroom. School enrollment grew to a peak of three thousand students in twenty-one schools, and teacher-training institutions were not able to produce enough staff for all the new schools. A teacher-training program was initiated at Namwianga Mission which "presented opportunities for not only teaching and converting the students themselves, but also national teachers and preachers could be developed and sent to teach and preach to their own people." The same writer added these comments concerning the status of the program in 1945:

> Most, if not all of the African missionaries, would no doubt heartily agree that one of the greatest needs, if not the greatest, on the African field today is a sufficient number of properly trained African teachers to carry on the work in the village schools, as well as part of the work on the mission station. We cannot say, to our chagrin, that the African is very keen to be Christianized. But we can say emphatically that he is keen for education. The cry is for more and more schools, which do give us incidentally perhaps the most effective means we have of evangelizing the African, even if many do not have this as an aim for going to school.

By 1947, another missionary wrote:

> Namwianga had grown in status, in knowledge, and in spirit . . . Teacher training had been added on the mission.
> Native teachers are going out every year opening schools and starting congregations in the villages. Our building program had made great strides (Rowe 1967:173).

The teacher training program at Namwianga produced a sizeable number of faithful and dedicated teachers who lived Christlike lives in the village communities where they were teachers. Some even became outstanding church leaders, but others did not fare so well.

As the school system grew and educational standards became

more rigid, the Mission discovered that it was becoming almost impossible to place dedicated Christian teachers in every school. Some were immoral and aroused resentment among the village inhabitants toward themselves and the Mission. Because teachers' salaries were by that time being paid by the government, it was difficult for the Mission to take effective disciplinary action. Relations between missionaries and national teachers became strained and it was quite apparent that the village primary schools were developing into more of a liability than an asset. Finally, in June, 1965, nineteen village schools which had been maintained and supervised by the Mission were turned over to the government. What had once proved a strength, and a program which had occupied the minds and energies of most of the missionary force, began to crumble. An air of pessimism and uncertainty pervaded the Mission as it attempted to evaluate the past and plan for the future.

John V. Taylor in his book, *The Primal Vision*, indicates that Churches and Missions all over Africa have depended upon an educational program but that times are changing and much reassessment is taking place regarding the Church's *real* role in Africa:

> For forty years and more the advance of the Christian Church in tropical Africa has depended more upon her virtual monopoly of Western education than upon any other factor. Today secular governments are taking that monopoly from her and it is a bitter irony that the factor which seemed to be Christianity's greatest strength in Africa threatens to prove its heaviest liability. For to a great extent, it has become a classroom religion (1963:20).

The year 1965 was a year of decision for the Mission. It had had an educational emphasis for so long that there seemed to be no alternative to more education. Some argued that "forty years of toil would be wasted unless we could offer a secondary school" or that "the government would no longer allow the Mission to work in Zambia if it did not offer a school or a hospital." The decision was made to open a new secondary school which would be operated with missionary personnel and money donated by overseas supporters.

By objectively analyzing the past mission strategy of the Churches of Christ, it is possible to make the following observations:

1. Direct evangelism, which failed to win the power structure, failed to teach those individuals won, and failed to form them into ongoing congregations, seemed a poor method of mission.

2. Teaching (i.e., education) replaced direct evangelism as the chief mode of mission.

3. Nationals interpreted this shift to mean that education is more important than church planting.

4. Missionaries became increasingly confined by administrative duties to mission stations.

5. They became isolated from villagers and their spiritual needs.

6. This minimized contact with Africans and enhanced the missionaries' feelings of racial superiority.

7. Year after year the young were educated and baptized while the older men and women were largely neglected and not evangelized.

8. Students have used mission-operated schools as stepping stones from the village to positions in the cities, where an overwhelming percentage has been lost.

MISSION STRATEGY: PRESENT

Churches and Missions are now operating in a different Africa than that of five to ten years ago. Their policies have been altered at many points, and changes have had to be made both voluntarily and under duress. Mission strategy of the Churches of Christ has not been unaffected by the winds of change which have blown and are continuing to blow across the face of independent Africa.

As was mentioned earlier, the hand-over of nineteen village schools to the government in 1965 brought with it the feeling that the Mission had run its course unless some new program could be initiated to take the place of village education. By July of that year all that remained of the Mission's educational program was one small predominantly white and two mission-station "African" primary schools, so plans were immediately laid for a Christian secondary school at Namwianga. Applications were submitted to the proper government educational authorities and with permission granted, Namwianga Christian College enrolled its first class in January 1966, using temporary facilities.

Appeals were made to churches and individuals in America to underwrite the expensive new project and a board of trustees was selected to publicize and raise support for the new "Christian college" in Zambia. American brethren responded generously and it was not long before enough money had been pledged to allow construction to begin.

Past experience had shown that when the Mission accepted government subsidies it also relinquished some of its control, so in order to forestall government control of "our Christian school" it was decided that all the funds should be raised by the Mission and its supporters. Construction of the $200,000 complex was thus begun in early 1968 and scheduled for completion in time for the opening of the new year in January 1969. The Mission has, therefore, with much sacrifice and financial expenditure, made the switch from the primary to the secondary level in its educational program.

The distribution of mission resources is still heavily weighted in favor of education. At the time of this survey in 1968, facts showed that 88.9 percent of the total missionary force of the Churches of Christ was engaged in one way or another in education and little direct evangelism was being done. The missionaries, who were confined to classrooms for five days per week, found that only their weekends were available for preaching and visits among the village churches. A few of them found this imbalance extremely frustrating. One remarked,

> There is nothing very spiritual about teaching eight classes of math every day. I do not have even one class of Bible and somehow this is not what I had planned to do before I came to the mission field. No time or opportunity is available to do what is most important.

Even though mission policy is still mission-station centered and to a large extent missionary controlled, there is evidence of a greater desire to identify with the nationals. Africans are being asked into missionary homes for meals and lodging and nationals are reciprocating by extending invitations to their white brethren. This represents a very recent trend and was seldom practiced prior to 1966. After being invited to spend the night in a certain mission-station home which had traditionally been off-limits to "black people," a national church leader was overheard to gasp incredulously: "I am amazed' Certainly a revolution must have taken place here if it is indeed true that I am to sleep in that house!" And as he thanked his missionary host for his invitation he was visibly moved by the new warmth which had begun to flow from heart to heart for the first time.

The following was typical of many statements made by young missionaries who now have an intense desire to identify and fellowship closely with the national people:

> We have not had the real fellowship with the African brethren that we should have had. We have been afraid to eat their food and sleep in their huts. We are above them

and they resent it.
   When we lived at Kabanga Mission, we invited one of the African preachers in to eat with us. He actually cried as he told us that this house had been built in 1927, but that this *was the first time he had ever been inside it.*

Case after case could be cited in which the air of colonialism and paternalism has pervaded many of our past missionary efforts, but this is an area in which present attitudes represent a decisive break from the past.

AN ASSESSMENT

I have described the missionary policies of the Churches of Christ since 1910. Of necessity this historical sketch is brief and somewhat critical, but my prayer is that as we missionaries courageously admit our past mistakes and rejoice in our victories we may be enabled to see more clearly the real goals and opportunities which lie ahead.
Living and working as we are in a radically new Africa requires some ruthless scraping of outmoded methods and principles.
Throughout the last forty-five years of its history among the Tonga, the Church has been very mission-station centered. The trend which began under colonialism has continued and Leslie T. Lyall rightly describes the colonial era as preeminently the era of mission institutions. He declares:

> . . . independent governments will scarcely tolerate indefinitely the education of their children by foreigners. They will be sensitive as well about foreigners caring for the health of their people because they have failed to do so themselves. In short, such institutions will certainly be taken over gradually from missions by the national governments (1966:71).

In the wake of these government takeovers of mission institutions many missionaries are wringing their hands in despair because they now have nothing to do. With no geography classes to teach, no patients to treat and no more buildings to erect, the institutional missionary often feels that he is no longer useful. He senses little appreciation for his long years of sacrifice and toil for the African people and usually foresees little hope for the future.
   Instead of feeling rejected, we missionaries should rejoice that the national governments are now willing and quite capable of assuming the responsibility for the education and health of their own people. Or, as F. B. Welbourn suggests:

Perhaps churches have, for many years, been expending men
and money on providing a secular education with very little
in the way of "religious" results. These resources might
be better used in other areas of society (1965:91).

Mission schools have so often been a type of bait which has
attracted students and then provided the golden key to the
middle classes. Students are willing to endure almost anything
to get an education and may even comply superficially with the
forms and rituals of their teachers, but afterwards reject the
faith of their teachers (McGavran 1965:140). Welbourn again
says that

> there is no evidence to suggest that the products of mission
> schools are any more firmly Christian than those of
> government schools. The supporters of the view that a
> Christian education can be given only in schools managed by
> the Church, must be asked whether the facts support their
> thesis (1965:88).

With the burden of schools and hospitals lifted, the Church
can advance unencumbered by these subsidiary activities which
sap her resources and blind her eyes to the real task at hand,
that of winning receptive men and women--and above all
receptive groups--to Christ and allowing Him to add them to His
glorious Body. Let us break out of the isolated cocoonlike
environment of our mission stations and *move to where the people
are who need the message of Jesus Christ!* The conflict for the
souls of men moves from one place to another on the field of
battle and we must, as faithful ministers of the Word and
courageous soldiers of the cross, shake ourselves loose from
our introverted stations and go quickly to where the battle is
really being fought.

6

Other Churches and Missions

Almost five decades elapsed after David Livingstone's journeys through what is now Zambia before a permanent foothold was gained by Missions among the Tonga. The tireless missionary had with good will and compassion certainly paved the way for others to follow, but because of debilitating disease and a multitude of discouraging episodes, Missions were hindered from really getting started until the Primitive Methodists established Sijoba Mission among the We of the Gwembe Valley in 1901. The Jesuits had previously been unsuccessful in starting their work among the Tonga.

Most of the earliest Missions began during the first decade of the twentieth century. Three years after the arrival of the Primitive Methodists, the Paris Missionary Society began working at Livingstone among the Leya. The seven years between 1904 and 1911 saw the opening of six more stations (Rotberg 1965a:152).

In this chapter we will look briefly at the history of each Mission or Church, describe the status of each Church as of 1968, and summarize the reactions and attitudes of the respective mission representatives regarding the future of their particular Missions.

THE ANGLICAN CHURCH (UMCA)

The Church of England founded its Northern Rhodesia Diocese in 1909 and entrusted the work of the Universities' Mission to Central Africa (UMCA) to it. J. E. Hine was appointed the first bishop and in April 1911, he established the headquarters for the UMCA at Mapanza Mission. A cathedral was built in 1912 but Mapanza and the surrounding area were estined to prove hard to crack. One of the UMCA bishops described the work at Mapanza as "an uphill job--probably one of the stiffest in the Mission." The Tonga just were not very responsive (Smith 1928a:92-93).

Smith records that in 1928 there were four out-stations situated around Mapanza, five European missionaries, six African workers, and a total of 118 communicants. Apparently the early years between 1911 and 1928 were discouraging times and were likely responsible for the switch to a heavy institutional program at the Mission. By 1928 one hospital, a dispensary, a day school and a college were already in operation (1928a:191).

The Anglicans have continued to emphasize social action for the past forty years and now have highly developed secondary and hospital facilities at Mapanza. They have realized comparatively small growth of their communicant membership. Whereas in 1928 they had a communicant membership of 118 they now have a total of 1609, most of whom are children attending their schools. At present four missionaries and twelve national ministers are taking care of the pastoral and parochial needs of their twenty-six churches.

I was informed that the UMCA Mission among the Tonga has relied heavily upon their schools and hospitals throughout its history, but that the Mission is now in the process of handing over all of its primary schools to the government. The Anglican sisters are also being withdrawn from the hospital and plans are underway for transferring its training centers to government control.

Two of my informants, who were responsible representatives of the UMCA at Mapanza, stated that the main problems facing their Church are polygyny and the equating of church and school by the people. When asked about the official policy of the Church concerning polygyny, the priest-in-charge replied:

> We are very severe on polygamists who become so after they are church members. The official stand of the Church regarding the baptism of polygamists is that in a polygamous marriage, the first wife is baptizable but the man and his junior wives are not.

He went on to add:

> The Church is dying because older Christians who were baptized many years ago have left the Church because they have become polygamous. The women who have married these men have also left the Church because they know what the Church believes about polygamy.

As a result, much of the adult membership is being eliminated and the small "school churches" have trained insufficient leadership and supplied inadequate nourishment. Consequently, the burden of pastoral care still falls upon the mission-station staff which already carries a heavy load of administrative and educational duties.

The fact that the people have come to equate "church" with "school" is a difficult problem for the Church. The older people regard it as an insult to be invited to a church which is composed almost entirely of children, and because of a misunderstanding of the differences between church and school, one generally finds that when the school closes for vacation, the church also ceases to assemble.

There is little conversion growth taking place among the adult pagan population. Adult members of the Church are generally former primary school students who were baptized many years ago in one of the "school churches."

Migration was specifically mentioned as one of the main causes of the numerical decrease in many of the Anglican congregations. Due to the fact that these congregations are composed mainly of primary school children, the size of each church is affected quite adversely when the children leave their villages in search of higher education. Secondary schools are still scarce and widely scattered in Zambia and the students may find it necessary to travel hundreds of miles to school. They are at an impressionable age and many of them lose their religious and social moorings while at school.

The following evaluation by an Anglican missionary concerning the present status of his Mission was very much to the point when he said:

> We have emphasized social work too much. The nationals are throwing off the shackles which we have maintained on schools and hospitals.
> When we ask our people "What has the Church brought you?" or "What difference have you seen in your life since the coming of the Church?" they answer, "Why the Church has brought us all these schools and hospitals." *They see nothing else!*
> We must begin to preach the resurrection morning, noon and night, and we need to start itinerating.

It was quite noticeable that he was dissatisfied with the paternalistic institutionalism which had been the policy of his Mission for so long. He predicted that

> with the present course of action there is little hope for the Church. It is an externally supported institution. It is totally foreign. We would do well to get back to the Bible. I think the Church is in for a bad future.

Three different informants said that their Church was dying.

Two of the missionaries could see no hope for the future unless the present course of action was altered. Having been heavily committed for so long to institutionalism, its ministers despaired of the future. With their schools and hospitals now in government hands, they felt unneeded and unwanted. One of the missionaries believes that there are two directions which are possible for his Mission to follow. The first course of action would be to offer some alternative social service, presumably in an area in which the national government is still unable to provide adequately for its people. This direction seemed to be the most favored by the higher officials of the Mission. The second possibility would be to institute and expand the "pastoral and parochial" programs; which was what one of the missionary informants desired. In other words, he was reexamining his role as a minister and felt keenly that he should be engaged in active and aggressive pastoral work.

While the Anglican Church has a greater communicant membership than do Churches of Christ (1909 communicants to 1200) and has perhaps had at least some better trained missionaries, they too appear to have experienced the detrimental deceits of school-based churches.

The detailed picture of the Churches of Christ in Chapter V reveals something of the character of most Churches and Missions in Zambia. Differences do exist, but it would be easy defensively to overestimate them.

THE BRETHREN IN CHRIST (BC)

Two women, Miss Adda G. Engle and Miss H. Frances Davidson, were responsible for starting the Brethren in Christ work in 1906. They courageously traveled northward from what was then Southern Rhodesia and began working at Macha, on the Plateau. Their efforts were particularly directed toward girls, and the Mission has been noted from its earliest beginnings for its contribution to the "forgotten ones" of Tonga society.

Seventeen years after the founding of the first Mission in 1906, a second station was started at Sikalongo to the south, also among the Plateau Tonga. Once again great importance was given to a program for girls.

Edwin W. Smith, in his 1928 summary of Northern Rhodesian Missions, reported that the Brethren in Christ had

> . . . two stations, seven out-stations, eight European workers (including two nurses), thirty-two African workers, 195 communicants, 100 catechumens, seven schools with seventy pupils. About twenty men go about evangelizing, without pay, one Sunday out of every month (Smith 1928a:91).

He also quoted the 1924 Macha Report as saying that

wherever there is a school we soon see a big difference in
the Natives. They become more open to the Gospel, and there
is soon a kindly love and feeling springs up among the
Natives and the missionary (1928a:91).

The Brethren in Christ Mission has followed this course
throughout its history and has committed most of its resources
to educational and medical services. Macha station started with
an evangelistic program in cooperation with a school and was
followed soon afterward with a hospital.

In 1968 the BC Mission had forty-eight preaching points,
forty-three of which are at school sites. Of the forty-eight
preachers, thirty-five are teachers--"the rest are just pastors."
One of the higher officials of the Mission in Zambia informed me
that

> all the way through our mission program there has been an
> educational emphasis. We are still managing our primary
> schools, we are operating Choma Secondary School in Choma
> and are making application for two more secondary schools.

Apparently, instead of de-escalating its institutional
program like most of its sister missions in Zambia, the BC
Mission is expanding its educational work and continuing its
management of primary schools.

The local churches which have been planted by the BC are
divided into two districts, each with its own superintendent.
In the Macha district there are twenty-nine village congregations and one mission-station church. There are seventeen
village and one mission-station church in the Sikalongo
district.

TABLE 1

Local Congregations of the Brethren in Christ Mission
1968

	Number of Village Churches	Mission Stations	Members	Average Church Membership
Macha District	29	--	484	16.7
(Macha Mission)	--	1	200	200.0
Sikalongo District	17	--	374	22.0
(Sikalongo Mission)	--	1	42	42.0
TOTALS	46	2	1100	Average 22.9

Map 4

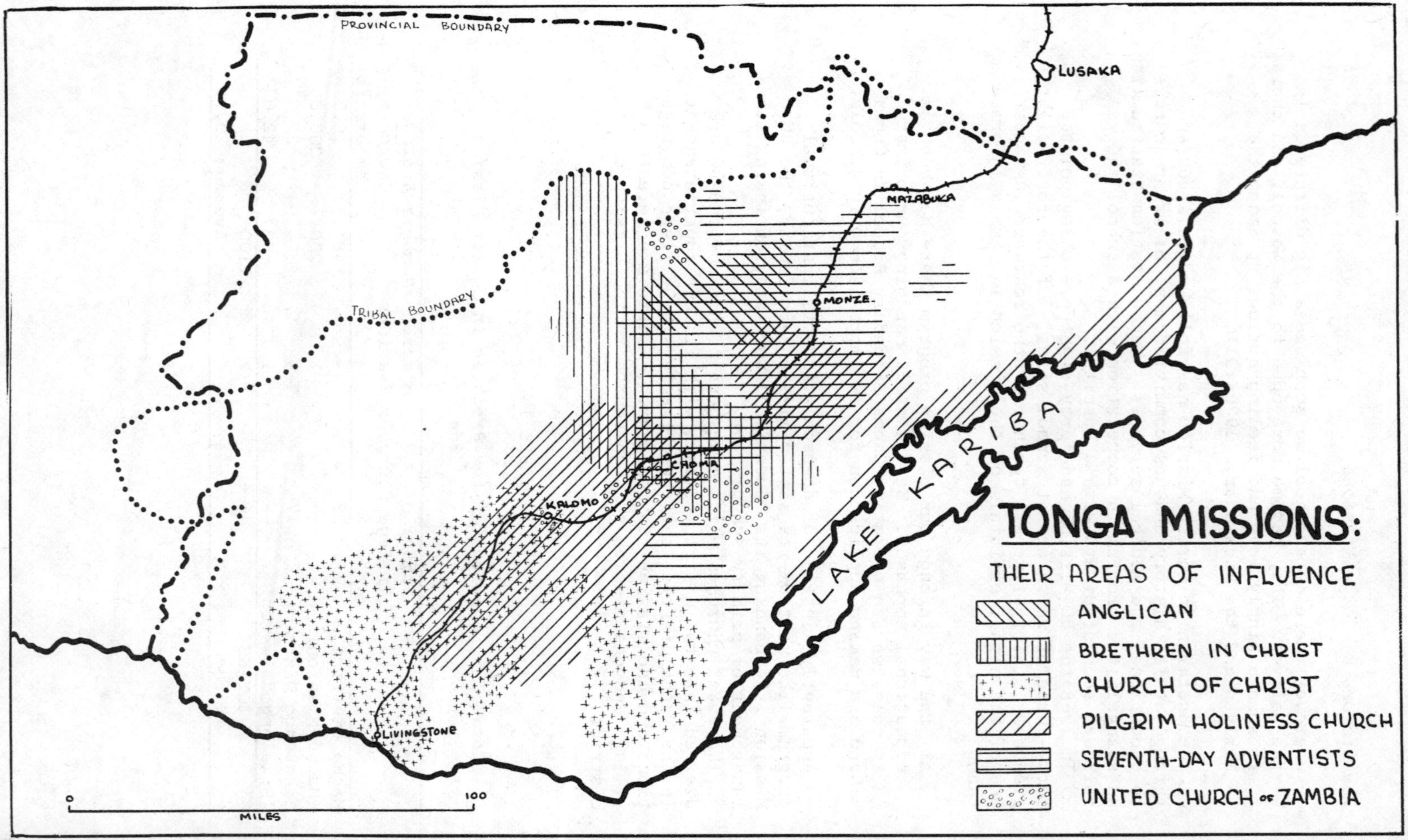

PROVINCIAL BOUNDARY
LUSAKA
MAZABUKA
TRIBAL BOUNDARY
MONZE
CHOMA
KALOMO
LIVINGSTONE
LAKE KARIBA
TONGA MISSIONS:
THEIR AREAS OF INFLUENCE
ANGLICAN
BRETHREN IN CHRIST
CHURCH OF CHRIST
PILGRIM HOLINESS CHURCH
SEVENTH-DAY ADVENTISTS
UNITED CHURCH of ZAMBIA
0
100
MILES

In October of each year the two district superintendents count their church members and submit these totals to the bishop at the Choma headquarters. The 1967 figures indicated that there were 1100 communicant members and 524 catechumens. Catechumens formerly were required to receive two years of teaching before membership was allowed, but I was told that "we are now beginning to relax this position."

The membership of BC churches is composed almost entirely of children because of the overwhelming emphasis upon schools, but the small adult element in the congregations is more male than female. The converts are predominantly Tonga because of the rural nature of the Church as a whole. Only in the city churches does s tribal intermingling occur.

The Mission is operating a large religious bookstore in Choma which is making a significant contribution to the dissemination of good Christian books, and certainly at a time when Africa wants to read, this vital provision must be made. It has often been said that Christian Missions have taught Africa to read, but communism has supplied the literature. The time is more than ripe for the Churches to step up their literature programs.

I encountered considerable diversity of opinion among the BC missionaries, for even while the Mission is planning a significant expansion of its educational program there is a growing reaction within their ranks toward the preponderance of social service at the expense of direct evangelism. One spokesman bluntly stated:

> Many of the younger missionary teachers are disillusioned about what they are doing. They want to get into the villages and preach, but cannot find the time to do it. Some have even said, "All we are doing is making clever sinners out of our students." Institutionalism kills one spiritually. Young missionaries come out to the field with great spiritual fervor and are thrust into a school. There they become frustrated and lose their "cutting edge."

The school system is still supported by the Mission, instead of the national Church assuming the responsibility and burden of its own institutions. Control remains firmly in the hands of the Mission, and nothing illustrates this better than the ratio of missionary to national minister. There are forty foreign to only forty-eight national ministers.

Due to the widespread receptivity to their message which some of the BC missionaries have experienced on their evangelistic visits to the villages, a good deal of reassessment is taking place in their minds with respect to the future role that they will play in the overall mission program. One said, "There is a revolution in the making and one of the most encouraging things we can observe now is the questioning of the status quo by some of the newer missionaries."

It is clear that far from a Christian program which has communicated the Gospel to a whole countryside in hundreds of churches, the BC has a few small sealed-off churches which, chained to the school system, seem powerless to spread the fragrance of Christ in the villages and *mukowa*s of the land. They will remain powerless unless very soon a new and effective form of evangelization is launched.

THE PILGRIM HOLINESS CHURCH (PHC)

This Mission, like the Brethren in Christ, was also started by two women. They arrived at Pemba in 1934. The next year Jembo Mission was established fourteen miles southeast of Pemba. Harry Reynolds was appointed the first missionary-in-charge of what was to become the largest PHC mission station in the world.

To indicate the early direction of the PHC work, by 1934 two schools had already been started, to be followed the next year by a mission school at Jembo. The PHC has always held to the conviction that education is the door-opener to the community. The school has opened the door through which the Church has entered.

Four mission stations were planted by the Church between 1935 and 1956 and around these central institutions were developed schools and churches. In addition to the stress on education, recent years have also seen an expansion of the medical program. From the inadequately staffed dispensaries of the early days, the Mission today has built hospitals at each of its four mission stations.

By December 1967, the Mission controlled fifty-one primary schools with a total enrollment of almost nine thousand students. During 1966 and 1967 alone the Pilgrims cooperated with the government in the erection of 250 new school buildings. But finally the decision was made to turn over the village primary schools to the government because they had ceased to be effective. The transfer was completed in January 1968. Only the four mission-station schools were retained.

The results of the handover have been far reaching. First of all, a large percentage of the missionary force which had been confined by administrative duties has been released to expand the evangelistic program. Secondly, the PHC Field Superintendent believes that the transfer of the schools has given the Church a truer picture of itself.

> The older people are beginning to ask, "Where is the Church?" They are really getting concerned. All the missionaries are getting out of unnecessary duties and devoting their time to evangelistic work. We have begun to put real emphasis upon evangelism now.

Most recent figures show that the PHC has forty national preachers ministering in fifty-five churches with a total communicant membership of 2,793. Although this figure was quoted by the Field Superintendent, he hastened to add that the rolls would probably be cut 50 percent following a closer examination which was in progress at the time of this survey. He implied that the evangelistic program had suffered considerably from lack of attention and organization but that now more of the missionary personnel would be free to devote their time to church planting. He was optimistic about the future of his Mission and was looking forward to revival in the churches and to the sharing of more responsibility with the national brethren. In his own words: "We desperately need revival. We have a large percentage of people who are unfaithful. We are moving toward local discipline in the local church."

National ministers are being trained on a small scale at the Pilgrim Bible Institute located at Jembo Mission. It presently provides three different courses: (1) a three-year ministerial course, (2) a four-year theological course, and (3) a two-year Tonga Bible course for the older men who are unable to read English. These older men are said to be lending maturity and stability to the student body which is presently made up of fifteen men and nine wives.

A new importance is being attached to stewardship in the village churches. Tithing is taught and national ministers are fully supported from these funds. The Mission encourages its preachers to give all of their energies to the ministry and they are not supposed to engaged in "private works such as farming or running a store." As of January 1968, only fifteen of the congregations met in their own church buildings, so the Church has initiated a new program in which the village members supply the bricks, sand, and water. The balance of the construction costs and other equipment is allocated from district funds collected on the field.

The Field Superintendent reflected excitement and expectancy as he outlined the plans for the future of his Church. To implement these plans the PHC is suggesting the following steps for each of its churches:
1. Start praying for revival.
2. Follow this period of prayer with special services which emphasize the need for revival.
3. Institute a training program in soul-winning.
4. Begin village and urban visitation.
5. Conduct evangelistic services designed to reach the unsaved community.

So 1968 will go down in the history of the PHC as the year of policy changes, from burdensome and unproductive educational commitments to a greater involvement in direct evangelism and church planting.

I found no evidence, however, that an *African* evangelism,

adjusted to the Tonga social structure, intent on baptizing groups without social dislocation, bringing power structures and parts of power structures into Christ intact, was envisaged.

If the revival is deep and true enough it can bring in better churches than we missionaries plan, but the revival would be helped enormously by resolving to win these peoples by groups, families, *mukowas*, and villages. (See Chapter X.)

THE SEVENTH-DAY ADVENTISTS (SDA)

The Seventh-Day Adventist Church established its first mission station among the Tonga in 1905 at Rusangu, near Monze, but found that the Jesuits had earlier in the same year staked their claim to the same general geographical area.

Schools provided the "can-opener" for the SDA, as was the case with most early Missions, but this Mission was one of the first to recognize the relative ineffectiveness of their schools. In an interview with the writer, David Swaine, SDA Field Secretary, commented:

> Schools were in the beginning an opening wedge for our Church as with most Churches. But education almost crowded the Church out. We saw many years ago that primary schools were no longer serving any useful purpose (1968).

In 1955 the SDA relinquished control of all except two of its primary schools and the secondary school at Rusangu.

According to information furnished by the Field Secretary, the SDA Mission has forty-nine organized churches with their own buildings, seventy-five "elders" or local church leaders, and an active baptized membership of 5,736 communicants. Around each of the "organized" churches are numbers of small congregations which are still too small to have their own buildings. Thirteen of the fourteen missionaries are engaged in educational and medical work at Rusangu Mission, therefore most of the evangelism is carried on by the national elders and eight paid African evangelists who itinerate widely among the churches.

Statistics show that in the last five years the communicant membership has increased 18.3 percent which represents a growth rate far exceeding that of any of the other Missions. This is significant in view of the fact that the SDA Mission has very strict codes against smoking, drinking, and polygyny, and any member who indulges in these practices is immediately dropped from the church rolls. The official stand of the Church on polygyny is that a man must do away with all but his first wife before he can become a member.

TABLE 2

*Five-Year Growth Figures
of the Seventh-Day Adventist Church*

Date	Active Baptized Members
December 1963	4,699
December 1964	4,694
December 1965	5,390
December 1966	5,789
December 1967	5,736

Local membership records are carefully kept by each church; every three months a district leader compiles the totals for all churches in his assigned area; these quarterly records are then submitted to the Rusangu headquarters.

The two hindrances to church growth are, in the words of the Field Secretary:

1. The disparity between the incomes of our missionaries and our paid national ministers.
2. The feeling on the part of the nationals that we have control of unlimited amounts of money but will not hand it out to them.

He then gave two reasons why he believes that the SDA Church has grown: "1. The Spirit of the Lord is working in the hearts of men. 2. We insist upon tithing to pay for local preaching and teaching." And the facts do show conclusively that the contributions in their churches have risen tremendously in the last few years. One clear sign of their giving is the fact that all forty-nine of the congregations have their own buildings. I was told that "tithing is an article of faith, but a man is not disfellowshipped if he does not tithe."

Asked about the future plans of the SDA Church, the Secretary replied, "We will emphasize the preaching of the Gospel. That has been our aim all along, but we have been sidetracked a few times."

THE UNITED CHURCH OF ZAMBIA (UCZ)

During 1965, four of the oldest Missions in Zambia joined forces and now work together as the United Church of Zambia. The Paris Evangelical Missionary Society (1885), the London Missionary Society (1887), the Methodist Missionary Society (1893), the Church of Scotland Mission (1905), and churches founded under their auspices now make up this largest Church in Zambia.

Only one of these Missions has engaged in missionary activity among the Tonga. The Methodists (formerly the Primitive Methodist Missionary Society) established the very earliest mission stations in what is now the Southern Province of Zambia, among the Ila in 1893. Even though the Methodists succeeded in founding two missions among the Ila before the turn of the century, it was not until 1901 that W. Hogg was able to open Sijoba station in the Zambezi Valley. Afterwards the station was moved downstream to Kanchindu.

The Primitive Methodists encountered a number of difficulties and the people were seemingly unresponsive. A PMMS missionary wrote in the late 1920's that "the work has been of slow growth, neither the Ba-ila nor the Batonga proving easy soil to till" (Smith 1928a:83). And certainly this must have been the case because the PMMS statistics for 1928 show only 225 communicants in the Ila and Tonga tribes combined. In contrast to the church growth picture, however, the institutional program was progressing very satisfactorily with fifty-seven day schools and an enrollment of 1,810 pupils (1928a:83).

The Wesleyan Methodist Missionary Society and the Primitive Methodist Missionary Society were combined under one synod in 1932 and have since maintained a unified program in Zambia.

The UCZ Mission in the Southern Province is carried on almost exclusively by the Methodist Church and is divided into four district church councils. Only two of these, however, are totally within the Tonga area--Kanchindu and Choma. Statistics for the Choma are contained in the following table. Figures for the Kanchindu district were not available to this researcher.

TABLE 3

Local Congregations of the
United Church of Zambia, Choma D.C.C.
1968

	Number of Churches	Number of Communicants	Average Size of Church
Village churches	13	195	15.0
"School" churches	5	195	39.0
Town churches	3	120	40.0
Mission-station churches	1	30	30.0
TOTAL	22	540	
			Average 24.5

The 1968 membership totals for the Choma D.C.C. show 550 members, 540 of whom were considered active communicants. Forty-eight preachers itinerated among the twenty-two churches, but fifteen of them were still "on trial." Much more tribal diversity existed among the UCZ ministry than was true in other Missions; eighteen were not Tonga. Probably this was due to the greater urban composition of its churches.

Village churches were composed mainly of women and girls, with an occasional older man. But in the town churches exactly the reverse was true. Asked why there were more women than men in the village churches, a UCZ preacher replied:

> The men are more interested in beer than religion. Materialism has taken over. Because of more money today they are able to purchase beer in even greater quantities.

Primary schools were turned over to the government in 1965 and the Church is now putting more time and energy into evangelism. However, actual growth is quite slow. One church agent explained his plight like this:

> All my time here in town [Choma and Kalomo] is spent trying to reclaim backsliders. There have been many converts made in years past, but many have fallen back. I am trying to reclaim many of these fallen Christians.

Regarding the future, there seems to be little planning being done beyond the "reclaiming of lost sheep." No bold church growth policies for discipling the Tonga are capturing the imagination of the Church or mission executives at the present time.

CHURCHES WITH NO STATISTICS AVAILABLE

Salvation Army (SA)

This Mission has engaged in quite an extensive industrial and educational program in the northeastern area of Tongaland, but unfortunately I have no accurate picture of its membership. There are two mission stations under its auspices, one at Chikankata and the other at Ibwe Munyama.

New Apostolic Church (NA)

Because of the highly indigenous nature of this Church, accurate communicant membership figures were not available. From all indications, however, the NA Church is growing rapidly throughout the Southern Province as well as in other parts of Zambia. The following information was gathered from a number of informants during the survey, but as a general rule, I was regarded with suspicion and treated as a "spy" for "organized missions."

1. The New Apostolics are extremely independent and follow indigenous church principles.

2. They have a hierarchy consisting of: (a) "bishops," (b) "evangelists" or "priests" who itinerate widely, and (c) local unpaid "pastors" of small churches.

3. They allow polygynists in the Church.

4. They believe strongly in a baptism of the Holy Ghost.

5. Their services are very emotional.

6. They erect very simple grass and mud buildings.

7. Local pastors receive printed literature from the Salisbury headquarters periodically.

8. Church leaders are usually well-respected and self-supporting members of the community.

9. The zeal and dedication of the evangelists is great (e.g., one of my informants was an evangelist and he visits all his churches within an area of 120 by 50 miles on a bicycle!).

This chapter has covered only the Protestant religious bodies who are laboring among the Tonga; no attempt was made to survey the Roman Catholic Missions in the area. Suffice it to say that they have also carried on a highly institutional type of mission with hospitals and schools. They are particularly strong in the areas around Monze and Livingstone.

PART THREE

A Depth Study of Tonga Villages

MAP 5

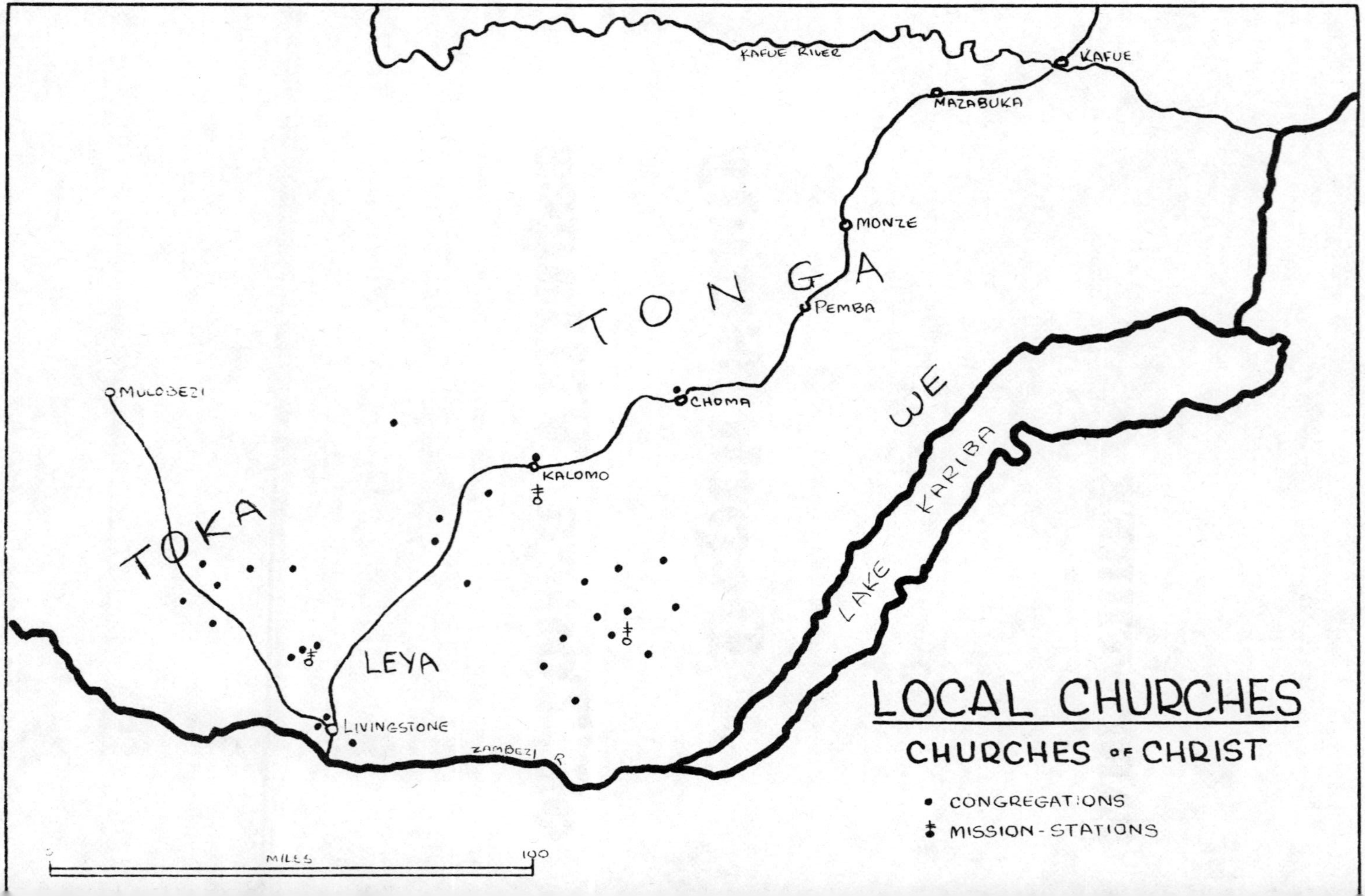

KAFUE RIVER
KAFUE
MAZABUKA
MONZE
PEMBA
CHOMA
KALOMO
MULOBEZI
LIVINGSTONE
ZAMBEZI R
TONGA
WE
TOKA
LEYA
LAKE KARIBA
LOCAL CHURCHES
CHURCHES OF CHRIST
CONGREGATIONS
MISSION - STATIONS
0
MILES
100

7

Growth of Tonga Churches of Christ

Prior to 1968, no detailed study had ever been made of Tonga Churches of Christ. No compilation of local congregations nor of their respective memberships was available. Ever since 1910, when the first church was planted at Mukuni Village, it had been assumed that the Church was growing, but no one knew where or to what extent. For example, it was optimistically estimated in 1968 that there were fifty congregations in the Kabanga area when in actual fact there were only twelve active churches. Guesses and estimates have clouded the facts regarding the real state of the Church throughout its history. So it is that the Church in this largest tribe of Zambia has provided an open field for a church growth survey.

Since 1923 Churches of Christ have spent over two million dollars in missionary salaries, church buildings, schools, and an orphanage. Thousands have been baptized, scores of churches have been planted, but never has there been an overall picture drawn of accomplishments and failures. Without this insight it is extremely difficult, if not impossible, to see victories and defeats in their proper perspective. One who is accustomed to very little church growth may be inclined to accept such as normal and biblical, whereas in actual fact, the receptivity of the people should make possible much greater growth.

Seldom, if ever, have large numbers of believing men and women been added to the Church without a strong emphasis on church planting and personal witness. Neither of these principles have been stressed by the Church of Christ among the Tonga. The churches which do exist are made up of believers who have been converted during public preaching services or in Bible classes in the schools.

THE CONGREGATIONS

There are thirty-seven churches of Christ among the Tonga scattered over an area of approximately ten thousand square miles. Only three of these congregations comprise more than 50 active, baptized members. The overwhelming majority are small, struggling bodies of believers made up mainly of women and children. They make an attempt to observe the Lord's Supper the first day of every week, but find it hard to maintain an adequate supply of the elements. The wine is carefully conserved so that not a drop is wasted. After the Christians have communed, the remainder is usually poured back into the bottle. To obtain wine in some areas involves a round-trip walk of sixty to seventy-five miles, so one church was reported to be using carbonated orange drink as a substitute for the "fruit of the vine." Some congregations meet together for Sunday worship even when they do not have the elements, but the Christians feel very strongly the absence of the Lord's Supper. Other congregations will not meet at all simply because they do not have or cannot secure the elements. To compound the problem, many of the church leaders come to one of the mission stations for their supply of wine instead of buying it at a local store. This adds to the "headquarter complex" which some already attach to the mission stations.

All thirty-seven of the congregations are led by unpaid leaders who may be farm workers, teachers, policemen, accountants, storekeepers, or self-supporting farmers. These leaders cannot devote much of their time to teaching and preaching, but this disadvantage is outweighed by the fact that there is little, if any, foreign control over their churches. Now that Zambia has her independence, more of the leaders seem willing to shoulder responsibilities. They want to be self-reliant but welcome advice. One put it like this:

> We want to do the work and govern ourselves not only in our country but also in the Church. But we do not know how to do some things; we need your brotherhood and advice.

The church which meets in the Mwaata suburb of Kalomo is the only church with a plurality of biblically qualified men who are serving as elders. This church, while recognizing the autonomy of all her sister congregations, has taken the lead in organizing and planning Bible lectureships and discussion groups.

It is now known that churches have existed in at least thirty other locations, but for one reason or another all have become defunct. Usually each of these little congregations was led by one man who may have died, moved away, or have been sucked back into the pagan community. Many of the members were school children whose unbelieving parents applied too much pressure

Depth Study of Tonga Villages 79

for their young faith to withstand. Other members were women who were subjected to ridicule and ill-treatment by their husbands. Still others lapsed because "there was no one to feed us the words of God."

Not one of the congregations has had an active planned outreach. The Christians feel little responsibility for the salvation of their relatives and fellow villagers. This deficiency must stem, to a large extent, from the dependency which has been fostered by the missionaries and national preachers. Missionaries and African evangelists have relied almost exclusively upon public proclamation in the villages. The audience plays a passive role. Following a hurried, weekend preaching trip by a missionary or national preacher, some believe, repent, and are baptized; then they wait for the next spiritual meal, which may be a long time coming.

Personal witness is practically unknown and one African put his finger on this weakness very well when he said, "I have never known even one missionary to take thirty minutes to sit down and, without being in a hurry, talk *man to man about Christ*. It must always be in a public way." Generally speaking, not only have the missionaries done very little personal work, but neither have the national Christians confronted others with Christ. The facts show that out of forty-one church leaders interviewed, *only two had been won to Christ by personal witness!*

So excited was one national (who earns his living as a government teacher) when he entered a pagan village and spoke quietly and persuasively to *family after family* instead of following the usual pattern of preaching before the village assembly, that he could hardly wait until he had another opportunity to return. The people were friendly, anxious to learn the "words of God," and invited him to come back as soon as possible. In his approach there was a personal touch, direct confrontation, and the results gratified and thrilled both the preacher and his hearers. The ground was prepared for a new church to be planted.

A close examination of twenty-six rural churches disclosed some rather startling insights. Only three of the little congregations had more men than women members, and four of the twenty-six had no men at all. It is no wonder, then, that there was a great lack of leadership in most of the churches. When I queried church members about the scarcity of men in the churches, the following three reasons were most frequently given:

1. The men like to drink beer too much.

2. The men object to going to school with children.

3. The men believe that prayer and worship are only for women and children.

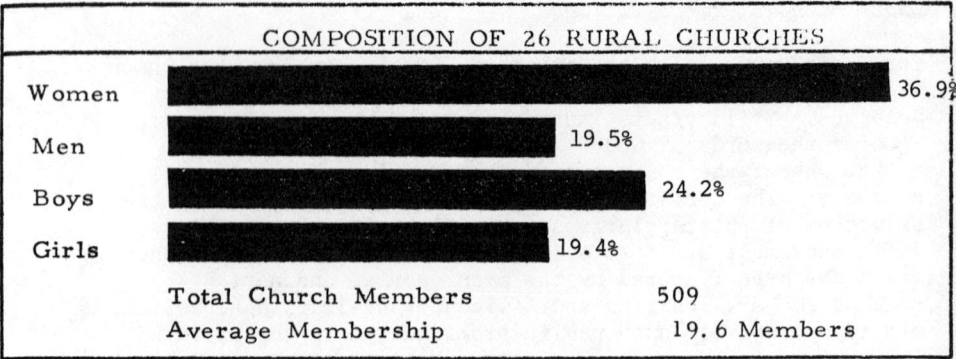

FIGURE 1

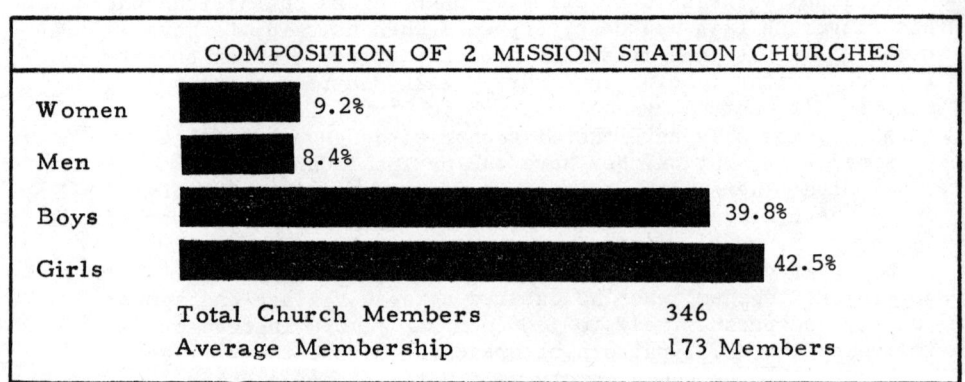

FIGURE 2

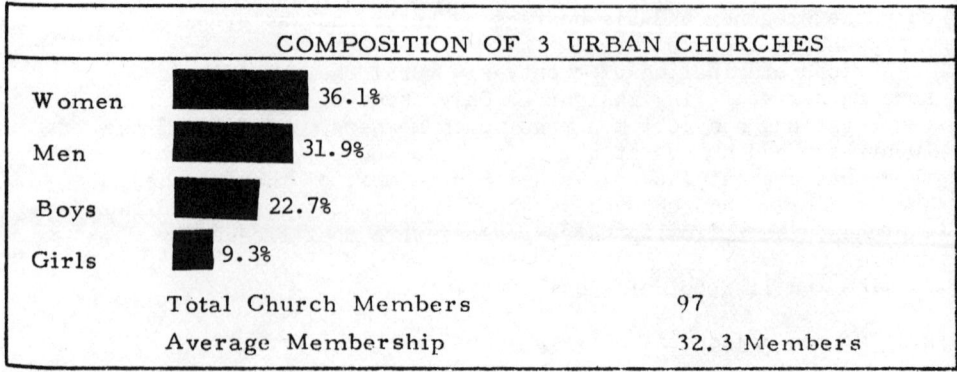

FIGURE 3

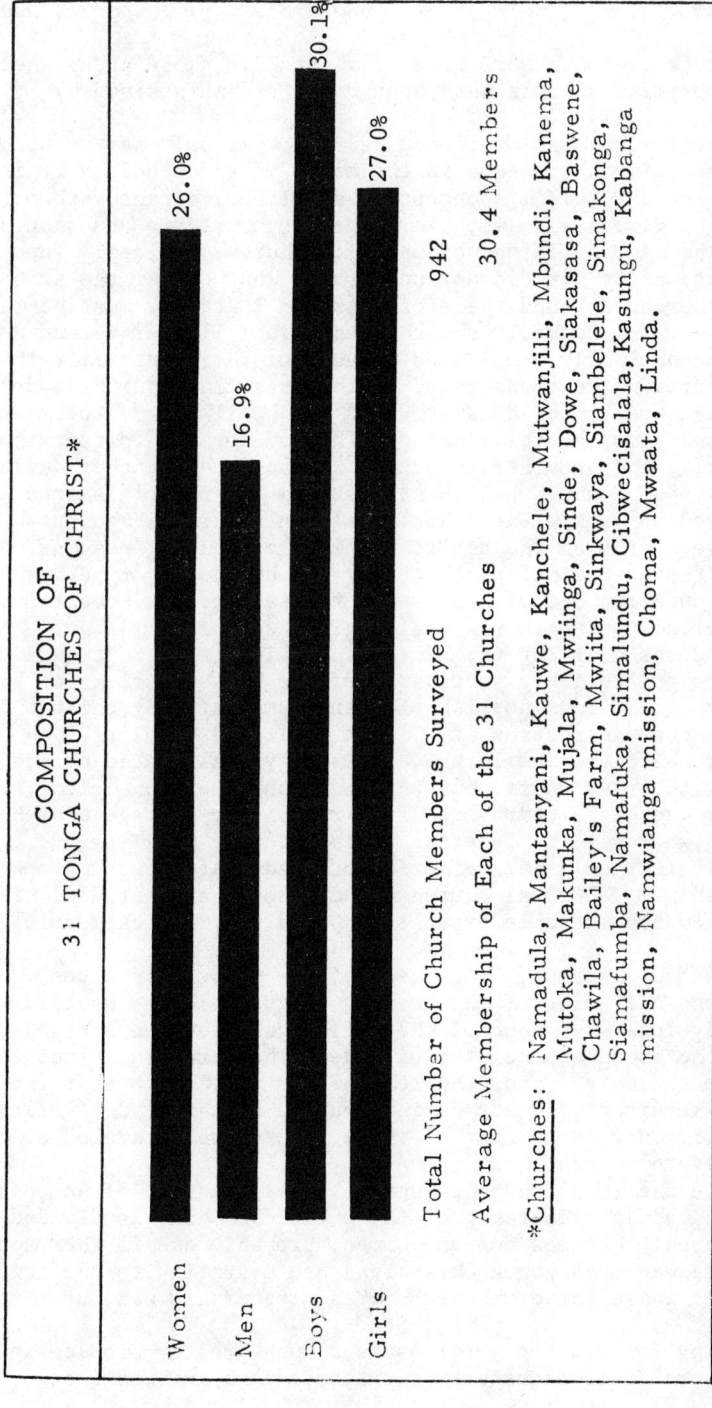

FIGURE 4

The last two reasons were generally cited in those areas where village primary schools have been built and maintained by Churches of Christ.

Apparently, as was mentioned earlier, "school" and "church" have come to mean the same in the minds of the people. It is easy to see why this misconception developed, because school was taught five days a week in the school building and then on Sunday the same building was used for church services. The illiterate adult men did not understand what either the school or the church was, and therefore assumed that they must be the same. In these "school" churches the older illiterate men were often unconsciously humiliated because of their inability to answer certain questions asked by the presiding church leader. It was an experience an adult would not be likely to tolerate the second time; he felt left out, he had nothing to contribute. Frequently, the preacher on Sunday was also the teacher during the week and he would ask questions from the materials studied the preceding week. The school children naturally had an advantage over even the adults who were capable of reading. Some of these adults feel that they are beyond any type of formal education and will politely refuse or offer some excuse when invited to the church building for worship.

Around the beer pot the adult man is in his element. He can listen to and tell big stories. Here he has an outlet for his virility and he runs no risk of being humiliated by children. Here, as one man phrased it, "I can tell very big lies."

The rural church buildings are usually constructed of mud and poles, with grass roofs, but a few are built of sun-dried bricks. One has a corrugated iron roof. The average church building, however, is inferior to the average dwelling, indicating either a lack of pride or inadequate teaching on stewardship. Two rural churches had gone to a great deal of effort and considerable expense to build their brick meeting houses.

In the rural areas, 76 percent of the membership lives within one-half mile of the meeting place, which is usually centrally located. None of the buildings have been erected within the boundaries of the village. The Christians want to separate themselves from the rest of the village so that the worship services will not be interrupted by the louder village pastimes. Only 10 percent of those interviewed traveled over two miles to church.

Unlike the rural churches which largely consist of women and children, adult membership of the urban churches was divided fairly evenly between men and women, probably due to the fact that more men than women Christians are migrating to the towns. In two of these three urban churches, leadership was outstanding.

Housing for worship services is a much greater problem in towns where it is necessary to purchase land and where any construction has to meet certain building standards. Consequently, most urban congregations are forced either to hold their Sunday services in vacant classrooms or to meet in their homes.

TABLE 4

Meeting Places

	Rural	Urban	Mission Station	Total
Church Building	9	-	2	11
Open Air	13	-	-	13
House Church	1	-	-	1
School Building	2	2	-	4
Other	1	1	-	2
TOTAL	26	3	2	31

In summary, it is possible to make the following observations:

1. The membership of rural churches largely consists of women and children (Figure 1).

2. Adult membership in urban churches is almost equally divided between men and women (Figure 3).

3. The reversion rate among young, urban church members is fantastically high (Figure 3).

4. The composition of mission-station churches is atypical of either rural or urban churches. Few conversions to Christ are taking place in the towns, pinpointing the rural orientation of the Missions, and emphasizing the crying need for urban ministries which are relevant and tailored to the complex city situations.

MEMBERSHIP

Even as recently as 1966, it was assumed by missionaries that there were as many as 10,000 members of the Church of Christ in Zambia, 98 to 99 percent of whom were Tonga by tribe. However, according to 1968 figures collected by this researcher during a survey, it was found that there were only 1200 active worshipping members of the Church. This figure includes only those regarded as faithful and active by the respective church leaders and does not include the many weak Christians and unfaithful members in villages where churches do not exist. "By their fruits you shall know them" was the principle followed throughout the survey. Local church leaders relied upon this one criterion more than any other and if a member was regular in church attendance, active in worship, refrained from beer drinking and adultery, his good standing in the church was usually unquestioned. The figure quoted above also does not include a small number of "dormant" Tonga Christians who are scattered far and wide throughout Zambia. However, due to the comparatively low incidence of external migration among the Tonga, it may be safely concluded that the number of Christians outside the tribal boundaries is insignificant. In the Copperbelt cities, for example, whose urban populations have been swelled by tremendous migrations of rural tribesmen in search of work, there are fewer than 100 active worshipping members of the Church of Christ from *all* the tribes.

When asked about their conversion, 89.8 percent of Tonga church leaders who were sampled stated that they had been converted from animism or, as they put it, had at one time "prayed to *mizimu*," but now they had become Christians. A few informants were reluctant to classify their former religious allegiance as "*mizimu* worship," preferring instead to have it referred to merely as an "unbelief in anything." Without question this is due to the stigma which has been attached to spirit worship and other animistic religious practices by missionary and national ministers alike. The ex-animist is sensitive at this point and feels that he will be regarded as inferior if he admits that he was once a spirit worshipper.

About 10 percent of the informants stated that they had been converted from other religious bodies, but without exception this change had occurred in their youth. One had become dissatisfied with the long delay imposed before baptism and had become a member of the Church of Christ because in that Church he could be baptized immediately, without a prolonged trial period. This delay before baptism was not an infrequent complaint leveled against some Missions and Churches.

Obedience to Christ in baptism has, too often in the past, been accompanied by scepticism and ridicule for many Tonga Christians due to the fact that they have been individually plucked from their own familiar functioning social organism into a "foreign" society. This approach is thoroughly Western, but not necessarily biblical. It has succeeded in building up resentment and opposition to Christianity in many quarters. One man testified:

> When I return to my village the people are no longer my friends. I do not stay very long in my village. I have become separated and not even my relatives will talk to me, so my visits are very short.

Depth Study of Tonga Villages 85

To the collectivistically minded African this ostracism is excruciating because his whole life is bound up in the social activities of the clan or kingroup. Sociological and psychological pressures which are unknown in Western society are brought to bear upon the individual Christian and are relentlessly applied day after day until the young convert cracks under the strain.

J. W. Pickett in his book *Christ's Way to India's Heart* believes that Western missionaries are unjustified in adhering to individual conversion as the only acceptable way to come to Christ. He says:

> Missionaries from the West commonly approach the Christian task in India with a strong preference for individual, as opposed to group, accessions to the Church. Yet the record shows that the Church has grown in India chiefly through group accessions. Nowhere does it appear that the Church has become firmly established in typical Indian conditions, so that it is capable of living and growing without foreign support, except where group movements have taken place (1960:26-27).

What Pickett says concerning Missions in India is certainly true of the methods employed in Tongaland. Not a single informant had been won to Christ as part òf a kinship group, large family, or village, yet this is precisely the type of society in which people could become Christians through multi-individual, mutually interdependent decisions. There is no reason why believing families, believing kingroups and, indeed, whole believing villages should not confess their allegiance to Christ and be baptized the same day. Tonga churches would be much stronger. (Individual vs. group conversion will be dealt with in greater detail in Chapter X.)

Figures 5 and 6 clearly show the methods which have been the most widely employed in evangelizing the Tonga. Missionaries have brought almost one-fourth of the informants to Christ by means of public preaching and religious instruction in mission schools. National preachers have used the same methods in winning 68.3 percent. Ministers, both national and foreign, have combined to win over 95 percent of the converts *by means of public proclamation*. We praise the Lord that many converts have been made through diligent and regular Bible teaching in schools, but this approach has seemingly set the pattern for practically all Christian witness. Consequently, personal witness has been responsible for winning only one-twentieth of the converts! Relatives have manifested little concern for the salvation of their kin. (Figure 5)

Biblical examples of the expansion of the New Testament Church should be restudied in order that the Zambian Church see more clearly its responsibility toward the unsaved. Great

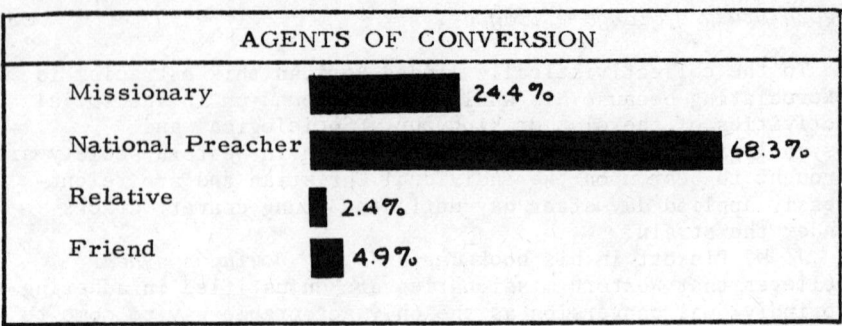

FIGURE 5

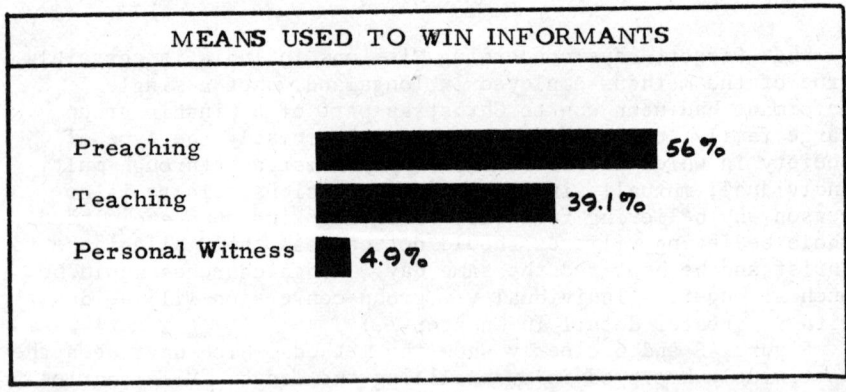

FIGURE 6

church growth is impossible when the Good News has to be funneled through only a select few of God's redeemed. Roland Allen makes a good point when he writes:

> The rapid and wide expansion of the Church in the early centuries was due in the first place mainly to the spontaneous activity of individuals . . . a natural instinct to share with others a newfound joy, strengthened and enlightened by the divine Grace of Christ, the Saviour, inevitably tends to impel men to propagate the Gospel. The early Church recognized this natural instrinct and this divine Grace, and gave free scope to it. Very many of the Christians in those local churches had no doubt become Christians, led by the spontaneous zeal of someone who was a Christian before them. The names of a few great apostles were known to the whole Church; but the first teachers of the majority of the Christians were probably unknown to any but those whom they had quietly influenced (1963:143).

One of the main reasons for this apparent lack of individual and personal involvement in the man-to-man sharing of the Good News is due to the fact that this method has seldom been used by missionaries. The *individual*, or family, or kinship group has been lost in the illusion that "we have been sent to preach the Gospel to all the nations but to no one in particular." The value of the person-to-person contact at the deepest level has too often been forgotten in the idealism which hopes to evangelize the whole world. In the last analysis, winning the world has to begin with winning families.

None of my informants had come to Christ simply by reading the Bible on his own or by hearing the Gospel over the radio. (Figure 6)

Ninety-five percent of the converts said that their relatives lived in the country, which bears out two observations which have already been alluded to previously: (1) Tonga Church of Christ churches are basically rural; and (2) there is a low rate of external migration among the Tonga as compared to some other Zambian tribes.

It would seem, then, that the main opportunities for the Church's evangelism are in the rural areas. The question of what lines of evangelism would be effective in urban situations is quite another matter.

The Gospel flows from the older to the younger person in Tonga society. Very infrequently does a son win his father or mother to Christ and even more seldom does a schoolboy or girl win an older person who is not a member of the immediate family. Therefore, to provide the necessary leadership in the churches and in order to clear the natural channel of communication (i.e., from elder to younger) it is imperative that the Church begin to concentrate upon the winning of adults instead of putting such an overwhelming percentage of its resources into the education of the young. This applies especially to adults with some standing in the community who are suitable for places of leadership in the rural church.

RECENT TENT MEETINGS

The idea of holding tent meetings at strategic locations throughout villages in the Kabanga area was originally conceived in 1966. These meetings were primarily designed to strengthen and revive existing churches, but secondarily they were to be a means of outreach.

In the planning stage, national Christians were invited to make suggestions concerning the purpose of the meetings and how to raise the necessary funds. They decided that if the "American brethren" could contribute the money for the tent and equipment, they would work diligently to reach a goal of one thousand baptisms the first year. A tent was purchased for $2100 and one church in the United States picked up the tab.

The first meeting in one location near the Mafuta River began on the night of July 25 and extended through the evening of August 2, 1966. Attendance is always better when the nights are not dark, so all of the meetings were scheduled to be held during the ten days of the full moon. Advance advertisement and contact work were done by a team of three missionaries and three national preachers.

TABLE 5

Tent Meetings 1966-1967

1966	Attendance	Baptisms	Restorations
Mafuta	2317	87	80
Siakuba	2928	84	93
Mwiita	1423	71	36
1967			
Mafuta	2057	28	71
Chawila	1276	36	32
Chidi	1151	26	47
Mukuni	3061	78	6
Kasungu	1397	33	30
Siakuba	1153	21	62
TOTALS	16763	464	457

The tent was equipped with electric lights, stools and benches, baptismal tank, and extra clothes and towels.

Attendance at the opening service of the first meeting was 150, but it climbed steadily during the ten days to 302 on the last evening. Visible results were eighty-seven baptisms and eighty restorations (Table 5). The preaching was done by graduates of the three-year Bible College at Nhowe Mission in Rhodesia. They were dynamic and relevant in their presentation, but the responses came mainly from children and women. Comparatively few adult men were baptized.

Two more meetings were held in 1966 and six in 1967; each was preceded by four weeks of preparatory work and followed by about four weeks of post-baptismal teaching. It was not uncommon for a number of people to be baptized by members of the follow-up team.

We are made to rejoice at the ingathering of 464 new Christians and the restoration of 457 more who had grown cold to their first love.

An objective analysis of the effectiveness of tent meetings reveals the following strengths and weaknesses:

Strengths:
1. They revive local churches spiritually.
2. They enable each individual member to see that he is part of a much larger fellowship than just his own small church.
3. They provide an outreach which is not normally present and is so desperately needed in most churches.

Weaknesses:
1. It is almost impossible to provide adequate post-baptismal teaching for the widely scattered new converts.
2. Because of this, there is a high reversion rate among undernourished babes in Christ.
3. There is a tendency to be drawn by the display and novelty of electric lights, noise, and equipment.
4. Due to the fact that a foreign church has underwritten the cost of the tent and equipment, nationals accept little responsibility for its upkeep and erection, preferring that these chores be performed by the missionaries.
5. So far the tent meeting has not enabled serious confrontation of the local power structure. No meetings exclusively for influential men have been held. No attempt has been made to suggest that it is normal for the men to decide first. But this lack can be easily remedied in the future.

Tent meetings can be effective tools in evangelizing the Tonga provided they do not become a substitute for engaging in widespread personal witness. Public preaching is not opposed to, but is often easier than, approaching the unsaved in a loving, man-to-man confrontation.

The strongest point in favor of the tent meeting is that it provides a larger fellowship for Christians and enlarges the personal vision of each individual member. Its weakest point is that it is very difficult to follow up adequately. This can be illustrated in the following manner. Suppose that twenty penitent believers are baptized at one of the night meetings; fifteen of them are teen-aged children, four are women, and one is a man. These twenty converts are scattered throughout six different villages which are up to two hours' walking distance from each other. One begins to see how difficult it becomes for the two to four converts to stand up against the remaining non-Christian structure of the village. When a strong church already exists in their home village, their path is not so rocky, but if the handful of new converts are the total church in their village, we should not be too surprised by the phenomenal reversion rate among the young converts.

CONVERSIONS AT MISSION SCHOOLS

When this survey was being made in June, July, and August, 1968, Churches of Christ were maintaining two primary mission schools and one secondary mission school. Practically all of the students above the age of nine years were communicant members.

Almost 100 percent of the students who attend the mission schools become Christians before graduation, whether it be on the primary or the secondary level, and this has been true for at least twenty-five years. Although there are no baptismal figures available for that period of time, it is safe to estimate that there have been at least 100 baptisms per year at the mission schools and an additional 200 per year in village schools. Add to this number approximately 50 baptisms from churches which were not connected in any way with schools and we arrive at an average annual total of 350 baptisms. Assuming that a minimum of 300 converts have been made every year for twenty-five years through schools alone, there should be a grand total of 7,500 Tonga members of the Churches of Christ, but in actual fact there are only 1,200. *This represents a reversion rate of 84 percent!*

Since 1942, the Church has grown very little among the adult population while tremendous resources have been increasingly poured into educational facilities for the young. Adults have, in the main, been neglected and the animistic power structure has remained intact after years of Christian education. Baptized school children have been sucked back into pagan village life and have reverted under pressure.

We cannot afford this phenomenal reversion rate for another twenty-five years, but must put the horse back in front of the cart and begin to convert parents and their children, headmen and their villages, village leaders and their households. The Church must make it possible for children to follow the example

Depth Study of Tonga Villages

of their parents in obedience to Christ.

We must plant churches made up of families! They not only have a spiritual but also a sociological cohesion. And this is quite biblical. For example Paul, the greatest church planter of all time, under the guidance of the Holy Spirit, planted family churches. The New Testament records how he planted the church at Philippi by beginning with the obedient families of Lydia and the jailer (Acts 16:15, 33). Paul and Silas started the church of God at Corinth around Crispus and all his believing household (Acts 18:8). Peter planted the family church at Joppa when he baptized Cornelius and his household (Acts 11:14).

In this chapter, I have tried to present an accurate picture of the state of the Tonga Churches of Christ, and of the methods currently being used. I have briefly analyzed them for effectiveness, noted strengths and weaknesses, and finally, offered some alternatives for the future.

8

The Power Structure and the Church

Unlike the Bemba and Lozi, with their highly developed hierarchies of authority, the Tonga have never had a well-structured leadership with various sub-chiefs, chiefs, and a paramount chief. Only during the few decades of colonial rule did there exist any semblance of clear-cut chieftaincies. The colonial government appointed responsible men to chieftainships and instituted a system of leadership which was uncharacteristic of traditional Tonga life in order to facilitate efficient administration in the more remote areas.

To a certain extent, the powers of the chief which were largely vested in him during colonial days have reverted to the village councils and headmanships, and the chief is now more of a figurehead than the locus of any real authority or leadership. Furthermore, under the nationalist government the chief has been divested of most of the former glory of his office, and it is likely that the future will witness the complete abolition of the chieftaincy. Probably a more democratic and individualistic pattern of government will gradually replace the present collectivism. In view of this loose formation of Tonga power structures, we may safely assume that the tribe will swing more readily toward individualistic decision-making, for Tongas have always cherished their freedom of movement.

Mos- of the 1968 survey was conducted in the chieftaincies of Nyawa, Musokotwane, Mukuni, and Simwatachela. Definite changes are taking place in the chiefdoms and sub-chiefdoms, and the structures of the matrilineal kingroups and clans are also undergoing modification. Inheritance rights are being transferred from kinship groups to the immediate family, and wealthy farmers are becoming more reluctant to divide their fortune among all the matrilineal relatives. They instead want their children to share the inheritance.

Internal affairs of the village are governed by a council of elders presided over by the headman. This village power structure has no authority beyond the confines of the village and is generally pagan. I know of only one village in the chieftaincies mentioned above that has a Christian council of elders. What this means is that either this vital part of the village has been neglected by the messengers of the Good News--or their message has been irrelevant to it.

If the Church is to grow in Tongaland, *the power structures or parts of them must be won for Christ*. The Church must be content neither to nibble at the fringes of Tonga society nor to pluck assorted malcontents from among the village population. The Church must solve the problem of winning converts without inducing in them a traitorous feeling toward the remainder of their social unit.

So often, it seems, there are only two alternatives for the church planter. Either: (1) he will immediately accept and baptize the penitent individual irrespective of the consequences for him or the rest of the village; or (2) he will concentrate upon converting the power structure *first*, knowing that the remainder of the people will be receptive (including the penitent individual) and will find it easier not only to follow but also to *remain faithful*. To delay the baptism of the individual penitent believer, however, goes against the most deep-seated convictions of the missionary whose entire methodology has been patterned after the pietistic church growth of the Protestant West (Pickett et al 1962:6).

Baptism is not the *end* in itself, it is really the beginning of the New Life. In the act of baptism the believer demonstrates his total surrender to Christ by dying to his old life, being buried with Him and then raised to walk in newness of life (Romans 6:3, 4). For the Church passively to ignore this fantastic reversion rate among the Tonga churches is inexcusable. We are unfaithful husbandmen in the Lord's vineyard! It is just as important that the individual Christian remain faithful after baptism as it is for him to be baptized in the first place, and this means being converted *with* his group. One individual babe in Christ without a group cannot long withstand the stress of ostracism, ridicule, and hate which he is called upon to face in a village situation.

If, on the other hand, a group is converted, the case is far otherwise. If the group converted includes an individual and the rest of his household he will not be quite as weak. If the group includes several families which are related, he and it will be strong; and finally, if the group has within it the older responsible and respected men of the village, the church resulting will be even stronger and capable of growing independently.

Sometimes objections are raised to group conversions on the basis that the individual is not given the opportunity to make his own commitment and to surrender himself personally to his Savior. But this is not true. A. L. Warnhuis argues:

> In group conversion, the individual is still as important as ever. Groups are influenced through individuals. The mistake occurs when the objective is only the individual who is separated from the group. Instead of separating him from the group, the individual should lead the way into the group (Pickett et al 1962:17-18).

The purpose of this chapter, however, is not to discuss in detail individual versus group conversion, but rather to provide a background for the ideas concerning how the Church can, in the interests of much greater church growth, go about winning and making use of the Tonga power structures.

THE HEADMAN

Every Tonga village has a *sibbuku* (headman). Sometimes he is also the *sikatongo*, or neighborhood leader, but there is always one man who has the final say in all village matters. He is a settler of disputes and judge in domestic disturbances. When the cattle owned by one member of the village get into his fellow villager's garden, it is the headman who presides over the proceedings and sets the penalty for the guilty party. Cases of domestic infidelity are also brought before the headman for settlement.

The authority of the headman does not extend beyond his village unless he is a neighborhood leader, in which case his jurisdiction includes only the neighborhood. If the crime is "too large" it is referred to the chief's court and generally the headman is the first to realize when the offense is too serious for him to handle. The headman wears the name of the village and is its ritual expert.

THE COUNCIL OF ELDERS

Council members are the wisest, most respected, and responsible men in the village, and they act in an advisory capacity to the headman. During his absence, they make the decisions. The village people respect the council of elders, follow its leadership, and accept its decisions.

Frequently they are polygynous and overwhelmingly non-Christian, and because of the traditionally negative attitude adopted by Missions toward polygamy, this particular power structure has remained intact, untouched by--indeed, rejected by--the saving message of Christ.

Despite the fact that both missionary and national preacher have written off or disregarded these polygynous elders, some still remain receptive to the Gospel. Others resent having been neglected by Christian missionaries and are much more difficult to reach now than they would have been thirty years ago.

Polygyny will be discussed in more detail in Chapter X, but it should be said here that our position with regard to this predominantly polygynous power structure to a large extent will determine the future rate and type of church growth that will occur in village churches, i.e., the future of Christianity in Zambia. This council must be won for Christ if the Church is to grow as God intends it to grow.

THE ASSEMBLY OF HEADMEN

In matters which affect more than a single village, there is an assembly of headmen which gathers to consider and render judgments upon the issues at hand. The meetings are informal and attendance is not compulsory, but most headmen make a special effort to be at all assemblies.

This group of men, like the council of elders, is responsible, respected, and has within it a high incidence of polygyny. Aside from the national political scene, it is this body which wields the most power at the grass-roots level. Ultimately, in order to effect group movements to Christ, it will have to be considered seriously in the planning and witness of the Church. It is imperative that the members of this group hear the message of Christ in a meaningful way, for their acceptance or rejection of the Good News will largely determine how the Church will grow across the country.

POLARIZATION WITHIN THE VILLAGE COMMUNITY

In the vast majority of Tonga villages, the membership of the local congregation constitutes only a small minority of the total village community. The typical little band of Christians has found it necessary to break completely with the remainder of the village. Christians refer to themselves as "worshippers of God" and "abstainers from beer" and label their pagan counterparts "spirit-worshippers" and "drunkards."

Thus, the church becomes isolated from the rest of the community, its members develop a persecution complex (often for good reasons) and it grows only be extraction. It is not uncommon for the Christians to care little about saving their fellow villagers and when this happens, a gulf has developed between the "just" and the "unjust," resulting in a polarization which is extremely difficult to overcome.

A good example of this unnecessary polarization has occurred in Mantanyani village near Zimba (Figure 7), where the "Christian sector" of the village consists of from forty to forty-five inhabitants. All are not Christians but it is apparent that they consider themselves very different from the "parent" village. Both settlements are called Mantanyani village, but the Christian suburb is about one-quarter of a mile from the main village.

The Mantanyani church, like most Tonga churches, is a small congregation made up mainly of women and children. The name of the local minister is Samuel Mantanyani, who was baptized in 1951 by an itinerating African preacher. Probably he is a son of the headman of the whole village. He says that "those who want to follow God live mostly in this village and not in the big village." He is literate, possesses a Tonga Bible, and is in charge of six vernacular hymnbooks.

On the day of our visit Samuel Mantanyani directed all the songs, led all except one prayer, and presided at the communion service. The only other adult man in the church was called upon only once to offer a prayer of thanks for the fruit of the vine. He was an older man who had been converted in 1935. It appeared that he had been faithful through the years, but he still did not own a Tonga Bible. All that he possessed was a pictorialized Bible storybook.

After the open-air services, the women were quite apologetic about the small attendance and expressed the desire to build a church building. They said, "We want someone to help us build, but we are only women." Their husbands were in the parent village drinking beer.

I also visited the larger non-Christian segment of Mantanyani village where practically all of the men were gathered about the beer pot. There was no doubt in my mind that *the real power structure of the whole village* was assembled around that beer pot!

ACCEPTING THE WHOLE POWER STRUCTURE

Had Christianity been advocated to the whole village and allowance been made for a group decision, Mantanyani today might very well be almost totally Christian. The church would have its own self-supported and well-respected leadership, its own church building, the village would not be divided, and Christianity would be a live option for every non-Christian member of the village.

As it stands, however, Christianity is probably viewed by the pagan inhabitants of the parent village as a divisive ideology and something to be avoided at all costs. Individuals have been pulled into the church from the periphery of the village, while at the same time the majority of men, because of

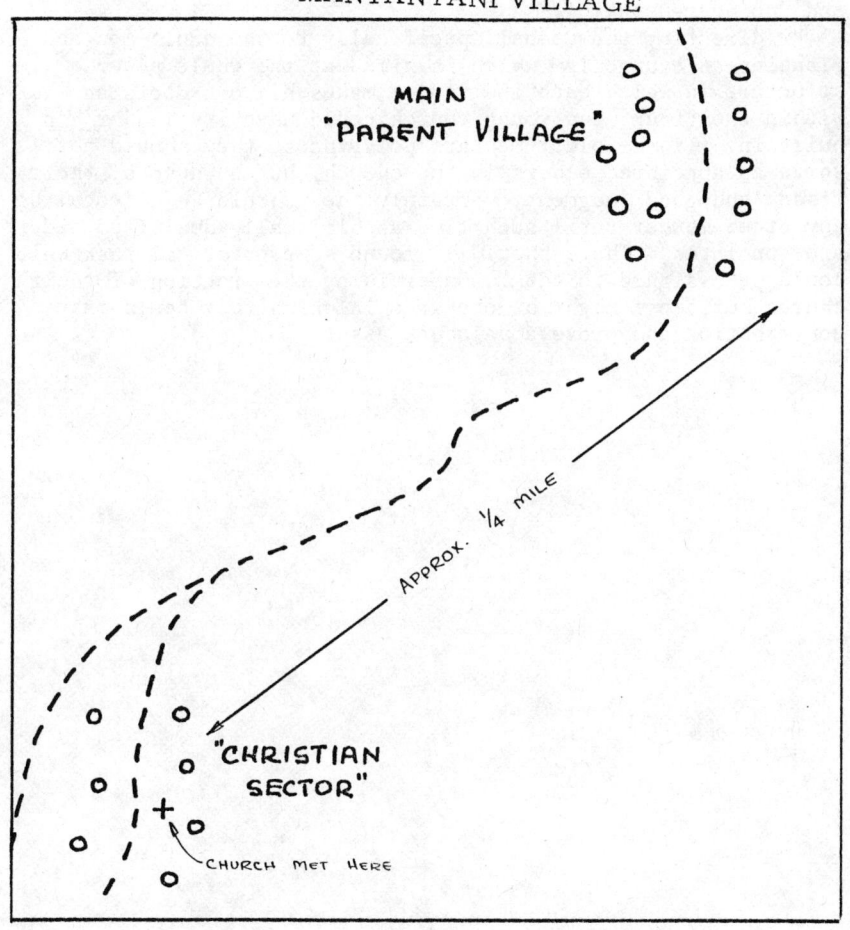

FIGURE 7

their polygynous marital state and their propensity for beer-drinking, have been kept out. Instead of hearing the wonderfully good news of salvation through faith, and obedience to Jesus Christ, they have heard only the bad news of "no polygamy" and "no beer-drinking."

By directing the Gospel specifically to the adult men and planning an evangelism which is aimed at the whole power structure in which each individual makes his own decision within the group, the young church could have its leadership built in. If the older men are polygynous, they should not serve as appointed elders in the church, but because of their wisdom and good judgment, certainly they should be as vocal as any other member until such time as biblically qualified elders are appointed. There should be found some practical task which could be assigned to them. Supervising the erection of their church buildings might be one area in which they could make a contribution and prove a valuable asset.

9

Obstructions to Church Growth

The path to conversion has, for many Tonga, frequently been fraught with obstacles or blocked by resistance to change. Sometimes the people have misinterpreted the primary purpose of the missionaries and instead of being viewed as a herald of a more excellent Way, the missionary has often been looked upon as a crusader against drunkenness and polygyny. The animist has seen little evidence of any congeniality between the new way and his old pattern of existence, nor can he detect anything that is distinctly better than what he already possesses.

We do not minimize the transformation which must take place in the life of every individual who wishes to accept, obey, and surrender to Christ Jesus as Lord, but in seeking to prepare the way for such a drastic change, it is our responsibility to remove every barrier that we possibly can from the path of the hearer *except the cross of Christ*.

At the cross the believer makes his decision to die with Christ, and to appropriate the blood of Christ to blot out his sins. There each person publicly confesses and demonstrates his allegiance to the King of Kings, and only then does the convert have the power to overcome the sin in his life. The Spirit of God will then be able to bear fruit in his life and perfect him.

Requiring a man to stop getting drunk, to put away all but one of his wives, or to desist from worshipping "evil spirits" *before* he becomes a Christian, is like asking a man to lift himself out of the mire by his own bootstraps. It is impossible for a man to demonstrate the fruits of the Spirit without the Spirit.

I believe that throughout Tongaland there are four major obstructions to church growth. They are: (1) the problem of widespread drunkenness, (2) polygyny, (3) the equation of "church" and "school" by many of the people, and (4) the slow growth resulting from over-institutionalized mission.

DRUNKENNESS

Almost invariably the problem of drunkenness has been mentioned at the top of the list by Tonga church leaders as the main reason for reversion and unfaithfulness in church attendance. It has also proved an obstruction to those who might otherwise become Christians.

Since the coming of the first Missions in the 1890's, drunkenness has been a widespread problem among the Tonga and there are definite indications that beer-drinking is on the increase. Wives have begun to make beer to earn cash and are now able to acquire things for which they had formerly been dependent upon their husbands. Women are discouraged from becoming Christians by those who say, "If you become a Christian you won't be able to make beer for profit anymore."

Few Tonga women drink the home-brewed *bukoko* (beer), but are content to remain sober while their menfolk lose all sense. Much fighting and bragging accompany almost every drinking party.

Elizabeth Colson, in her book *The Plateau Tonga of Northern Rhodesia*, describes in detail the significance of beer-drinking in ritualistic sacrifices to the *mizimu* (1962:50ff.). Beer-drinking does have religious meanings in Tonga society and we must be fully aware of the fact that in preaching against the practice, we may be condemning the whole religious system rather than an isolated sin.

I personally find it extremely difficult to determine the extent to which beer-drinking is involved in Tonga religious rites and rituals, but I believe beer-drinking is losing its religious connections and is now being engaged in more out of sheer pleasure than anything else. To the women it is a source of income and independence, but to men the beer party means association, story-telling and a place to pass the day.

Alcoholism has spelt the downfall of many a Christian. One informant observed:

> Most of the Christians [Tonga Christians in the Ngwezi area] were baptized many years ago. The delinquent Christians say, "The beer has taken us; we cannot return." If all of those who have been baptized were still faithful Christians, we would have strong churches all over this area.

The same man also cited a frequent excuse used by non-believing men when approached about Christ: "We are beer-drinkers; we have no time to listen to the words of *Leza* [God]."

Asked about the obstructions to church growth, another Tonga informant responded simply and unhesitatingly:

> Beer. The men like beer very much, but there are few women who drink. Many of those who are converted in tent meetings remain faithful for about one month, but then most of them go back to drinking beer because they do not have sufficient teaching. Non-Christians say to the new converts, "Let us see if you can stop drinking beer, then we will believe."

In order to get to the root of the problem of drinking, we must try to uncover as many of the reasons for this practice as possible. Powdermaker, in her book *Coppertown: Changing Africa*, suggests that heavy drinking is one means by which a man of low estate thinks that he achieves higher status:

> In the past chiefs drank more than commoners, elders more than young people, and men more than women. They were "showing off" (a traditional and contemporary value) in their display of wealth, necessary for heavy drinking. Important, too, was the fun and conviviality which accompanied the drinking.
>
> But there are also unconscious functions in getting drunk, and the major one was probably the usual relieving of anxieties, caused in this situation by living in a world of change and being unable to change with it (1962:302).

Africans generally lack self-consciousness in talking about getting drunk. There is no stigma attached to the practice (Powdermaker 1962:302-303). This, in itself, is enough to warn us that this problem has deeper implications than meet the eye.

There are, in my opinion, at least five reasons for beer-drinking and drunkenness in Tonga society:
1. It has religious significance in the performance of certain rites, rituals, and sacrifices.
2. It is one attempt to achieve and maintain status.
3. It is a display of wealth.
4. It is an attempt to overcome the anxieties and strains of a people whose culture is undergoing change and upheaval.
5. The village beer party is an occasion for association.

Obviously, through beer-drinking and drunkenness *these people are trying to satisfy felt needs*. They are desirous of human dignity and purpose, and of peace with the supernatural. They want others to like them and crave fellowship and association. They long for security and peace of mind in the face of a rapidly changing environment. This many-faceted problem cannot be resolved by castigation and negative preaching.

I sincerely believe that Christ through His Body can provide an answer to every one of these needs. They can be satisfied within the Church. People must be led to see that Christianity *is more than just "no beer-drinking."* By sensing the needs of the Tonga heart we can lead him into a new relationship with Christ, and his deepest desires will be fulfilled within the fellowship of the saints.

Perhaps non-alcoholic substitutes could be found to take the place of intoxicating drink. *Mukande* (sweet beer) might fill the void left by the removal of *bukoko* (alcoholic beer).

It might also be better for the Church, while warring earnestly against drunkenness and outlawing religious drinking, to cease insisting on the non-biblical prerequisite for baptism: that penitent sinners renounce beer-drinking.

THE CHRISTIAN ATTITUDE TOWARD POLYGYNY

For decades there has been a basic conflict between Christianity and African traditional life on the subject of polygyny. Frequently the fact that a man has been involved in a longstanding polygynous union becomes a seemingly insurmountable barrier to his becoming a Christian. Missionaries cannot agree upon what course they should follow.

I think that it is about time that Western missionaries take a hard second look at this problem regarding which we know so little and upon which the New Testament is silent.

> At no point has the Christian message and ethic broken more radically into the life of Africa than in the demand on the family structure that it should accept monogamy as the marriage pattern for those of its members who become Christian (Beetham 1967:41-42).

Walter Trobisch, a missionary who is well-known for marriage counseling in Africa, writes regarding polygyny:

> We have made ourselves fools before the world with our policies. Let us admit honestly our helplessness. We are facing a problem here that we just do not know how to solve.
> Maybe our mistake is that we want to establish a general law for all cases. We want to be like God, knowing what is good and evil and have decided that monogamy is good and that polygamy is evil, while the word of God clearly does not say so. The Old Testament has no outspoken commandment against polygamy. And the New Testament is conspicuously silent about it. Instead of dealing with polygamy, the Bible has a message for polygamists (1967:10).

Fortunately there does not appear to be the high incidence of polygyny among the Tonga that exists in many other African societies, and polygyny seems to be on the wane. This decrease is probably due to the effect of education upon marriageable young people, the higher brideprice, and the inability of most husbands to support more than one wife. However, it is an obstruction to church growth and must be dealt with.

When Christianity was brought to Africa it was confronted by this unique problem. Never in its history had it faced such a view of marriage, for Greek, Roman, and Anglo-Saxon societies had all been predominantly monogamous before they had become Christian. It therefore "came as a shock to missionaries to discover that African society valued polygamy" (Welbourn 1965: 117).

Not every missionary took a negative stand against polygyny. For example, one early missionary writing in the 1897 *Missionary Review of the World* indicated his sympathetic and understanding view of the polygynous man who had entered into such a union innocently when he said:

> It seems to be very much in the spirit of the Gospel, and in accordance with apostolic practice, to admit into the Church very imperfect elements, trusting to the working of the spiritual life present in it to eliminate the elements of evil. So slavery was dealt with. There must have been not a few slave-owners in the early Church. And one can not help feeling, that I Tim. 3:2 distinctly hints that there were in the early Church some that had more wives than one. If a man is kept out of the outward church because of his having more than one wife, many dangers may arise in his family life. He worships under a stigma that lowers his self-respect. His wives and children may very well feel it so much as to be deterred thereby from coming to worship at all. If, on the other hand, his wives and children should follow him in making a Christian profession, and are baptized while he is not, the man will feel that an injustice is done him by which his rightful influence as a Christian man over his household is greatly weakened, just at the time when he has begun to desire to use it for good (Gifford 1897b:191-192).

This missionary's application of I Timothy 3:2 does not necessarily prove the existence of polygyny in the early Church (it could mean digamy), but he does manage to point out the cohesion which is possible within polygynous households, and that one evil (in this case polygyny) should not be righted by resorting to another (the destruction of the household).

Polygyny has been called by some "permanent adultery." With this I disagree. In African society, a man who has paid the compensatory brideprice to the wife's kinship group and has fulfilled the necessary rituals is legally married to the woman. Polygyny "is legal under Native Customary Law" (Taylor and Lehmann 1961:85).

The question then arises, "Would the separation of a polygynous husband from his second wife be a divorce?" "It depends," states Walter Trobisch,

> upon whether we consider polygamy also as a form of marriage. I believe we have to. Let us be fair. It is not "permanent adultery." Adultery is never permanent. It is a momentary relationship in secrecy with no responsibility involved. Polygamy is a public state, based on a legally valid contract, involving life-long responsibility and obligations. If polygamy is marriage, separation is divorce.
>
> Our dilemma is that we want monogamy and we do not want divorce. Yet we cannot have one without the other (1967:13).

Generally speaking, one of three positions has been most favored by Missions in Africa regarding polygynists: (1) some refuse to baptize husbands, wives, or children in a polygynous household; (2) others would baptize the wives and children but refuse the husband, and (3) a very few permit the baptism of the polygynous husband and his family in the first generation only (Barrett 1968:117). I firmly believe that we should accept the third position.

By accepting the man in the state in which he has been called (I Corinthians 7:17-24) we do not indiscriminately destroy his household, create fatherless children, drive his *divorced* wives into adultery or prostitution, or alienate forever the lineage of his divorced wives.

If we adopt the second view, however, Christianity becomes (in the minds of pagan people) an ideology to be resisted at all costs for it destroys households and tears apart the tribal solidarity. Two more heinous crimes could hardly be found in African traditional society. Many will be unable to see the blessed Christ because His servants have placed an unnecessary barrier before the polygynous pagan. One church growth writer from Liberia speaks to this point very concisely when he says:

> For the pagan community the danger is that the emphasis on polygamy will conceal the real "offense" of the Gospel. For the pagan the distinction is apt to be, not between those who follow Christ and those who do not, but between those who practice polygamy and those who do not. The missionaries have tried to reject polygamy by rejecting polygamists.
>
> By the very stringency of their method they have unwittingly guaranteed that polygamy will remain in the society as a respected alternative to Christianity. This accepted social norm will unite a segment of the community and

insulate its member from the Gospel. They will not even think of themselves as potential converts--the Gospel's decision will not be a possibility for them. This group of rejected polygamists will form a social backwarer, a reservoir in which the old religious sacrifices and fears will continue to breed, a pocket of resistance to the Gospel. These pockets are particularly susceptible to conversion to Islam. By enocuraging a man to give up his wife, the Church is in the position of encouraging a man to turn his back on responsibilities. Surely the Gospel should not force him to choose between honor--that is, his responsibility to a wife and children--and his own salvation.

The grace of God will not be bound in the cultural box of Western social patterns. If uncircumcised, pig-eating Gentiles can receive the Holy Spirit and be baptized, then by the grace of God polygamists can become Christians without being forced to thrust a wife into adultery or break a serious and honorable promise to a wife's father and family. They can become Christians with the full assurance of salvation that comes from believing and being baptized, and communing with the faithful. To deny this is to doubt the power of God's grace (Wold 1968:180).

Lest we should be inclined to dismiss polygyny as an isolated sin upon which we should concentrate and root out of society at the expense of everything else, let us first consider the functions of polygyny in tribal life. Louis J. Luzbetak, missionary anthropologist, lists the following eleven functions which reveal the complexity of this social institution:

The functions of polygyny . . . would include: (1) prestige derived from the fact that a man has several wives while the majority of men must be satisfied with only one wife; (2) prestige derived from the fact that a man has a large potential offspring; (3) prestige and the satisfaction of fulfilling a social or religious obligation; (4) a means of supplying a strong labor force for the family, e.g., necessary for cattle raising; (5) a means of reducing the work load for the women; (6) a way of providing a defense for the family, e.g., in areas where feuding is common; (7) a way of providing social security for widows; (8) a way of providing companionship for women where there is a strict separation of sexes; (9) a sexual adjustment, e.g., if taboos require long abstinence; (10) a way of fostering intertribal or interfamilial friendships; (11) personal reasons, such as lust, incompatibility, revenge, etc. Since monogamy cannot fill many of these needs, polygamy will most likely not be displaced until ways are found to fill the needs in some other manner or until the functions themselves lose their value and disappear. Merely to preach against polygamy is futile (Luzbetak 1963:246-247).

There can be no doubt concerning the New Testament ideal for Christian monogamy. In the Bible marriage is depicted as a spiritual-moral tie between man and wife; two who become one flesh (Mark 10:6-9). The sexual relationship is an essential element, but certainly not the all-determining factor.
Marriage in the Bible also reflects the closeness of the spiritual relationship between Christ and His Church (Ephesians 5:29-33).

This high view of the worth of woman in Christianity does not exist in traditional Tonga society. The basic evil in pagan marriage is *the low view of woman*. It is not confined to polygynous unions, but also exists in monogamous marriages.

I believe that we should teach the obvious monogamic ideal of the New Testament to those who have obeyed Christ as their Savior and who have become members of His Church, but that such teaching should be a part of our *post-baptismal instruction, not our pre-baptismal requirements*.

Polygynous members who were baptized in the state of polygyny should denounce the practice to their children. They must teach their children that polygyny is wrong and allow Christ through His Spirit to enrich their homes, to forgive them of their grossness, and to increase their love for their families and their children.

It is just as impossible for a polygynist to straighten out everything before he becomes a Christian as it is for a murderer to restore the life of the person he killed before he became a Christian. There are some things which cannot be restored to their former state and we need to be thankful that our Father is willing to take us in whatever state we are called.

EQUATING CHURCH AND SCHOOL

There is almost no distinction between "church" and "school" in the minds of many Africans. Christianity has become a classroom religion in Africa, a misconception which is largely responsible for the disproportionate ratio of school children to adult members in local congregations throughout Africa.

A common response by adult men when invited to church is, "I cannot go to school with children. Church is only for children and women." He is saying that he is *above* what he conceives the Church to be. It would be an affront to his social position to require him to learn along with the children of his village. As long as he continues to conceptualize the Church in such terms, this equation of church and school will remain an obstruction to church growth. This is a problem of meaning to which solutions must be found as soon as possible.

It is particularly acute in those areas where the school emphasis has been the strongest.

History shows that often the first thing that missionaries brought to a community was a school. After it was established and operating as efficiently as could be expected under the circumstances, a few children would usually be converted by the Christian teacher, and perhaps an adult or two would also accept Christ. But the place where they met was always in the school building, where there were enough chairs for everyone and the little congregation could find shelter from rain and cold.

In many of the Sunday services the schoolteacher is the monolithic director of all of the worship activities. He leads the singing, presides at the communion, preaches the sermon and teaches the Sunday school lessons. Sunday services are built around him; he is in charge of the hymnals, Bibles, and the order of worship. So much depends upon him that when he vacillates the whole congregation wavers. When school closes for vacation, church services are discontinued until school resumes.

As we have already noted, the Churches of Christ turned over their village schools to the government in 1965. Shortly after this handover, many of the village "school churches" were defunct and so-called "Christian" teachers no longer felt any responsibility for the church. Some even forbade the congregation to meet in their school buildings for services. As the teacher went, so the church went, in so many cases. At least ten churches died overnight.

During a visit to Siambelele Village (near Zimba) I located six women who had recently been baptized and who now form a living church in that little village. I asked them if a church had ever existed in their village, to which they replied, "Yes, we used to assemble in the school building, but when school was discontinued several years ago, we stopped meeting." The amazing thing in this instance was that the church had been recently started by an itinerating preacher who lived in a nearby village and was managing to meet without depending upon the schoolteacher to feed it. The handful of members had been able to make the transition from school church to church, and their misunderstanding of the place of the Church and their relationship to Christ had, to a large extent, been overcome. They had come to realize that *they* were the Church, and they felt a certain independence.

In village after village, I found that when the schoolteacher stopped leading, the school church folded. Too many things depended upon him.

Hundreds of people (mainly schoolchildren) have been baptized by Christian teachers in village schools and for this we must thank God. Some of them have remained faithful in the face of overwhelming odds. But the Christian schoolteacher is also a man in need of Christian fellowship. He does not find the spiritual buttressing which he really needs from among his students. He is often a stranger in the village where he is sent to teach, and unless he is an exceptionally mature Christian he frequently reverts under pressure or dies of spiritual hunger.

The basic misinterpretation of the relationship between the church and the school still exists in many villages where schools have been operated by the Church at one time or another and it may be years before the church assumes the preeminent position in the village. I do not know the answer to this dilemma, but perhaps what one Christian schoolteacher has done may be a partial solution to the problem. He has concentrated on planting a church in a nearby village where they do not have a school, and he is encouraging the church members to erect their own church building and meet in their own village.

Another way to overcome this obstruction to church expansion is to begin preaching Christ and persuading *winnable units* to accept Him at one time. This will involve starting with adults instead of children. They will begin to see that God has a message for *them* and that *they* are in a position to make the decision to accept or reject.

The school church has an extremely limited power of penetration within its village environment, and unless a concentrated effort is made to convert the pagan power structure and the winnable adults within the village, congregations with this school-church complex will continue to be dependent upon the Christian teacher or upon visits by missionaries to keep them infused with life.

INSTITUTIONALISM AND MISSION-STATION CENTEREDNESS

Introversion, isolation, and a centralized sedentary organization usually characterize *institutionalism*. This inward-looking kind of mission work is better known in mission theory as *mission-station centeredness*. The Church is faced with this obstruction in Tongaland, and if it is to minister Christ to 270,000 Tongas, it must grapple with this obstacle to church growth, and then find and implement radical new methods by which it can break out of this deadening centralization.

Mission-station centeredness closely resembles the church-building centeredness which afflicts most American churches. Instead of the building or mission station serving as a base for outreach into its immediate area, it becomes a place where its members or missionaries find security, speak the same theological language, enjoy one another's association, and from which they make periodic appeals to the world to come and learn of Jesus Christ. As introversion increases, contact with the totally lost decreases. Conversation and fellowship among the saved takes precedence over witnessing to the lost.

The longer this church continues its inward emphasis or extends its period of consolidation, the greater is the tendency for it to begin erecting a bigger, more comfortable building, padding its pews, installing softer and thicker carpets, organizing itself into committees and planning programs, and losing sight of the pressing human needs of salvation and compassion which abound on its doorstep and around the world. The church which has turned its eyes toward itself becomes sedentary, selfish, and isolated. It becomes an institution, not the living body of Christ.

Similarly, when a mission station becomes self-centered and introverted it begins to concentrate upon the erection of bigger and better buildings, its missionaries find association among themselves instead of with the nationals and devote practically all of their time to administrative pursuits, negotiations with contractors and management of building, and teaching and healing projects. Like the home church, the sensitivity of its missionary personnel to human needs and to the thousands of precious people for whom Christ died who live within its area of influence is lost in the hustle and bustle of an isolated and introverted institution.

Roland Allen, writing from his own missionary experience in China, describes the plight of "mission-station centered" missionaries very well when he says that

> their attention is distracted from their proper spiritual work, their energy and power is dissipated, and their first contact with the people whom they desire to evangelize is connected with contracts and other purely secular concerns. It is sad to think what a large proportion of the time of many of our missionaries is spent over accounts (1964a:53).

And then he adds:

> In creating these missionary establishments we not only overburden our missionaries with secular business, we misrepresent our purpose in coming to the place. It is of the utmost importance that the external manifestation of our purpose should correspond with the inward intention and rightly express it (1964a:54).

The mission station becomes the domain of the missionary, where he generally exercises strict control over the activities of the station. It usually represents a permanent base of operations, consists of a complex of buildings, foreign in style and expensive to maintain. A static mentality toward aggressive evangelism generally pervades the missionaries who have become rooted to their station. The church is only one of the many activities of the station, and not infrequently it becomes the least prosperous and least important of all (Lyall 1966:73).

A close friend of mine who has recently concluded a nineteen-year missionary career in Africa said that institutionalism has a way of making a spiritual man immoral. That is a strong statement to make, but he substantiated his assertion by recounting how missionaries in a certain field were actually fabricating glowing stories of success in order to keep funds coming from sincere donors in America.

Having lived or worked for a total of twenty years on various mission stations among the Tonga, there are several reasons why I believe that institutionalism and mission-station centeredness almost always obstruct rather than propagate the Church of Jesus Christ.

The institution tends to become an end in itself. Instead of the school, hospital, or Bible school being the fruit of (and the responsibility of) the national churches, the institution becomes the tree which supports the churches. The institution, in this case, grows out of the desires of the missionaries for the people, rather than out of needs which the national churches recognize and for which they assume most of the responsibility.

The primary goal of discipling the Tonga tribe to Christ is lost in the shuffle of efficient administration, good teaching, erecting nice-looking, permanent school buildings, and maintaining high standards of hygiene--all of which coexist with the vague notion that "we are training leaders for the Church of the future."

Reports back to American churches call for more missionaries and more money so that the school can be expanded or a larger water system installed. An institution which has become the end in itself has an insatiable appetite for missionary personnel and resources.

Institutions take priority over evangelism in the deployment of missionary personnel. By their very nature mission institutions demand routine, consistency, and continuity. Schools do not open and close their doors at random. Schedules have to be made and met. There have to be enough teachers and sufficient funds to enable a school to function. When the need for an additional worker in an institution arises, usually a missionary is either persuaded to offer his assistance "on a temporary basis" or he is transferred from evangelistic work to the institution. The institution comes first, it must go on, evangelism and post-baptismal indoctrination can wait.

Where institutional work or the mission station is still the center of a particular missionary effort, young missionaries have gone to the field inspired by indigenous church principles and anxious to put them into practice, only to find that the existing institutional organization dictates otherwise. Tensions and frustrations arise because these new missionaries feel that they are surrendering their primary objective by giving so much of their time to less important duties.

Institutions receive financial priority over evangelistic and church-planting budgets. It is often argued that the institution must be perpetuated because so much time, energy, and money have already been invested in it. "We cannot give up now" or "we must hang on" or "let us keep as much control as possible" are statements frequently heard in missionary circles which are heavily committed to an institutional program. The investments in an institution are too great to be expendable, so if anything suffers, it must be something other than the institution.

Lester P. Westlund, in his article "Avoiding the Dangers of Mission Institutions," voices another argument which is employed to justify continued support for institutional work (irrespective of its effectiveness) when he says:

> One mistake often made by missions using the personalized system of support is to justify the cost of supporting missionaries in institutional work by saying that the people who support these would probably not give the money to the mission for anyone else, so the loss to the mission is small compared with the cost of the service. This, of course, is a false view. All money spent in missions contributed by Christians at home is the Lord's money and must be expended with great care. One dollar is as valuable as another (1968:236).

The fact that the institutional programs of Missions in Tongaland have received financial priority over direct evangelism and church planting has raised another problem which hinders the numerical growth of the Church. An evangelistic missionary recently phrased the problem like this:

> The money which is being sent from America to build the secondary school at Namwianga Mission is actually hurting the work elsewhere in Zambia. The national brethren ask us for money to help them build church buildings. When we refuse they cannot understand why so much American money is available for a school in the Southern Province and not for church buildings. It appears to them that the school is more important than the Church.

When institutions receive top priority in terms of missionary personnel and money, it is extremely difficult, if not impossible, to convince people that Christ and His Church are more important than our nice-looking school. Not only do we, as missionaries, forget our main goal, but what is more tragic, the nationals see external manifestations which do not correspond with our inward intentions. This severely impedes church growth.

Institutions fail to produce church growth proportionate to the financial investments in them. Supporters of a large secondary school operated by the Churches of Christ have argued that their institution is training a large percentage of the Christian leadership for both rural and urban churches throughout Zambia. This should be true simply by virtue of the fact that in 1968, 88.9 percent of the missionary personnel in Tongaland was engaged in the secondary school program. (See Chapter IV.)

Dissenting opinions were expressed by two missionaries who have been devoting themselves to direct evangelism. They made the observation that the "strongest leaders in the churches had been converted as adults and not as schoolchildren in 'our' schools."

In 1968, over 90 percent of the money contributed by American Churches of Christ and individuals for their missions in Tongaland was expended on the secondary school at Namwianga. Of course, one might point out that 1968 was a year of construction and that the costs were unusually high. But, unless the proportion changes drastically in the future, this one institution alone will continue to consume by far the largest slice of the financial pie.

I believe that a number of questions need to be raised concerning this tremendous expenditure in terms of personnel and money and the overall effectiveness of such an institutional approach:

1. Are the teen-aged graduates of this Christian secondary school *actually* becoming the leaders of the churches?

2. Are they planting churches or forming the nuclei of churches where they work or live after graduation?

3. Are we training the children of Christian parents who want a Christian education for their children or are we using the school as an evangelistic tool?

4. Is the institution maintaining a high level of spirituality and evangelistic fervor?

5. Is it helping to build strong churches?

6. Is it possible, within five years, for national churches to assume its support and operation in view of the nationalization of education by the Zambian government?

7. Provided the Zambian government permits a church-supported educational institution to exist, would national Christians be willing and financially capable of taking over the school within five years?

8. Do the national Christians consider the school theirs, or do they view it as a foreign imposition?

If these questions cannot be answered in the affirmative, it would be my conviction that this Mission should take a long, hard look at what its real goals are. The legitimacy of such an expensive school approach must be weighed in the balances with such statements as that made by an articulate national Christian church leader who says:

> The school is good, but it is totally on American support with American teachers, which will not be tolerated in Zambia for long. The school administration is now asking the Zambian brethren to take over support of the school, but this is impossible because the churches which should support the school do not exist! We have neglected for fifty years the most important part of mission work--evangelism. We must plant churches and teach Christians to give before the school will succeed.

He is saying, among other things, that the tree (the Church) does not exist to support and produce the fruit (the school). When the school precedes the Church, the growth of the Church is obstructed.

Institutionalism may have harmful effects upon missionary personnel. Living and working within an isolated community such as an introverted mission station or institution can contribute to spiritual stagnation. This does not happen to everyone, but in talking intimately with many missionaries and having had some years of personal experience, the following harmful attitudes may develop:

1. Routine and the environment of slow growth in the institution rob missionaries of their sense of urgency to proclaim the Gospel.

2. Inward-looking mission stations insulate missionaries from the actual line of conflict where souls can and are being won to Christ.

3. Isolation from village nationals often fosters racial superiority.

4. Local loyalties to a particular institution increase the missionary's desire to maintain control.

5. Language study is thwarted because missionaries usually have contact only with English-speaking students and staff on the mission station.

6. Routine and pressing duties of the mission station often crowd out time for God, and the spiritual life of the missionary suffers.

7. Missionaries become conditioned to slow growth and consequently are not sensitive to areas of receptivity.

Institutionalism may have harmful effects upon national Christians. It became apparent to me during the 1968 church growth survey that mission-station centeredness had adversely affected the attitudes of village Christians toward Christ and toward the Mission.
1. They failed to see that Christ was the real purpose for the existence of the institution.

2. Church planting was relegated to a role secondary to the operation of efficient mission institutions.

3. Village Christians resented the neglect by missionaries who claimed they had the Words of Life but who were too involved in duties at the mission station.

In exposing some of the dangers of institutionalism, I have attempted to point out ways whereby it hinders and threatens to continue impeding the growth of the Church in Tongaland. But having acknowledged the weaknesses of such an approach, what are some possible solutions to the dilemma?

This has been a highly critical chapter. The reader may feel that I see no possible good in mission institutions. I believe that a mission institution which does not lose sight of its missionary vocation can be a useful instrument of evangelism but this chapter is written as a result of my conviction of the truth of what I have written. This is not speculation; it is the conviction which comes from observation and investigation.

There are at least two important factors which demand a critical assessment of current missionary involvement in mission-station-centered institutions. The first is the pressure which is being applied by the nationalistic governments of emerging African nations. Government takeovers of medical and educational institutions which were formerly operated by Missions are a manifestation of the rising national pride of independent nations. The second factor which necessitates a different direction for over-institutionalized Missions is the growing emphasis upon church growth as the main criterion for mission. Missionaries who regard the calling of *multitudes* of men and women to responsible obedience in Christ Jesus as their goal will not long remain satisfied with the gradualism of mission institutions. Many are questioning the validity of institutions which fail to produce leaders for the churches.

Dr. Alan Tippett lists four criteria, with which I heartily concur, which should be applied to every mission institution. He believes that:

(i) The function of a mission institution is to provide in some way for the growth and strengthening of the local Church.
(ii) A mission institution should provide a course or programme relevant to the local situation where its graduates will live, and to the Christian encounter in that situation.
(iii) A mission institution should train its graduates as catalysts in the local congregations.
(iv) A mission institution should be one which can be taken over by the indigenous Church (1968a:125-127).

When any mission institution becomes an end in itself and fails to meet these four important criteria, it compromises its purpose and renders itself a liability rather than an asset.

PART FOUR

A New Direction for the Church

10

Changing Attitudes

It is evident that the Church has not yet achieved its potential for growth among the Tonga. It is also apparent that the time for change is *now*, and that both national Christians and missionaries will have to make a clear-eyed assessment of the past, admitting its mistakes and courageously setting about to make the changes that are prerequisite to growth and strength.

It will be the purpose of this chapter to suggest a number of attitudes which will best manifest a spirit of love between Africans and missionaries and will also help bring into being more vital, growing, independent churches. To illustrate the great need for this spirit of love and close fellowship, I quote the following representative statement by a middle-aged Tonga Christian:

> I am glad to see the *luswaangano* [fellowship] which is beginning to be experienced between the white missionaries and the African children of God, but we are still at the door. This is only the beginning, we must go farther. Most African people are still afraid of white people, and the only way to dispel this fear is to have fellowship between black and white. When the black man retreats, the white man should go forward with his hand extended.

This man has expressed the general feeling of many members of the Church. He believes that a step in the right direction has already been taken, but longs for even greater advances toward real, unfettered fellowship.

MISSIONARY ATTITUDES

Fraternalism vs. Paternalism

Perhaps because of a lack of faith we have feared and distrusted any independence on the part of national brethren. We have been thoroughly paternalistic, even with the best of motives. We have desired that our converts turn to us for the final authority, much as a child would to his father. In a sense we have said, "Just obey, or follow the rules, and everything will be all right. We know what is ultimately best for you."

What has been true in most of Africa is also the case in Tongaland. The coming of Missions has roughly corresponded with the expansion of colonialism and, as a result, oftentimes missionaries have become identified with the colonial administration as agents of imperialism. Unfortunately some missionaries did quite frequently adopt the general attitudes of the white administrators toward the governed and, from this viewpoint, it is not difficult to feel superior when you begin to convince yourself that the nationals are incapable of responsibility or self-government. Nor is it hard to doubt whether the national Church will ever be capable of functioning without the fatherly hand of the missionary to guide and administer its discipline.

We have conditioned ourselves to the position which holds that our converts must be submitted to a long probationary period (which may extend over several generations) before they can be expected to stand alone. Somehow, as mature Christians, we doubt that the Holy Spirit can bring about the same spiritual growth and development in the lives of our converts as He has effected in our own. This is a lack of faith in the power of God. Roland Allen points out that the two principles which underlie all of Paul's missionary practice are: "(1) that he was a preacher of the Gospel, not of law, and (2) that he must retire from his converts to give place for Christ. The spirit in which he was able to do this was the spirit of faith" (1964a :148).

In response to our ethnocentrism an African newspaperman writes:

> What we need is a heart-to-heart fellowship, but that isn't possible before the missionary looks at us as human beings because he himself is a human being. We are not mechanical things. We don't want to be pushed, nor led by him, but we want him to walk together with us at our side, and transfer the leadership to the only One who has the power and the insight and thus will give His spirit to those who don't have enough in themselves (Jensen 1964:147).

New Direction for the Church

The Tonga brethren desire fellowship with the missionaries now more earnestly than ever before. They believe that it is possible for an association of real equality to exist between foreign and national Christians. One of the most touching and humbling experiences that I have ever had was when an elderly Tonga preacher told me with tears in his eyes:

> I have been a Christian for many years and I am an old man. Today [as we sat at his table for a meal] is the first time that a white man has ever eaten *insima* [hard porridge] in my house. Although I have prayed that this would happen for a long time, I thought that I would not see it before I die. Truly, this is a wonderful day, to see white and black eating together in fellowship.

This man has been a Christian for fifty years and has served as interpreter for many of the missionaries who have come to Tongaland. His picture has been flashed in churches all over America during the film presentations of missionaries on furlough, but he had always been regarded as a "lesser" brother in Christ.

Identification with Nationals

Upon close examination one always finds that missionaries have been most successful in communicating the Gospel in meaningful terms when they have been willing "to be all things to all men." On the other hand, where missionary work has been ineffective, one frequently finds at its very core the failure to identify (Nida 1954:250-251).

We find it next to impossible to really understand, much less to judge, the customs and mores of others unless we appreciate their point of view. Their methods appear clumsy while our's seem so efficient. What we overlook is that we see things this way because we ourselves are also culturebound.

Identification is not achieved by "wearing a breechcloth, eating manioc and termites, or dwelling in a grass hut." Eugene Nida has said that "what really counts is having a mind which can understand, hands which join with others in common tasks, and a heart which responds to others' joys and sorrows" (1954:257).

Dr. Kenneth D. Kaunda, president of Zambia, has made it clear that identification is not achieved by becoming a "white" African. He says to Europeans:

> We do not expect, as the price of identification with our society, the abandonment of all that is a genuine part of their own culture. We recognize that Zambia will be all the richer for the wealth and variety of human types within it . . . Identification need not mean absolute uniformity (1966:74).

It has been my experience that there are four very important ingredients which help missionaries to identify with nationals: (1) eat without reservation what is set before you; (2) sleep without fear of being contaminated by disease in their homes; (3) know and use their language out of the motive of love, and (4) join empathetically with them in their moments of sorrow and fear. To some these might seem obvious, but in actual fact there has been much opposition to the first two elements just mentioned.

For years missionaries have carried their canned food and sometimes water supplies on all their village tours. Lest they destroy the temple of God's Spirit (their bodies) they have consistently refused to eat what was offered in a spirit of love and generosity. They have overlooked the fact that just as there is a gracious Christian way of presenting a gift, there is likewise a gracious Christian way of receiving what is given, especially where it is given in the name of Christ. Thus the real joy of joining hearts in a common fellowship meal has been denied most Tonga Christians. There should be nothing amiss in following our Lord's example when He ate with the publicans, the sinners and outcastes in what must have been the most unhygienic conditions. Some of the greatest truths of all time were taught by Christ around a fellowship meal. The unity of believers can be demonstrated not only in a formal worship service, but as we daily eat together with glad and generous hearts (Acts 2:46).

When invited to sleep in the home of a national brother we should not recoil in disgust because of the disease and "carriers of sickness" that we might encounter during the night. Bugs and insects may be an unpleasant inconvenience, but must we allow mere discomfort to stand in the way of real identification and communication? If we refuse such an invitation, no matter what excuse is offered, the damage is already done. Our air of superiority drives a cold wedge between two brethren who at any other time of the day would enjoy one another's association. We have a clear injunction on this matter from the apostle Paul in Romans 12:15-16, especially verse 16.

It was in the closeness of a dark room that an African brother told me of his innermost love for me simply because we were together. It was a relatively new experience for both of us, but in the darkness of that room we prayed together and then he said that he felt like he could tell me anything that was in his heart. I told him that I felt the same way toward him. Such mutual love is possible only when we throw down the fears and distrust which we have toward one another.

Most missionaries will agree that we should know the vernacular language of the people among whom we work. We cannot appreciate people fully until we can understand and speak their language, for it is only then that we are able to enter the inner circle of their lives. Then, instead of ridiculing some strange custom, we may come to see its function within its cultural context.

The fourth important element in identification is empathy. What was said concerning one missionary should be true of all. This missionary never passed a village in which a funeral was taking place. He joined with the people in their mourning and sorrow and did not leave until the rites were complete. Although he left the field twenty years ago, the fact that "he cried with us and was with us in our sorrow" has never been forgotten. Today he is remembered as "the one who ate with us, slept with us, spoke our language, and shared our sorrows."

Regarding the importance of empathy in times of sorrow one informant said:

> The people fear the *dilwe* [funeral] very much. People are much distressed and often have to be restrained from committing suicide. They are very sad. If the missionary wants to show love when passing through a village where a *dilwe* is taking place, he should not pass on until the funeral has been finished. He should even give a hand in covering the body. He must shake the hands of as many people as possible, expressing his sorrow and his involvement in their suffering.

Language Mastery

Someone has said that the key to a man's soul is his language. One of the main tasks of the missionary is to unlock the door of men's hearts so that they can hear, receive, and respond to the message of Jesus Christ. To be an effective church planter, a mastery of the language is imperative, and the earlier in his career the missionary can learn the language, the sooner he can really begin to communicate. People cannot respond to a message they cannot understand.

> Thought forms, idioms, proverbs must be mastered, and unless the missionary resolutely sets out to do this in the early days of his service, he is very unlikely ever to reach his goal. Multitudes have given up their struggle and crippled their ministry (Harris and Parrinder 1960:58).

Certainly an evangelistic missionary must have an adequate knowledge of the language of the people among whom he lives and works. He should know all of the traditional and ritualistic terms which are employed in the sacred rites of the tribe, else he will be unable to present the truth of Jesus Christ. Only when people see and hear something which is clearly better than what they already possess will they be constrained to make a change. Without a good grasp of the language we may be tempted to destroy something before we have a functional substitute to replace it. Language mastery will help us to avoid creating cultural vacuums. He needs to know the language well; not merely well enough to write a sermon which he reads, but well enough to engage in dialogue with men face to face by the evening fireside.

Language study is extremely demanding and requires real self-discipline, but it is absolutely basic to identification. To regard language as unnecessary and time-consuming will ultimately result in frustration, isolation and the feeling of inadequacy. If one is to survive the shock of cultural differences and begin to overcome his revulsion toward what are actually intelligible happenings, he must understand the language of his people.

Knowing the language sets people at ease and builds bridges to communication. This was demonstrated very well during a recent conversation which an African companion and I had with an old Tonga chief. We approached him as respectfully as we could, he ordered stools for us to sit on and, as was the custom, we waited patiently for him to speak first. After conversing at some length with my African friend he turned to me, extended his hand, and said in Tonga, "How are you, my *lord*?" I replied in his own language, saying, "I am not a European, only my skin is white; really I am a Tonga." His eyes brightened and with a smile he stretched his hand forth a second time and said, "Truly, you are a Tonga, my *son*!" The gulf had been bridged. Instead of a strained lord-servant relationship between the chief and me, there came to exist a father-son kindredship. The Good News flows much more easily in the latter.

Placide Tempels, a missionary who was able during a long tenure in the Congo to get into the inner circle of African thought has written this concerning his experience:

> One lives their life with them, sharing their difficulties, their feasts, their games, their hunting, their palavers. Speaking their language, one learns more by listening to their intercourse one with another than by pursuing systematic investigations (1959:28-29).

Not only does a proper use of the language open the hearts of non-Christians, but it also helps expose the ethnocentric heart of the missionary to the hopes and needs of his adopted people.

Church Planting as the Goal

Constantly as missionaries we must reconsider our goal. Fog swirls in from every quarter to cloud our vision and divert us from our course. For missionaries who are laboring in receptive fields there can be but one goal: the winning of men and women to Jesus Christ and organizing them into autonomous churches.

Ministers of God who lived in New Testament times were never content with proclamation for proclamation's sake. They were not indifferent as to whether men obeyed or not. An air of expectation pervades all of the accounts of Paul's preaching. We find in the New Testament not only that Paul expected results, but that others expected them also. Today we must pray and work for great church growth and we must expect results. It is certain that our labor will be in vain if we lack the faith to even pray for such an ingathering.

Because of our religious and cultural background we have conditioned ourselves to slow growth. In America, a church which adds fifty new members per year through conversion from the world is admired for its zeal and faithfulness. But some missionaries have been sent out from churches which are converting less than fifty per year, and therefore they have come to expect no more when they go into ripe fields. If the national Church grows too rapidly, we doubt its quality; if it grows slowly, we cast about for biblical justification for such stagnation. Donald McGavran says:

> This glorification of slowness, this deep-seated conviction that God works slowly, this investment of literally hundreds of thousands of lives by foreign and national churchmen that a relatively few persons might come to a more genuine Christian faith, has built up a mental structure which cannot acknowledge the importance of great church growth. The tremendous challenge of the open door often cannot be even seen (1963:20).

It is too easy to be detoured into the conviction that service alone, without any regard to bringing men to Christ, is good mission work. Efficient schools and clean hospitals are not enough if they minister only to the physical needs of man. We will defeat the whole purpose of Christian service if we allow it to become paternalistic or superior. Too often we have proclaimed the Good News like a rich man casting a penny haughtily into the outstretched hand of a beggar, and thereby we have made him all the more a beggar, and by our very superiority cut off our identification. Service is true Christian service only when it brings people into touch with Christ. I have used the word *touch*. It is not enough for a school to impart knowledge, even knowledge of religion, or for a hospital to teach cleanliness (that may even accentuate the gulf between the hospital worker and patient). But if the motivation, planning, and definite actions of school and hospital are directed to the one goal of bringing people into *touch* with Christ and confronting them with His appeal for acceptance, they are within the orbit of the Christian mission.

But when service (a legitimate aspect of the ministry of the Church) becomes a *substitute* for mission and these institutions fail to see the "fields which the Lord is bringing to harvest," they settle down to an acceptance of slow growth.

Customs and Religious Beliefs

It is quite useless, and sometimes dangerous, for missionaries to go into a mission field to "convert the heathen" about whom they know almost nothing. In some cases we have pleaded for a restoration of New Testament Christianity among a people when the New Testament is hardly known, not to mention Christianity. Ignorant of the language, national customs, and deep-seated religious beliefs, we have all too frequently assumed that the successful American evangelist will meet the same favorable response in the heart of the Republic of Cameroun as he did back in Texas.

The missionary who has learned the language of his people soon finds that their religious system is extremely complex and their values quite different. He should then seek to become acquainted with every sacred tree, stone or grave, and to acquire all the knowledge he can about local customs, beliefs, and tribal history. *His first task is to know the people, not to preach the Gospel.* "There are far too many enthusiasts who rush around, often in luxurious cars, 'sowing the word,' preaching to people of whom they know nothing . . ." (Harris and Parrinder 1960:58-59).

We cannot emphasize enough the point that the people to whom we go are not living in a spiritual vacuum. It is no secret that animists are more aware of the spirit realm than the majority of Western Christians, and we must be extremely cautious about calling another man's light "darkness." Paul recognized the deeply religious nature of the Athenian Greeks and used this as a stepping stone to begin his message about the God who was to them unknown (Acts 17).

Due to what has often amounted to an indiscriminate condemnation of their religious beliefs and practices by missionary and national minister alike in Tongaland, it is now a common practice for the people to hide their belief in the power of the *mizimu* and the efficacy of the diviner. By having denied the existence of such "superstitious beliefs" or by deriding those who believe in such, we have not helped our converts overcome them, but rather have merely encouraged them to conceal these beliefs from us; thus we have prepared the way for syncretism at a deep level of their experience.

Our preaching must uphold the supremacy and lordship of Jesus Christ; we will then find that our hearers are capable of making the application to their own lives. We must give them the real antidote, a real Savior who helps them in their dark hours to *overcome* their fears instead of driving them to deeper levels of their psychological make-up.

Reading a Necessity

Missionaries who do not read enough can grow stale and become isolated from everything outside their own little part of creation. Administrative duties, village itineration, counseling with new Christians, and a myriad of other tasks can consume so much of the missionary's time that he may find few opportunities to read and study.
The missionary must have daily quiet time with God for his very ministry depends so much upon the power of the Holy Spirit working through the Word. We may be on fire for the Lord when we leave our homeland thinking that we know all the truth and possess the best methods, but that flame can quickly be quenched. To neglect Bible reading and study is to dry up the very fountain of living water in our lives. It is spiritual suicide!
But in addition to Bible reading and prayer, there are numerous other areas of special concern with which we will need to keep abreast. There is nothing that I regret more about my first five-year missionary tour than the fact that so little of my time was spent in reading either the Word of God or books on other subjects.

Building a Ministry Through Prayer

During the apostolic era, the Church of Jesus Christ multiplied exceedingly. Our Lord built His short earthly ministry upon the strength derived from the close communion which existed between Him and His Father. Repeatedly we read that He "withdrew into the mountain" or "arose a great while before day" to pray. A sorely troubled Jesus went into Gethsemane the night before the crucifixion, threw Himself totally into communion with the Father, and emerged confident and resigned to bearing the suffering and reproach of the cross.
Not only did Christ seek and find consolation and power in ceaseless prayer to His Father, but we read accounts of how the apostles also knew the necessity and worth of prayer in their ministries. They were well aware of the urgency of their task and jealously guarded their time in prayer lest other important work should encroach upon it. So engrossed were the apostles in their most demanding task that they appointed men to take over the duties of ministering to the poor so that they could devote themselves to prayer and to the ministry of the Word (Acts 6:4).
E. M. Bounds in his book *Power Through Prayer* describes the dedication and preaching of the Early Church:

How these New Testament preachers laid themselves out in prayer for God's people! How they put God in full force into their churches by their praying! These holy apostles did not vainly fancy that they had met their high and solemn duties by delivering faithfully God's Word, but their preaching was made to stick and tell by the ardor and insistence of their praying (n.d.:78).

If our missionary ministry is not built upon a constant surrender to God in prayer, our witness will lack authenticity and spiritual fire. Water cannot be drawn from an empty well. Let us give ourselves to a life of prayer that we may more closely approach our full potential as stewards of God's grace.

Avoiding Money Problems

Such a disparity usually exists between the incomes of most missionaries and the average African national that it is easy for us to enter into financial arrangements which jeopardize the success of our work and theirs. The missionary sometimes gives the impression that he has access to unlimited amounts of money, and when the time comes to encourage the village congregation to build its own church building, he finds himself in an untenable position. Then again, if the missionary supplies the funds for constructing the church building, he pauperizes the converts. They come to rely more and more upon him to supply their every need. Paternalism breeds paternalism.

By giving or lending money indiscriminately we foster dependency and destroy initiative. In so doing we unconsciously create for ourselves a father image which we may subsequently find difficult to get rid of. Cash transactions have a way of making one individual feel superior while at the same time casting the recipient in an inferior role.

Each missionary will have to make his own decision about the level he wishes to live on. It is possible to have too much money and too much can do more harm than good. As missionaries we should resist the idea, whenever we encounter it, that given enough money, practically anything can be done. One missionary with whom I am acquainted actually wrote to his supporting church to request a *decrease in his monthly support* so that he would not be tempted to live on too high a standard and separate himself from the village people.

We must not lose sight of the success which the Early Church enjoyed in the first century. The Gospel spread like a flame by the witness of poorly supported men, and financial entanglements were kept at a minimum.

Employer-employee relationships are to be avoided as much as possible lest we suddenly find that by having discharged one of our employees we have alienated a whole community by virtue of the fact that they are all related in some way to the fired worker.

Nationals must be given the opportunity to see us get blisters on our hands from helping them hoe in their fields, or take notice of the sweat on our foreheads while we give them a willing hand in building a hut. Many Africans do not know that a white man is capable of manual labor. Perhaps it would be feasible for us to exchange labor instead of employing nationals so often to do our work for us. For example, in exchange for the energy and time needed to dig the missionary's well, the missionary might reciprocate by helping the nationals plow and plant their fields.

This is an area which cries out for critical evaluation.

Annual Work Evaluation

Making an objective evaluation of our work is probably one of the most difficult tasks we could ever face, but it is absolutely essential. We must remain aware that we are God's stewards or husbandmen, and, as such, we should not needlessly fritter away our short years of missionary service in unproductive activity. Our eyes must be open to the line of conflict for by becoming too absorbed in some work or project which continues year after year without examination, we may find that the battlefront has moved somewhere else and we have ceased to be frontline soldiers.

There are too many receptive fields waiting to be reaped for us to be content with an area in which people are stubbornly resistant to the Gospel. It is of no great merit to continue hanging on just for the sake of being persistent. Far too much is at stake for us to disregard priorities in mission. There is biblical instruction on this point (Luke 9:1-6).

To submit ourselves each year to a conscientious and objective evaluation may not only involve some modification of our methods or the substitution of other plans; it may even mean making a major move to another area. Today's missionaries, particularly in Africa, need to be mobile and ready to move quickly to the ripest areas *as they become ripe*.

One of the greatest handicaps to located institutional programs is that they almost always defy objective evaluation. Vested interests and the immovability of brick and mortar make it almost impossible to analyze the approach and then to act, regardless of the consequences. Rationalization usually wins the battle.

By periodically retreating from our particular work and viewing it from a distance, we missionaries will have opportunities to meet and cross-fertilize ideas and methods with workers from other fields. This will result in greater efficiency, better approaches, and renewed vigor for all concerned.

NATIONAL ATTITUDES

Initiative and Responsibility

Since independence was attained in 1964, there has been a noticeable upsurge of initiative among the churches, but much remains to be done. A few local congregations are beginning to plan meetings and lecture series in which speakers are invited from other churches to deliver messages or teach classes.

In 1967, one of these churches took the lead in extending an invitation to leaders of her sister congregations throughout Tongaland to assemble and discuss the role of the Church in independent Zambia and other topics of import. Such initiative is not the rule as yet, and churches should encourage one another to take more responsibility for the organization of similar affairs.

It is just as important for the African brethren to pick up the reins of self-government as it is for missionaries to relinquish them. Leaders of the church at Kasungu Village talked to me in 1968 concerning the possibility of conducting a lectureship in their village. I suggested that they plan the meeting, send out invitations to speakers, and host it themselves. They were amazed that such an idea should be proposed, for meetings of this nature are generally planned and held at a mission station, where they can be supervised by missionaries and where adequate facilities for housing and feeding the guests are available. Whether any action was taken upon the suggestion, I do not know.

To be truly indigenous and independent, the leadership of each Tonga church must assume its rightful responsibility and authority. Churches will do well to emulate the spirit of national political independence in this regard, for why should the churches continue to rely so heavily upon foreign missionary supervision when the nation of Zambia itself has thrown off the shackles of foreign domination? The Church should be following the lead of the country, not going in the other direction.

Feeding Others

There is widespread spiritual hunger among national brethren who depend upon itinerating missionaries or Zambian preachers to feed them. They seem to have little confidence in their own ability to teach others and have been conditioned to the role of receiver rather than that of giver. National Christians should be taught that greater blessings always come to the donor than to the recipient and that the teacher learns more than the student. The Christian who shares his faith grows more by giving it away than by merely trying to accumulate more knowledge concerning it.

I do not wish to minimize the need for trained, well-grounded leadership, but I am suggesting that national brethren take more initiative in teaching others rather than meekly wait for the missionary to provide all of the spiritual answers.

The African Christian who knows the essentials of the Gospel of Jesus Christ, and has accepted and obeyed his Lord, is in possession of the pearl of great price. He is no longer a beggar looking for food, but instead has laid hold of a treasure which is far superior to anything that natural men possess. He is a member of a chosen race, a royal priesthood, a holy nation, and to commend Christ to others he must not by his attitude and actions suggest that he is still in darkness.

Taking Stewardship Seriously

The most effective answer to missionary paternalism is improved local stewardship.

The early Christians rose to the physical as well as to the spiritual necessities of their needy brethren. Paul encouraged the wealthier churches to contribute to the needs of the poorer brethren in Jerusalem and Judea. When they were presented with the challenge their response was immediate; collections were made when the church assembled on the first day of the week, and the gifts were sent by responsible men to the brethren in Judea.

As the needs arose, they were met--so much so that they had all things in common and no one had any need. Luke writes that "there was not a needy person among them" and "no one said that any of the things which he possessed was his own, but they had everything in common" (Acts 4:32, 34). Such a sense of interdependence and commonality does not exist in most Tonga churches at a time when the lesson of Christian communal solidarity could be most easily taught within the indigenous collectivism of the society. Villagers, the majority of whom are interrelated, already feel a responsibility toward the welfare of other members of the kinship group, so it is likely that the village could be taught to assume an even greater sense of responsibility toward their "family in Christ."

One probable reason for this lack of feeling of responsibility within the Tonga churches is that the congregations are made up of a mixture of individuals who do not necessarily possess a close natural kinship. Some may be related only by marriage, and still others may be from another tribe. Future village churches should result from interrelated, interdependent believers who accept Christ at the same time. In such churches, no one Christian would experience physical need without immediate and appropriate action on the part of the members of the church in response to that need.

Furthermore, in such a congregation, prompt and unified action would be forthcoming with regard to the more far-reaching necessities of sister congregations. Ultimately, these independent congregations would want to support their own ministerial training institutions and send their own missionaries to surrounding tribes.

Another reason for poor stewardship in Tonga churches is that due to paternalistic mission policy they have not been challenged, nor do they have real goals to meet. The majority of village churches give only enough to purchase the wine for the Lord's Supper! This apparently is the only reason they have for giving. At the same time, they may be meeting in the open air under a shade tree without even a crude shelter for a church building.

The most feasible solution to this problem would be to encourage the contribution of *kind* instead of *cash*. In areas where currency is relatively scarce, a Christian could give a goat, another a bag of corn, and another his labor of love. All of these contributions should be made with a definite purpose and goal in mind. Stewardship would then mean more than merely the collection of enough money to buy a bottle of wine every month or so.

National Christians must, within their own local congregations, begin to respond to such immediate needs as: (1) the rehabilitation of members who suffer loss of property by fire or theft; (2) paying the hospital bill for one of their members, or (3) helping elderly Christians plant, cultivate, and reap their corn crops. The needs are infinite, both in and out of the church, to which national Christians should respond.

Donald McGavran believes that the teaching concerning stewardship should take place early in the new life of the convert:

> As ingathering takes place, it should be on the basis of self-support. As people become inquirers, the Church should let them know that Christians give largely. New villages especially can be led to give largely (Pickett *et al* 1962: 81).

Erection of Church Buildings

Closely akin to the basic principle of stewardship is that of the erection of church houses in which the saints can assemble in all types of weather.

At the present time, several Tonga churches are meeting in school facilities or in the open air. Under these circumstances, school regulations or bad weather often force a curtailment of regular worship services and attendance fluctuates considerably.

National Christians must build houses of worship on their own level. They should see that a pole and mud building with a grass roof is just as acceptable to God as something more elaborate. Many of the village Christians were once students on the mission station or in village schools and believe that only a burned-brick building with a corrugated iron roof is acceptable or "good enough." Consequently, little congregations struggle on, year after year, without much hope of ever being able to construct their own expensive permanent structure. It would be much better for them to begin with a temporary building and then start contributing toward more adequate facilities.

* * * * * *

These are only a few of the attitudes which require modification or drastic change. All of us are not guilty of all of these attitudes, but my prayer is that we will be open and courageous enough to "wear the shoe if it fits our foot," learn from past experience, and make the necessary changes.

African brethren should realize that their relationship to our Father is not mediated by the fatherly missionary; instead, we are all brothers in Christ, each with his own strengths and weaknesses. Churches which depend upon their own resources to not only take care of their own needs, but also to plant other churches, are following a plan which is biblical and infinitely reproducible.

In summary, we state the universal principle of mission that *missionary paternalism and local stewardship vary inversely*. As long as missionary domination, control, and general "fatherliness" exist in mission policy, just that long does the lethargy in giving, lack of initiative, and widespread childishness continue in the local congregation. We must recognize that the survival and growth of the local church are in the hands of the local church, and pray that the local congregation will emerge from paternalism, grapple with its own immediate problems, make its own decisions, assume its own financial responsibilities, and become aware of its own autonomy. Only then will it be dynamic and truly indigenous.

11

New Emphases for the Church: Theological

Someone has said that the first step toward bringing about a solution to a problem is to recognize the fact that the problem actually exists. In the foregoing chapters we have observed a number of problems which have obstructed church growth; criticism has been leveled at ineffective and outmoded methods, and specific documentation has been introduced to substantiate the censures. However, to admit that a problem exists is not enough. God wants us to make disciples of lost men, baptize them, and bring them to the fullness of Christ. But to merely intensify our castigation of present mission policy will not in itself bring about this greater ingathering. We need some new emphases, both theological and practical.

Today Christian missionary work is being carried on amidst numerous nebulous theologies of what the mission of the Church really is. Some say that the mission of the Church is fulfilled by going into the world to do good to all men, or by operating hospitals, building schools, administrating, raising the standard of living, making nations friendly toward one another, or in just being there to offer the cup of cold water for Christ's sake when the child asks for it. Without a clear definition of what we are setting out to accomplish, it is very easy to get lost in activities which absorb our time and energy, but which fail to carry out God's will for *lost* men.

IMPORTANCE OF CHURCH GROWTH

By the term "church growth" we mean the spiritual process by which new congregations are reproduced and formed. The Church of early New Testament times grew rapidly and new congregations were formed as a result of this process of spiritua- reproduction.

One well-known church growth writer has classified the growth of the Church into three categories: *quantitative, qualitative,* and *organic* (Tippett 1966, 1968a, 1968b). The New Testament Church grew *quantitatively* by numerical expansion and the incorporation of converts into its fellowship (Acts 2:41, 47; 4:4; 6:7; 8:6; 9:31, 35, 42; 10:44-48; 11:21; 13:48, 49; 14:1. 21; 16:5, 15, 33, 34; 17:4, 12; 18:8; 19:18). *Qualitative* growth occurred as the fellowship was edified, taught, indoctrinated and built up into the fullness of Christ by the ministry of the Word (Ephesians 3:19; 4:11-14; Galatians 5:22). J. Y. Campbell says that this type of growth

> is an ideal, not for the individual Christian, but for the Christian Church as a whole; the Church is to become a "larger incarnation" of Christ, an organism through which he can work perfectly (Richardson 1966:89).

The third essential kind of growth which took place in the rapidly growing New Testament Church was *organic*. An organized, indigenous type of church growth accompanied numerical expansion and maturation in the New Testament Church. Elders were appointed in the newly planted churches (Acts 14:23) as overseers of the flock (Acts 2:17-38; I Peter 5:2, 3), and deacons were selected as special servants to care for the needy (Acts 6:1-6).

The Church grows quantitatively today when new converts are persuaded to accept their Savior and are added by Christ to His Church. This type of church growth depends upon the winning of converts. Converts are won by men and women whose own faith in the Lord Jesus is warm and vibrant enough to kindle faith in others (Acts 11:20, 21). Churches grow quantitatively from nothing but converts.

Churches which grow are those which recognize the limitless power of God and believe in it strongly enough to tap this power. They are churches whose members believe that they now enjoy a life which is on a higher level than that which they had before.

I urge that we accept the church growth point of view in mission today. This point of view holds that the Church should be doing many good things in the world, but that as long as there are more than two billion men who have never yielded themselves to Christ (in addition to the millions of nominal Christians), the proclaiming of Jesus Christ by word and deed as divine and only Savior, and persuading men to become His disciples and responsible members of His Church, *should be given top priority* (McGavran 1967). Church growth must become as important to us as it was to Paul and Barnabas and Silas.

We must recapture the missionary passion of the first century.

The church growth point of view is founded upon the Bible and is rooted in the very nature of God Himself. Our Father wants His lost children found. This was the reason for the Incarnation and the Cross. For persuading men to become followers of the Way, men and women have paid with their lives down through the centuries.

A necessary part of the Great Commission as recorded in Matthew 28 is the "going," but no one would claim that it is the main thrust of the Commission. The "going" is for the purpose of "making disciples." Christ's injunction is not fulfilled when we merely change our area of operation--it is obeyed when we persuade men and women to become His disciples. Proclamation, also, is an essential part of the Commission, but even proclamation in itself is not enough. It would be possible within five years to proclaim the Gospel to almost all of the world's population by equipping slow-flying aircraft with loudspeakers and thousands of tracts, to be dropped at strategic locations; but even after having successfully completed such a task, no one would argue that the Great Commission of our Lord had been carried out. Men have to be persuaded to become disciples of Christ. There must be a vast multiplication of churches.

Bearing in mind that we are slaves of Christ, we are not free to choose the philosophy or theology of mission we will follow. God is concerned with the salvation of sinners; He is not willing that any should perish, and it cost Him His Son to demonstrate this tremendous concern for mankind and to make possible the bridging of the gulf between Himself and us (II Corinthians 5:18, 19). The missionary imperative lies in the nature of God Himself (John 3:16). What other aim in mission could be more important than the discipling of all of the peoples of the earth?

The second essential element of the church growth viewpoint is its insistence upon the establishment of priorities. Winning men to Christian commitment can never be one of many equally good ends, because it was for this cause that our Lord went to the cross. It has eternal urgency. Everything that we do or plan must be weighed in the balances to ascertain whether or not churches are in fact being planted.

Regarding the question of priorities in mission, McGavran has written:

> Missionaries and mission organizations today, faced with many human needs, often defeated by resistant populations, always bound by previous patterns of action, cumbered with institutionalism in advance of the Church, burdened with cultural overhang which leads them to proclaim Christ in Western ways, committed to a non-biblical individualism, not understanding multi-individual accession as a normal

way in which men come to Christ, and deceived by their own promotional efforts (whatever missions do is "wonderful") engage in "splendid church and mission work." They are not frequently engaged in specific, purposeful, well-planned, and efficient church planting. This is true of both liberals and conservatives. Bitter experience teaches them to entertain small expectations of church growth, and they spend most of their time and missionaries for other things. They claim that these other things contribute to church growth, or are intended to do so: but they almost never evaluate what they are doing or revise their programs in the light of whether churches are in fact planted (1967).

Missionaries who are being sent to the field today find themselves under constant pressure to produce "results." Under the strain they frequently find it necessary to begin to cast about for some means of justifying their efforts to the supporting churches. Church growth is often pushed into the background in favor of the relief of suffering and the provision of the loaves and fishes, because "results" of this nature are more readily available. Large schools and hospitals are built with foreign money to enable home churches to be proud of what they are doing for the poor unfortunate natives. Clean, English-speaking students make a better impression upon the supporters than village illiterates. Generally, supporters see more future for the bright young man who speaks fluent English than they do for the illiterate elder who is a recognized leader in his village community. As a result, even the missionary begins to place great emphasis upon improving the person's physical condition prior to his conversion to Christ.

Leslie T. Lyall believes that if there is "one truth [which] has emerged from the confusion and turmoil of recent years it is this: the only permanent thing in any situation is the local church" (1966:74). This has been stressed also by church growth writers. Missionaries may have to leave their schools and hospitals very suddenly and if these schools and hospitals have overshadowed the local community of believers which consists mainly of schoolchildren and staff, no one may be left once the institution closes. Lyall goes on to say that

> All missionary work must be geared to establishing a strong local church community under wise and experienced leadership, prepared to survive vigorously when missionary activity is gone (1966:74).

Priorities have to be established when we are attempting to decide what areas are most receptive. It is perfectly possible for dedicated missionaries to work for decades among resistant people and realize very little church growth. Church growth occurs when Christians work hard among responsive people, provided we accept potential for church growth as a valid criterion for determining where we will work. The receptivity of Indonesia's millions should have priority over Afghanistan's few hundred thousand violently resistant Moslems.

The church growth viewpoint insists that in the twentieth century world with its numerous repsponsive peoples, a faithful reaping of these responsive tribes and peoples as they become ripe be assigned a higher priority. Our task as ministers of reconciliation is to pay attention to the reconcilable now while they are responsive, not to doggedly continue our proclamation to the obviously resistant. Even our Lord instructed His disciples not to waste time on those who would not listen (Luke 10:10, 11). Frequently where the harvest is great, the reapers are too few.

The point is that our Heavenly Father wants as many as possible of His children to be saved and brought to the fullness of Christ. In order for us to bring our wills into coincidence with His divine purposes, we must earnestly desire a great quantitative increase of Christians on this earth. If the world is to become Christ's and is to experience the fullness of the abundant and eternal life, churches must multiply enormously.

The farmer who heard the tornado warning on the radio did not stand at the door of his house and shout warnings to his twelve children who were widely scattered across the farmland. Rather, he ran from barn to barn persuading his children to run to the security of the cellar before the storm approached. He drove his car rapidly across the far reaches of his farm warning his children that a storm was coming. Only when he had accounted for his wife and twelve children and had brought them safely into the cellar did he believe that he had fulfilled all that was possible for him to do.

Our Heavenly Father wants His lost children found and brought into His fold before it is too late. He is not satisfied by merely shouting from the door or by finding only a few. His love is far greater than even that of the earthly father who did not rest until all of his children had been found. The eternal importance of church growth must be seen. McGavran makes this point very clear:

> When our Lord commands us to make disciples of the nations, He surely does not consider the job successfully concluded when one in 100 has yielded Him allegiance. Burying even 1 or 2 percent in a napkin to return to Him after thirty years, still 1 or 2 percent, will scarcely merit His "well done" (1963:14).

Calvin Guy has observed that some people become very indignant at the mere mention of "the cost/result ratio." Their objection is that since "one soul is worth all that can

be spent on it" one should disregard the cost/result ratio.
Their objection might contain some validity if the Church had
at its disposal unlimited resources and if it was necessary to
pour out these huge sums to send one soul. However, in view of
today's mounting responsiveness in land after land, the
lavishing of large amounts of money upon the conversion of only
a few seems hard to justify. Furthermore, widespread soul-
hunger among so many peoples suggests that it is not necessary
in our day (McGavran 1965:141).

EVANGELISTIC MISSIONARIES

Active participation in evangelism by large numbers of Tonga
Christians will come only when large numbers of missionaries
really start to evangelize. This means that unless the medical,
the educational, and the philanthropic missionary joins with
the evangelistic missionary in regular and enthusiastic
evangelism, we can expect comparatively few national Christians
to become really concerned with dynamically presenting the
Gospel and with persuading men and women to become children of
God.

We should cease to rationalize that so long as we operate
and administer our school or hospital efficiently, we have done
our specialty well and there is no additional need to witness.
A dynamic faith will kindle a like faith in other hearts.

It is constantly necessary to stress the need to evangelize.
It is so easy for the best of missionaries to get caught up in
office work and administrative duties that he might as well
live in suburbia for all he sees of the people. A close
missionary associate told me not long ago as he fingered
through his Bible that he scarcely had time to read and study
the Book anymore, so demanding had his administrative and
teaching load become. Another missionary said sadly that he
was not spiritually prepared to engage in evangelism. He felt
that at the present time he would have to confine himself to
his teaching position in the mission secondary school.

Melvin Hodges, a missionary to Latin America, has made the
statement that:

> The missionary is the planter of churches and the sower of
> seed. But he is more. He brings with him and creates
> around him the atmosphere, the climate, in which the church
> is to grow. This depends directly on the theology he lives;
> on his own "godliness." We communicate our faith or lack of
> faith, and nurture our converts with our own spiritual
> vitality. If we ourselves are New Testament Christians with
> New Testament experience and faith, we will create the
> climate for the growth of a New Testament church (McGavran
> 1965:28).

If we, as missionaries, want the Church to grow, we must be vital Christians who will inspire in our converts the true spirit of sacrifice for the Gospel and the burning passion for lost souls. The radiant personal faith of the missionary is an irreplaceable factor. Every other ingredient may be present, but if this quality is missing, very little church growth ever occurs. History has shown that wherever there has been authentic spiritual fire in the lives of missionaries, all kinds of difficult barriers have been hurdled. Missionaries who have gone to the mission fields from zealous and growing churches in the home country have generally ignited the spark of faith in the lives of their national converts. Missionaries on fire for Christ can turn their section of the human mosaic upside down. Conversely, they can affect it very little.

Some missionaries have said that "we should let the nationals reach their own people." By adopting this attitude we rationalize our evangelistic role once again. The apostles were committed men, filled with the Holy Spirit, who expected their converts to be equally committed and filled with God's Spirit. They preached Christ and Him crucified and they expected men to respond in the same manner in which they had answered the call. We have no right to expect our converts to be either more concerned about evangelism or more dynamic in their witness than we are.

If we are to practice methods which are anywhere near the Pauline methods in power and directness, it is imperative that we first have this faith. Without faith in God and faith in the Holy Spirit in our converts, we can do nothing. We cannot possibly act as Paul did until we recover this faith.

Missionary evangelism is extremely demanding. The missionary must learn the language, the customs and religious beliefs, and endure physical discomfort. National Christians need to be inspired by missionaries who are willing to walk the dusty paths with them as they seek to persuade men to become children of God. Nationals should see Spirit-filled missionaries burning out and spending their lives to win their people to Christ, or in the words of one elderly national Christian, "we need missionaries who will come to us and die for us, if necessary, to tell us the words of God."

INDIVIDUAL VERSUS GROUP CONVERSIONS

Present within most African societies is the strong sense of communal solidarity. Tonga society is no exception to this rule, except for the comparatively small segment of the tribe which has become detribalized or socially dislocated in some other way.

In such societies people are accustomed to making individual decisions *within the context of a group*. Although each person

New Direction for the Church

makes his own decision on a certain matter, the group finds it much more satisfying to act as a group once the consensus of opinion has been reached. This type of group decision-making may at times occur on a relatively small scale within a family, a household, or a particular segment of the village which is composed of blood relatives. On other occasions whole villages, clans, kingroups, or various cooperative groups may be involved in the palavers. Decisions within these groups are taking place constantly on a wide variety of subjects and concerning many activities.

Westerners place strong emphasis upon individual action in decision-making and find it extremely difficult to imagine that people can act as a unit. Yet in highly integrated societies people act together with amazing cohesiveness. Agents of change and church planters must not underestimate the importance of such socially conditioned decisions or, on the other hand, fail to appreciate the individual's role.

When first confronted with the concept of group conversion, I reacted to it negatively. My own conversion had been very personal and my Western individualism had rebelled at the thought of a "group decision." What I had failed to realize was that the Christianization of groups does not exclude individual conversion in the least. In the strictest sense of the word, individual conversion is the only kind possible. No group has a mind of its own; only individuals within the group possess minds and are capable of making decisions. No group can believe in Jesus, confess His name, nor repent of its sins. *Only individuals within the group* can make such decisions.

Really what is meant by the term "group conversion" is what has been referred to by most church growth writers as *multi-individual conversion*:

> It is many individuals believing on the Lord at the same time in shared knowledge of the joint action and mutual dependence on each other. Such multi-individual action has very different marginal meanings and results from lone individual action taken in the teeth of group disapproval (McGavran 1965:73).

I now believe that thousands of Tongas could be persuaded to accept Christ and become "responsible members of His Church" through multi-individual conversion. Where the Church grows in such a fashion, individuals acting within the group are able to reconstruct their lives, both individual and corporate, around Jesus Christ.

If the Tonga people, both Christian and non-Christian, could realize that becoming a Christian means that a believer can be baptized along *with* the rest of his believing family, household or village, and that they could continue to live in the same village, cultivate the same gardens, and marry within the customary framework, more would accept Christ and fewer would revert after their conversion. Christianity would then be more successfully integrated into everyday life. Instead of the ostracism, ridicule, and isolation which resulted from the individualistic pattern of the past, Christians would make up the majority segment of the village and not merely the non-conforming fringe. The Church would no longer be considered a foreign organization which belongs to the missionary, but as Christ's Body, with the members of that Body responsible only to Him as its Head. As long as Christianity remains outside a people it will make slow progress, but once it has been integrated into it, it will flow unhindered through it.

We have been wrong in insisting that the only way to build the Church is by converting individuals and extracting them from the families, clans, villages, and social groups, thus separating converts from their relations and cutting them off from their roots. As Warnhuis shows, such a Church is merely a conglomeration of individuals "often held together only by the cement of foreign money" (Pickett *et al* 1962:20). Conversely, the few Tonga churches which do consist of whole family units or households, are the most united and spiritual of those which I surveyed.

Missionaries should begin to think seriously about the question that John V. Taylor has posed:

> Until our vision is aligned to the African way of looking at things, until we have felt our individuality vanishing and our pulses beating to communal rhythms and communal fears, how can we guess what that Lord looks like who is the Savior of the African world (1963:35)?

We must become more aware of the ways in which the Good News is best advocated in tribal social structures. We must develop greater alertness toward the *winnable units* which surround us on every hand. The units of pagan society can and must be won for Christ.

The church growth point of view insists that more attention be focused upon the patterns of the social entities within which people organize themselves to satisfy and supply their human needs, solve their problems and make their decisions, for it is within this context that they will make their decision for Christ or against Him. As Tippett says,

> It behooves us as His missionaries, to make ourselves aware of cohesive social segments, *winnable units*, within which we may perform our ministry (1968b:42).

The concept of multi-individual decision is soundly biblical. Throughout the Bible we read accounts concerning the responsibility of the individual to the group. From the early history

of the nation of Israel we recall where the leaders made their
proclamations within "the assembly of the congregation of
Israel" (Exodus 12:6; 16:9, 10; 35:1; Leviticus 8:3; Numbers
1:18; 8:20) and the decisions were arrived at within the
context of this assembly (Numbers 14:2, 10, 36; 15:36; 35:24;
Judges 21:10). Moses and Aaron frequently gathered together
the elders of the people to deliver to them the word of the
Lord or to allow these elders to make their individual decisions
within a group for the good of all (Exodus 34:31; Numbers 4:34;
31:13-20). The *congregation*, the *assembly* and the *people of
God* were all terms which demonstrated the solidarity of the
Israelites in the Old Testament. This people acted cohesively
under their princes, elders, and tribal leaders. Each member
of the assembly had the freedom to make his own decision within
the congregation; this was not a group decision in which the
individual counted for nothing. The individual was important,
but once the concensus of opinion was achieved, united action
was taken by the group (Tippett 1968b:43-46).

Multi-individual responsibility toward the group is indicated
clearly in the New Testament (Acts 1:13; 2:44, 45). Group
action in response to the preaching of the Gospel took place in
large groups on Pentecost (Acts 2:1, 41) and in Samaria (Acts
8:12-14). *Whole villages* turned to the Lord (9:35); *households*
accepted Christ and were baptized (Acts 16:15, 33, 34;
I Corinthians 1:16); and the Word of God found acceptance
within *kinship groups* such as the one gathered in the house of
Cornelius (Acts 10:24, 44-48).

Group action in conversion is still the best pattern for
most non-Western peoples just coming out of paganism. The
above accounts clearly show that God was pleased with multi-individual decisions in all three areas of church growth:
quantitative, qualitative, and organic. It also indicates
conclusively that young churches founded in this manner grow
more rapidly in the areas of leadership, fellowship, grace and
unity when they grow in this manner. All three must be kept in
proportion.

Let us pray with one accord that God will help us to shake
off the Western individual sin which restricts us from
accepting multi-individual accessions to the faith.

A POSITIVE THEOLOGY

The message which has been brought to Africa has, for the
most part, been very negative. This is in a way understandable
in view of the tremendous cultural differences which confronted
the early missionaries. Coming from a Christianized society in
America or Europe, they were appalled and repulsed by the dark
and sinister practices of polygyny, idolatry and spirit worship.
Their preaching was aimed at these sinful indulgences as well

as at other forms of "heathenism" or "superstition." The long history of negative preaching and teaching which followed has created voids. Christianity has come to mean a "religion of don'ts" to many Tonga, and comparatively few have experienced the positive blessings of being redeemed children of God.

Our goal must now be to develop a *positive* theology, a *relevant* method of presenting that body of truth, and a *greater reliance upon the power of the Holy Spirit* in the lives of believers.

The initial step toward a more positive message is to study the culture of the people we seek to win.

> Such customs and beliefs constitute the culture of each group of people and *understanding this culture can spell the difference between success and failure in introducing new ideas and methods* (Arensberg and Niehoff 1964:4).

Religious beliefs of a people are an integral part of their culture, not merely a compartmentalized aspect as Christianity so often is in Western culture. A culture is much like a brick wall; each brick is necessary to preserve the solidarity and strength of the wall. If a brick or a number of bricks are removed from the wall, its strength is weakened.

People, however, adjust and react in various ways when their culture is tampered with. If the agent of change removes an essential part of the complex of life and does not replace it with a *functional substitute*, the society adjusts to this new state of affairs by either tolerating the cultural void, by providing its own substitutes, or by resenting the agent of change.

It is important then that we understand what *function* a particular element fulfills within the cultural whole. Instead of preaching vehemently against the "terrible evils of spirit worship," for example, we need first to be aware of the extent to which spirit worship is intricately bound into the whole culture. We need to ask, "What are the basic religious needs satisfied by worshipping ancestral spirits?" Once we know what the fundamental needs are and have a better replacement for the "brick" that we want to remove, *only then should we advocate a change*. It is absolutely essential that we provide something distinctly better, or lead the people to suggest their own functional substitute. "Legislating or ranting against socially harmful practices," writes Eugene Nida, "is not likely to have much effect. Preaching itself is relatively useless *unless it offers something distinctly better* [italics mine]" (1954:179).

There are probably scores of areas within the Tonga culture into which the Gospel needs to penetrate and transform but I should like to mention here only a few of what I consider to be the essentials of a positive and relevant message. These are theological principles which should have a wide application among the predominantly animistic peoples of Africa.

The Origin of Man

Much of traditional African religious belief centers around the creation myths: the beginning of things and the origin of man. The whole conceptualization of God often refers to these myths which attempt to explain the nature of things. According to some of the myths, it was during the early period of mankind that God the Creator withdrew from the affairs of men because He was insulted by a woman.

The biblical view of the beginning of man's existence, then, is a very important part of our message. Some basis must be given for the presence of the clan which means so much to most Africans. When, where, and how did the clan begin? These are questions which need answers. (See Genesis 1-2:25; Job 33:4; Psalm 86:9; 146:5, 6; Nehemiah 9:6; Jeremiah 27:5; Malachi 2:10; Acts 17:24-26.)

Western missionaries who come to Africa often forget that they have accepted certain presuppositions concerning the origin and creation of man which are not present in African mythology and this first essential biblical concept needs to be taught and learned well. We must link ourselves with the beginning (Sundkler 1962:100-101). The stories of Genesis should provide the content for many of our sermons. The imagery and customs in this first book of the Bible will find open and receptive hearts which will readily identify themselves with the people of God. In fact, they more readily associate themselves with the Genesis narrative than do we Westerners.

The God of the original creation is still active in history and in our lives. We must tie together two very important events in the minds of our converts: (1) God created all things (Genesis 1), and (2) He is creating within His obedient children a *new man* (II Corinthians 5:17; Galatians 6:15; Ephesians 2:10; 4:24). God still creates!

The Relevance of the Old Testament

In so-called "Christian" countries, the employment of the New Testament in our teaching is assumed as the part of the Bible to start with, but among people without a Christian heritage the New Testament has to be undergirded first with the Old Testament.

Animists are very conscious of power encounters. Although we presuppose the powerful encounters of the Old TEstament and take them for granted, to them the account of Elijah and prophets of Baal (I Kings 18) on Mount Carmel says a great deal. In this bit of biblical history, God emerges as the only True God, Creator and All-Powerful. Among animists a weak, watered-down version of God will have little appeal. As God's servants and ambassadors of Christ, we must lead our people to the God of Power. Nothing will more clearly demonstrate this power of God to the African than these Old Testament passages.

We must not grow weary of telling the dramatic accounts of God's great acts in history: the creation, the flood, the calling and preservation of the People of God, the Incarnation and the Resurrection. For the Christ to be really meaningful, much time and patience must be spent with the people in the Old Testament. We may find our listeners more apt at discovering Old Testament theological concepts than are we.

Relationship between the Living and the Dead

African traditional religion is closely bound up with fertility, vitality, the continuation of the clan or lineage, procreation, birth, marriage, death, and communal solidarity. It is precisely at this point that we need to speak out; this is where much of the conflict takes place between Christianity and the African view of life and death.

The survival of the clan and the continuation of the lineage lies behind the strong emphasis upon fertility and the desire for offspring. For an individual to break the lineage or solidarity of the clan is a great sin and it is almost unthinkable for a man to die without offspring; he will have broken the chain. "We must have many children," said one Tonga man, "because six of my children might die in one night." He had ten children and felt reasonably secure that his line would go on. His concern was not focused so much upon problems of feeding and clothing his children as it was upon maintaining the lineage.

When a man or woman dies, her *muzimu*, or spirit, joins a large body of other spirits which remain very close to the living members of the family for about three generations. Only the *mizimu* of the most prominent are remembered and worshipped for more than three generations. But even though the clan is going on, it really is gradually fading out as the living forget the distant dead.

Our theology must include teaching on life after death, where the ancestors are, and an assurance of the future. A denial of the fact that ancestral spirits exist is unfounded and unbiblical. They *do* exist, they *are* real (Luke 16:19-31), but they are awaiting the judgment and have no power to affect the life or circumstances of the living (vs. 27-31). We must emphasize that both the living and the dead are subject to the "Judge of the living and the dead" (Acts 10:42; II Corinthians 5:10; II Timothy 4:1); that Christ has power over the spirits because He is their Creator (Colossians 1:16, 17). We are surrounded by a "cloud of witnesses" (Hebrews 12:1) who are concerned with how we run the race of life.

The message we preach must constantly hold forth the promise

New Direction for the Church

of a resurrection (Job 19:25-27; Psalm 49:15; Daniel 12:2; Hosea 13:14; Matthew 22:31, 32; Luke 20:35; John 5:21, 25, 28, 29) and an assurance of an after-life for those who believe and obey Christ (John 3:14-16; 6:47; Romans 6:23; I Timothy 4:8; I John 2:25). The hope of eternal life is a dimension which does not commonly exist in animistic religious belief. To the African,

> The survival of the man and his clan is a matter of primary importance to him and to his people, and the survival of the dead, the after-life, is a matter of existential interest to him and to his Church (Sundkler 1962:114-115).

The Love of God

Most Africans will readily agree that the Supreme Being (as they conceive of God) is Power and Spirit, but only Christianity can demonstrate the *love* of God. Not only did God not remove Himself in a huff when a woman stuck her pestle in His face (as the African myth goes) but He does not want us to continue running from Him. God stands at the door of His house longing for the return of His prodigal children. Animists must hear about this God--the One who cares and is mightily concerned.

The love of God in our positive message must overwhelm the animistic ideas of a detached, unconcerned, and angry Supreme Being (Psalm 103:13; Isaiah 38:17; John 3:16; 14:21; 23; Romans 5:8; I John 4:8).

Edwin Smith has said that Africans have agreed with the Jewish concepts of God as Power and Spirit, but

> it did not ever come into their mind to say: God is Love. Only the Lord Jesus was able to make men see that. Only He was able to make that belief possible (1936:156).

The *vertical* relationship of love between God and man is articulated best when there exists an open and sincere *horizontal* love between men. This all-giving horizontal love between missionary and national brethren must exist if the love of God for man is to be taught effectively.

David Barrett lists as one of the causes for the rise of schism and the formation of over six thousand contemporary religious movements in Africa the *failure in love*. He says that

> In regard to most of the components of love--service, sacrifice, forgiveness, caring, compassion, charity, peace-- missions had exemplary records, as is evident from the large and flourishing mission churches that have resulted. But at one small point only--love as listening, sharing, sympathizing and sensitive understanding in depth between equals-- missions in many areas appeared to the more critical observers to have failed (1968:269).

Telling *about* the love of God is not enough; it must be *demonstrated*.

The Nature of God

Among animists there is a widespread belief in a creator God (see Tonga Ideas of God, Chapter III), but He is distant and unloving. Christ, however, has given God a face; in Christ, God is no longer distant, unseeing and unconcerned (Nida and Smalley 1959:62). He enters into everyday life where He seeks men to be reconciled to Him and to become His children and friends (Romans 5:10, 11; II Corinthians 5:18-21; Ephesians 2:16; Colossians 1:19-22).

To know God we must know the Son (John 14:6, 7). We can identify with Jesus and through Him we can realize our sonship. We have access to eternal life through no other channel. Jesus Christ is the way to God.

In Christ, God is brought near and is ever-present in time of need. I am convinced that there is enough in animists' view of the Supreme Being to serve as a stepping stone to a biblical knowledge of God.

The Mediatory Role of Christ

There is no need for the African to go to God through human priests and religious practitioners. No longer is it necessary to offer the blood of black chickens at the door of the house. Christ has made a sacrifice sufficient for all time, and it is He who now stands as our Mediator, Priest, and Savior.

It is a basic tenet of animistic thought that the spirit of a respected member of the clan knows the problems of the living and is in a position to be understanding and helpful, because he has experienced the same difficulties. In Christ we have a Mediator of Power and Love who has also experienced the trials of humanity (Hebrews 4:14-16). Christ does understand and has the power to help in time of need.

Animists want a mediator to go between the realm of the living and the High God. Christ fulfills this need and does it fully because He was both fully human and is fully divine. This role of Christ must be stressed in our preaching to saved and unsaved alike.

Malevolent Spirits and Sorcery

One of the greatest blessings that the message of Christ can bring to the animistic heart is the release from fear. The fear of vengeful spirits and sorcery is at times almost paralyzing to many animists. The message for which the animist is waiting and to which he responds so often is that Jesus is our Deliverer from fear, and through His powerful name devils fear and fly (Harris and Parrinder 1960:60).

The need for deliverance from fear is often desperate. We must persuade men to accept Christ, for it is in Him that we receive the Spirit of power (Acts 2:38; I Corinthians 2:12-14). When we receive the spirit of sonship we are no longer slaves to fear (Romans 8:14, 15; Hebrews 2:14, 15). Christianity is a tremendous relief from age-old taboos and fears. In the past we have laughed at these as superstition and of no real consequence. I am calling for an attitude whereby we will say, "Here is the power by which we can overcome this fear." Because it does not threaten us is no valid reason for us to deny its existence.

Finally, not only must we have a positive message but for it to have real sticking power, it must be presented in a relevant manner. Drawing upon many years of experience as a missionary, anthropologist, and linguist, Eugene Nida succinctly states:

> In general, three internal factors most influence church growth: (1) the effectiveness of the minister or missionary as the source of communication (i.e., his understanding of the people, degree of identification, spiritual leadership, and possession of a winning personality); (2) the relevance of the message; and (3) the qualities of those who receive it--e.g., their fidelity to the message, their spiritual growth, and their aggressiveness in witnessing (McGavran et al 1965:99).

A major part of the missionary effectiveness which Nida refers to has to do with his flexibility toward the *form* that Christianity in Africa will assume. While preaching the brotherhood of all men we have unconsciously clung to a *white* Christ, son of a *white* mother, teacher of *white* disciples, worshipped almost exclusively with *European* music in *Western* church buildings. Our literature and films almost invariably depict *white* characters. It is small wonder that Africans complain of an imposed white man's religion.

For the message of Christ really to become integrated into Tonga life, the forms of its expression will have to become African. The missionary, who is himself a product of a culture and whose religious expressions have a Western configuration, will have to vigorously proclaim the essentials of the Universal Gospel and allow his non-Western converts the freedom to express their worship in African terms.

12

New Emphases for the Church: Multiplying Congregations

The quarter-million Tongas live in approximately two thousand communities--villages, neighborhoods, and kingroups. Their society is experiencing rapid and deep-seated changes. Young people are moving to towns and cities in search of education and employment. Rural people are laying hold of Western innovations and techniques which have managed somehow to filter back into the village situation. Few are completely unaffected by the upheaval.

Churches and Missions among the Tonga must turn with intelligence and determination to church multiplication. Although I have mentioned this goal throughout this study of the evangelization of Tongaland, it is proper here to emphasize the radical change that is imperative. Past patterns of mission work do not, indeed cannot, meet the challenges of independent Africa.

OUR PRIMARY OBJECTIVE

The goal of Missions should not be to educate the Africans-- though service to his fellowman is something dear to the heart of every Christian. The missionary goal cannot be to plant a few congregations at or near the mission stations and hope that, with the passage of the years, the "younger churches" will be able to overcome the obstacles which have defeated us and transmute our failures into successful evangelization. Committed to the principle of transferring all power and control to national Christians, we must not take shelter behind that worthy goal and divest ourselves of our own responsibilities.

We missionaries must be good stewards of God's grace, and we must also help our African fellow disciples to be good stewards themselves.

The primary aim in missions must be the planting of an ongoing church in *each* of the Tonga communities in city, town, and countryside. The primary goal: To multiply congregations until every man, woman, and child in Tongaland has had a chance to say "yes" to Jesus Christ and to become a living stone in the great temple which God is erecting there. Every redeemed individual must say so. The Good News will reach comparatively few if its communication depends entirely upon the planning and direction of foreign missionaries.

Most of the foreign missionaries in Tongaland at the present time are engaged in institutional missions. Even if all of them were to suddenly redirect their energies toward evangelism, it would still be virtually impossible for every Tonga to be personally confronted by Christ *through the efforts of these missionaries alone*. Our African fellow disciples must see that the Christ we proclaim is indeed Lord of each of our lives, and that the Good News about Him is the most important message that they could tell to their kinsmen. A fervent and relevant witness to the transforming power of Jesus Christ in the life of one Tonga is the most effective vehicle for the transmission of the Gospel to another Tonga. Tongas must win Tongas.

HOW AND WHERE CHURCHES SHOULD BE PLANTED

In Tonga society the Gospel flows most freely from the elder to the younger. Conversions take place rapidly in villages and towns where the parents or guardians have *preceded* the children of the household in becoming Christians.

Churches are strongest when composed of family or kinship units which have become Christian at about the same time. Unfortunately, among Tonga Churches of Christ, there have been very few instances where this type of conversion has actually been sought or encouraged by missionaries or national preachers trained by them.

We must begin immediately to concentrate upon the winning of *adults*. These persons may be largely illiterate, given to beer-drinking, and often polygynous, but this older segment of society must be won first. Once these parents have made the decision to become Christians, their children will find it much easier to complete the family movement to Christ. But to continue the conversion of individual students in our mission schools in the anticipation that they will win their pagan parents is futile. The words of schoolchildren or teen-agers usually have little positive effect upon their parents. Certainly the thirty years during which all of the Missions have reaped relatively meager results should be sufficient to convince us of this fact.

In village after village the initial decision to accept Christ must be encouraged and expected to come first from within the power structure. This decision, which will subsequently revolutionize their lives and society, must rest in the hands of the adult members of the community. Any course of evangelization which fails to convert these responsible men will limp along until sometime, somehow, into some Church, the responsible adults are won in significant numbers.

Missionaries have frequently been repulsed by the unpredictable and obnoxious behavior of drunken men at village beer drinks. It is an affront to our moral code; we are reluctant to get involved with this kind of lost individuals. But we must now turn our attention to these "hedgerows and byways" where lost men are. One concerned Christian leader went so far as to say, "We must go to the men around the beer pots; there resides the authority and leadership of the village. Those are the important men."

Since 1968, most local church buildings have been erected outside the immediate village perimeter because church members complained of excessive noise and distraction during worship, or cited instances of ridicule. The reason for these annoyances was that the members of these churches, mainly women and children, did not command the respect and attention of the major part of the village.

On the other hand, the headman and the council of elders within the village have had no difficulty in capturing and maintaining the rapt attention of the villagers. This conclave does not find it necessary to meet outside the village confines, but assembles in the middle of the village to settle the important and serious issues of day-to-day living. This is the traditional way.

The very location of the church building in most Tonga communities, outside the village, is a clear indication of the place which Christ occupies in the lives of the majority of the community. Until the message of Christ penetrates the heart of the power structure, we will have to be content with a collection of schoolchildren and women (precious as they are) in local churches, while the major part of the village remains intact and untouched by an irrelevant message couched in foreign terms. The appeal must be made to the adult men. There is no need for the Church to continue this fringe existence.

The power structure must be given every opportunity to move toward Christ. The rest of the village observes the deliberations and awaits the decisions of its leaders and "old people" before it acts. The surrender of these respected adults to Christ as Lord may trigger much larger movements.

Our goal must be to plant a church in every receptive community in Tongaland. There is no need for Christians to

walk several miles to worship. With a church in every village
Christians would be able to meet for fellowship and prayer
every single day. God's people could start every morning with
dawn prayers and meditation and end the day with songs, prayers,
and Bible study. The Christian life would become a total
existence, instead of merely a weekly observance. It would not
be long before churches would begin to thrust forward their
natural leaders for further specialized Bible training.

The question now arises as to *where* churches should be
planted first. It is agreed that the ideal for which we are
striving is a congregation of worshipping Christians in every
receptive community in Tongaland, but where should we start?
We have considered several disastrous sociological ramifications
of church planting without converting the male adult segment of
villages. This leads us to the conclusion that our initial
efforts to evangelize the Tonga must begin where these important
men are, i.e., in the rural areas. By concentrating upon
adults, the present paucity of capable leadership might well be
overcome.

On the following map I have pointed out the rural to urban
migration of many young people to cities and towns. Their
ties with the "old people" back home are not completely severed.
Their roots are deep and they return for frequent visits. If
these young people have come from strong rural churches where
their parents, along with the headman and wise men, are
Christians, it determines to a large extent whether their faith
stands or falls.

Schoolchildren, particularly on the secondary level, are
discovering that the animistic beliefs of their parents are not
sufficient to cope with the advancing tide of science and
technology. Hence, many are making the transition from animism
to materialism or secularism. It is my contention that young
people who come from Christian villages where Christ has become
Lord of everyday life will be more able to withstand temptation.
Only then can strong urban churches be planted. Urban youth
must be buttressed by Christian "old people" back in the village.

The consistency of rural traditional society is more
conducive to multi-individual conversions. Evangelization in
village communities is more collective and people act more as
groups. Churches would have strong natural cohesion and an
inherent unity. I believe more of the lost can be won by
igniting the spart of the Gospel in areas where the message can
flow from village to village and from family web to family web.

THE FUTURE DIRECTION OF "MISSION WORK"

Our goal is not to perpetuate good "mission work." We are
not in the business of building better mission institutions or
of installing more efficient water systems as ends in them-

PATTERNS OF RURAL TO URBAN MIGRATION

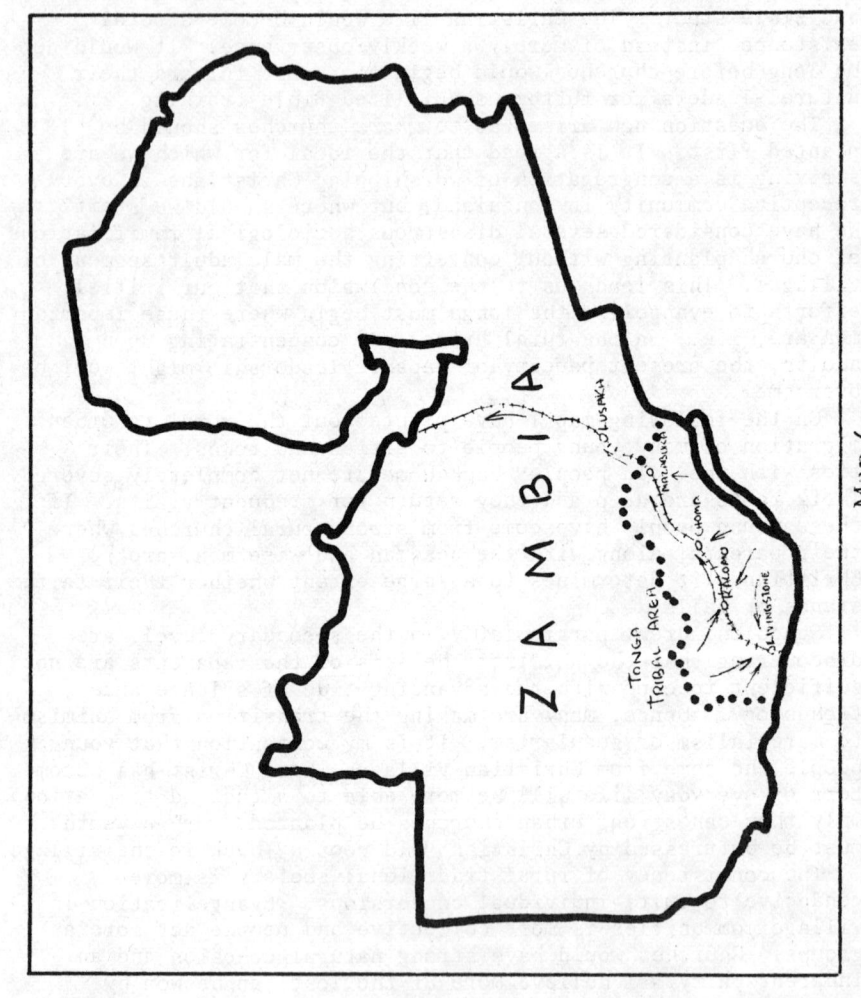

Map 6

selves. "Mission work" can include everything from plowing to plumbing, making bricks to milking cows. It does not necessarily involve church planting.

My plea is for a more specific goal, a more direct approach to the conversion of the Tonga people. With 87 percent of the tribe still uncommitted to Christ, our goal must be to win the multitudes. Another generation of a slow and gradual mission-station centered "mission work" will be disastrous. Unless a radical new approach is adopted which will bring in large numbers of believers, the Church in the next generation will be confronted by a multitude of confirmed materialists whose faces are set against the message of Christ.

What must be increased is the Church--the pure Body of Christ. I enter no plea for baptizing pagans who remain pagans. An indefinitely reproducible pattern but be used which the new Christians themselves, the newly Christian power structures themselves, the chiefs and tribesmen alike, can understand and duplicate in the hundreds of villages to which they will carry the message and in which they will plant the Church. This pattern must include churches made up of families, of adult men, of at least parts of village power structures.

Finding this pattern, multiplying it, adapting methods in view of how they work, overcoming obstacles to church establishment, developing Bible-based education which can be carried out in local churches without missionaries being present and without cash assistance, training the leaders of two thousand Tonga congregations, mounting campaigns against the social evils of the country--these are what "mission work" in the future must be.

In conclusion, I should like to strongly emphasize that the multiplicity of good ends must not be allowed to take the focus off the chief end which is *that churches be multiplied*. We should settle for nothing less. We should be diverted to nothing lower. Given a multitude of living churches, everything is possible. But as long as we are confined to a few little static, mission dependent churches, out of touch with the heart of this great people, very little real advance is possible.

13

New Emphases for the Church: Practical

For the Tonga Church to grow as it should there are any number of problems which need to be explored and solutions found, but I would like to suggest what seem to me to be five important and practical ways of speeding up a stable kind of growth.

DEVELOPING AN INDIGENOUS HYMNODY

This is an area in which the Western missionary will need to grant more freedom and independence to his African brethren simply because he knows so little about African rhythm and song.

Many years have passed since the first English hymns were translated into Tonga and still the hymnals used by the Churches contain relatively few indigenous hymns. The hymnal, *Inyimbo Zya Ivangele* (Gospel Songs) used by the Churches of Christ, for example, contains only nineteen completely Tonga songs set to indigenous tunes, from a total of 130 selections. The remaining 111 hymns are translations of English songs which also retain their Western tunes.

Table 6 demonstrates vividly the paucity of indigenous hymns in present hymnals being used in Tongaland. Even the highest percentage--14.6--in one of the hymnals is far from adequate. A concerted effort needs to be made to collect and preserve on tape the many Tonga hymns, before they are lost forever.

TABLE 6

Tonga Hymnals

Name of Hymnal	Total Number of Hymns	Number of Indigenous Hymns	Percentage of Indigenous Hymns
Inyimbo Zya Ba-Kristo (Methodist)	199	29	14.5%
Inyimbo Zya Ba-Kristo (BC)	200	14*	7.0%
The Salvation Army Citonga Song Book	202	0	0.0%
Inyimbo Zya Ivangele (CC)	130	19	14.6%

*Several of these hymns are not indigenous *Tonga* songs, but are translations from *Zulu*.

I recall meeting two old Tonga Christian men during my survey who have done much of their teaching in song. The songs they sing are stories set to music. The song lasts as long as is necessary to tell the story, and rhyme plays no part in the structure of the hymn. These old men have a tremendous contribution to make in the area of indigenous music. They should be encouraged to teach these oral renditions to as many Christians as possible, and their hymns should by all means be collected and included in a newer version of the Tonga hymnal.

The spiritual vitality of a congregation is clearly indicated by the extent to which all of the congregation joins together in the singing of spirited and moving songs. The feeling and intensity of expression with which a group of Christians sing their praises and thanksgivings to God is an accurate measure of the spiritual temperature of that church.

Our freest expression in song is attained when not only our hearts and souls are in tune with God but when a conscious effort does not have to be expended during the song upon the correctness of tune or upon the meaning of certain words or phrases. When an African Christian is worshipping God in song, he should be able to sing words which have the most meaning to *him* and which stir *his* heart. A mere translation of the beautiful hymn "When I Survey the Wondrous Cross" fails to evoke the same response within the African Christian as it does within a Western Christian. The English rhythm is foreign and the words, which have a tremendous impact upon the Western Christian, lose their power in the translation process.

If a more independent attitude were adopted toward the

development of indigenous hymnody among the Tonga churches, it would involve more Christians in creative worship. I can see four advantages to having a greater freedom of expression:
1. The thought forms and words would be Tonga, hence more meaningful.
2. Participation would not be limited to those who could read the words from the hymnal. Illiterates could quickly learn the Tonga tunes by rote.
3. Tonga hymns with indigenous words and tunes would provide a possible substitute for the obscene dances and beer parties which occuply such an important position in pagan village life.
4. The worship services as a whole would become less Western and more congenial to African Christianity.

APPOINTING ELDERS AND DEACONS

The second element which is essential to the establishment of a strong, independent Church capable of propagating itself, is *good leadership*.

This will require not only a significant force of itinerating evangelists who are well-trained students of the Bible, but also a substantial number of older men who are biblically qualified to be elders. They must be sufficiently self-supporting to lend stability to their local churches and take a lead in perfecting the Church.

These elders should be above reproach, married to one woman, temperate, sensible, dignified, hospitable, able to teach; gentle, not drunkards, quarrelsome, or greedy for money. They must be good managers of their households, keeping their children submissive and respectful in every way. They must be well-grounded in the faith and not recent converts, lest they become conceited (I Timothy 3:1-7; Titus 1:5-9). Ideally there should be a plurality of elders in every church to feed and oversee the flock.

At the present time, however, there are unfortunately very few Tonga men who would meet these qualifications. This is mainly due to the fact that we have taught only young people, converted them, and waited for them to develop into "elder material."

It is my contention that if we will now follow the group-conversion method of evangelism, which more often than not will include the power and leadership structures of the village, the men will meet the biblical criteria much more quickly. Secondly, the congregations will not be absolutely leaderless during the interim while the older Christian men are in the process of being given post-baptismal instruction.

In Chapter VI, I mentioned the fact that only one of the Tonga C. of C. churches has a plurality of elders. It is also,

incidentally, the only church which is exercising its
independence to any significant degree. The leadership in most
of the remaining churches falls into one of two other
categories: (1) uncertain and weak indigenous leadership which
is not very conscious of its own authority and assumes little
responsibility; or (2) missionary-led and dominated churches.
Churches with these two kinds of leadership will have very
little quantitative, qualitative, or organic growth.

Leaders (particularly elders and deacons) must be found
among the adults and trained at the level of their capability.
No longer should we focus our whole attention upon the bright-
eyed and eager youngster if our goal is to develop leadership
for the Church. We must plan materials and devise methods for
teaching *whomever the church selects from among its members to
receive this leadership training*. We must be in a position to
offer the required instruction to *anyone*, from the illiterate
Christian headman to the progressive Christian teacher with a
secondary education.

If we are to tackle this problem of leadership realistically
and effectively, we must train the men who are selected by each
local congregation, regardless of our first foreign impressions
of such candidates. The fact remains that the local Christians
know who their leaders are. We so often do not.

In Tonga society, decisions and tribal education flow from
the older to the younger. The Gospel follows the same channel.
It is erroneous to believe that the teen-aged students from
mission schools are going to plant churches and preach the
Gospel effectively when they return to their villages. The
Gospel does not flow uphill in Tonga society.

By concentrating upon the conversion of winnable units
instead of isolated individuals, the problems of leadership will
be alleviated to a large extent. Furthermore, the present
reversion rate among mission-school converts will be reduced
considerably. The students, most of whom come from pagan homes,
will have Christian homes to return to which will reinforce
rather than destroy their faith.

Provided the traditional kinship structure with its mutual
responsibilities is not disturbed too radically, there will be
very little need for specially designated deacons in village
churches. Since in Tonga society it is customary for adult
offspring to support their old parents, and for younger parents
to take care of the orphaned children of kinfolk, the close
communal structure does not make allowances for widows, orphans,
or the elderly. In small village churches there would be very
few, if any, duties which deacons would need to perform; hence
the office of deacon in a village situation would be
superfluous.

City congregations are different. Here the kinship interdependency is not present; there is more individualism, more
specialization, and greater needs which would require qualified

ministers (or servants) to do.

HOLDING LOCAL LECTURESHIPS

A third important area which needs a great deal of attention and creativity is that of decentralized religious instruction.

The term "local lectureship" is being used in a general way to refer to decentralized religious training as a whole. From the early efforts of John Nevius, who held "month-long Bible training classes" for pastors of the Presbyterian churches in China in the late nineteenth century to the "extension seminary" concept being used in Latin America in the 1960's, the Churches have attempted to provide an effective leadership training program. (See Dr. Ralph D. Winter's article on extension education, Appendix E.)

As Tonga churches have been planted over an increasingly large area, the problem of leadership training has become more and more acute. We have noticed a number of times in this analysis where churches have either grown or become defunct on the basis of the quality of their leadership, and it has become unmistakably clear that education by "extraction" has had extremely limited success. Today the crying need is for trained and capable leaders in local congregations.

Calvin Guy stresses the essentiality of decentralization and of mobility when he writes:

> Lay training in local institutes demands a high degree of mobility on the part of the training staff. By getting out where the people are, it is possible to train many without separating them from their environment (McGavran 1965:210).

This concept of religious instruction emphasizes that the *missionary* or *national instructor* be the one to do the going. The training is thus *extended to the church leader* who is reaping his crops, operating a store, teaching school, and therefore is unable to come to a central location for his religious education over a long period of time.

By making use of well-planned programmed religious textbooks which the church leaders may use for their own self-directed study, teacher-student contact time is reduced considerably. Using programmed books which are written on his own level, the church leader may progress at his own pace under the direction of a competent teacher who visits his group periodically to check on progress and answer questions.

Local congregations should be encouraged to plan their own lectureships, invite speakers for the occasion, and make arrangements for housing and feeding the guests. If these gatherings could be centrally located, with perhaps five to ten congregations taking part, the problems of transportation and finance would be more easily overcome. The main objectives of this type of meeting should be: (1) to share religious knowledge and experience; (2) to bring in national Christians from distant churches to challenge their fellow Christians; (3) to have fellowship; (4) to conduct special classes of interest for the women, and (5) to learn new indigenous songs.

A lectureship was held at Kabanga Mission on July 9-11, 1968. The whole program was planned by national brethren and they did all the lecturing and preaching. (See Appendix F.) The attendance was good, fellowship was rich, and many of the speeches were outstanding. Some Christians walked twenty-five miles to attend the meetings.

If the number of lecturesehips was increased considerably, Christians from remote areas would also be able to derive the spiritual strength and power which result from such gatherings.

The local lectureship and the extension training program would be supplementary; one would not be a substitute for the other. The former would be specifically designed to be inspirational and the latter mainly instructional, although they would certainly not be mutually exclusive in their respective intent.

In all of the planning and implementation of such lectureships, the missionary should insist on his position as an ordinary member lest he end up drawing up the schedules, inviting the speakers, and furnishing the transportation. His role would be like that of any interested Christian.

KEEPING RECORDS

A fourth area of importance to church growth is that of *keeping records*. It has not been the policy of the Churches of Christ to keep accurate and specific membership figures. Three reasons (there may be others) generally given for such a policy are: (1) we will usurp the autonomy of local congregations if we "require" that they send their records of membership to a central office; (2) we will become too concerned with "mere numbers" and lose quality for the sake of quantity, and (3) God knows His own and man has no right to judge who are God's children and who are not.

There is validity in the numerical approach to church growth. We ought to use the methods of statistical analysis to assist us in deploying missionary personnel to areas of greatest potential growth. We should be vitally concerned with whether or not the Churches of Christ are growing numerically. If one soul is worth more than all of the world it behooves us to be urgently interested in every soul won. This involves *quantitative* as well as qualitative and organic concern.

Good records of church membership should be meticulously kept by the local church leaders for these reasons:

1. Statistical evaluation of the rate of growth of churches in the various segments of Tonga society (e.g., village, urban, cooperative) will indicate areas of greatest receptivity.

2. Such information will have a bearing upon the deployment of missionary personnel and resources. It is poor stewardship and husbandry in God's sight for us to go on planting the seed among the rocks when just a few yards away the soil is fertile and ready to bear fruit.

3. Local church leaders will have an accurate picture of their congregations. Good membership records will enable them to know at a glance how many they are winning to Christ, how many are faithfully attending worship, who is absent or sick, and how many are reverting (Appendix G).

4. By studying the membership rolls with local church leaders the missionary will also get an accurate picture of each congregation and then be in a position to encourage and advise his national brethren. The missionary may learn productive new methods and approaches from one church which he can suggest to other churches.

5. Membership rolls kept in every church will make possible the compilation of accurate and meaningful reports to be sent back to supporting churches and individuals in America. Sending churches need to know what is going on in the mission field so as to be inspired to pray and support an effort that they can visualize. By receiving a comparative growth report each year the home churches can learn much more about actual progress on the field. Good reports will cut through promotional fog and give substance and expectation to their prayers.

Individual congregations should be encouraged to keep membership figures, but in no way coerced. The advantages of such a system should be suggested to the leaders, but they must be allowed to make the decision. This will preserve their congregational autonomy.

It has sometimes been argued that church growth statistical analyses are unscriptural on the basis that David was punished for counting the people of Israel (I Chronicles 21). Notice, however, the motivation for David's action. The Bible says that "Satan stood up against Israel and incited David to number Israel" (vs. 1). The devil tempted David to trust in his own strength and the might of his army (vs. 5). The numbering in this case was a sin because it was self-glorification. David was wrong because he failed to recognize that the strength of Israel lay in God, not in the number of fighting men.

Self-glorification, however, is not the motive for

establishing a system of keeping church records. The welfare of the flock of our Lord is at stake. The seriousness of the commission requires careful numbering. Elders in the local churches are under-shepherds of the flock under the headship of the Chief Shepherd. The good shepherd of Luke 15 had an *exact count* of his one hundred sheep, and only after making an accurate tally did he realize that one precious lamb was missing. The woman who lost one of ten coins knew *exactly* how many she had and that one had to be found.

Tippett has discussed shrinkage in church membership due to removal or wandering. He says that

> Its discovery and correction depends on correct counting and recording. Church statistics ask questions and demand answers. They demonstrate facts that require urgent notice. The Good Shepherd knows his sheep, even by name (John 10:3) (1968a:19).

Finally, by stressing good church record-keeping we will add the important elements of permanence and organization which so conspicuously absent in most Tonga churches at the present time.

BINDING CHURCHES TOGETHER

Individual Christians can sometimes become provincial and introverted until they somehow discover that the Church is much larger than just their own small congregation. The fifth suggestion is that we need some means of informing and binding churches together.

Probably the best way to rid Christians of their narrow view of the Church and widen their vision would be to start a vernacular church newspaper. It would necessarily be written in simple Tonga, so as to reach as wide an audience as possible. Such news items as accounts of conversions, the erection of church buildings, local lectureships, announcements, and other matters of interest would be included, with pictures whenever possible.

The newspaper might also contain a sermon outline or Bible story contributed by national evangelists and missionaries. The editorship and publication should be in national hands from the beginning. The cost of such an operation could be taken care of from the voluntary contributions of churches or individuals.

Other means of binding churches together could be developed as money and interest increased. Recorded programs could be submitted to government radio stations for broadcasting to Tonga areas. Local lectureships, which have already been mentioned, are an excellent way to bind churches together which are within walking distance. Slides and motion pictures of interesting events like church meetings, baptisms, and celebrations could be shown to churches in other areas of Tongaland. All of these means would be specifically designed to impress upon each church member that he is a member of God's family, a family which extends far beyond his own personal experience.

Only five of the more practical solutions to the problems of limited church growth in Tongaland have been mentioned. None of these are to be considered ends in themselves. Rather, it is hoped that they will stimulate us to search for and find many other ways to bring about more rapid ingathering.

14

Conclusion

THE TONGA TRIBE

In the absence of any clearcut tribal boundaries, I have somewhat arbitrarily confined this study of church growth to the Tonga-speaking Leya, Toka, We and Tonga peoples. Statistics and other information from Ila and Lenje areas (also Tonga-speaking) did not relate directly to the missionary efforts of the Churches of Christ, which have been the main concern throughout this thesis.
Frequent reference to the Tonga-speaking people as a tribe is in no way intended to perpetuate tribalism in the face of Zambian nationalism. Instead, the tribal culture has provided a rather constant and consistent whole within which church growth could be accurately measured. The Tonga tribal culture is in a period of transition and more of its people are capturing the wider vision of nationalism and seeking the economic benefits of Western contacts.

ACCULTURATION

This largest and oldest of Zambia's seventy-two tribes is undergoing the stresses and strains of a society in cultural change. Materialism is on the increase, the young are deserting village life for the wider economic and educational opportunities of the cities; villages are scattering, marriage patterns are less traditional, and tribal folk are becoming more interested in national politics.
During this period of uncertainty and insecurity, the Church

has an unprecedented opportunity to present the claims of
Christ and to assist many in finding meaning and peace in Him.
To those who sense the loss of cohesion in tribal society, the
news of the oneness of the people of God in Christ is welcome.
To the uprooted and dislocated, a fellowship of the saints
should be readily available both to proclaim and to demonstrate
to them the Gospel of Christ. This necessitates both urban and
rural church planting on a much larger scale than heretofore.

MISSIONARY STRATEGY: PAST AND PRESENT

Neither past nor present mission policy assigns top priority
to evangelism and church planting. The Church has been mission-
station centered and school oriented throughout most of the past
fifty years. Thousands of *individuals* have been baptized in
our schools, for which God should be praised and thanked, but a
vast percentage of these precious sheep have reverted to the
world. I am advocating the *planting of churches* instead of the
baptism of individuals who are never incorporated into a body
of believers. Involved in this approach is the winning of
adults, parents, and older people in their kinship groups,
families, and households. These units will form the nuclei of
churches in their respective village communities.

It is a grave mistake to continue investing such an overwhelming percentage of our missionary resources in schools
where a few individuals are baptized who revert under pressure
from their pagan parents or village associates. The money
which we invest in these unfruitful institutions is God's and
we will be held responsible for our poor stewardship.

The Church must come before the school. The right kind of
school will come only after enough churches have been planted
to support it. The mission of the Church is to reconcile men
to God in Christ, not to provide secular education. As
Christians we are to proclaim God's redemptive act and persuade
men and women to become responsible members of His Church.
This is God's mission; will we participate with Him in it?

NEW ATTITUDES

Admittedly, it is a generalization to suggest that every
missionary and every national Christian needs to develop a
whole set of new attitudes. Nevertheless, I have listed some
areas in which appropriate action should be taken to make us
more effective communicators of the Word and ministers of Jesus
Christ.

Our attitudes determine to a large extent our level of
identification, language mastery, empathy, prayer life,
fraternal relationships, observation of customs and beliefs,

Conclusion

and most important, the ways in which we present the message of Jesus Christ.

FUTURE CHURCH GROWTH IN TONGALAND

At best this has been only a brief survey of what God has done through some of His servants among the Tonga. The writer hopes, however, that there will be profit from the lessons of the past that were dealt with in this book, and that as we seek to apply new methods, based on sounder principles, more rapid church growth in Tongaland will result.

May those of us who sincerely seek to plant growing and independent churches among the Tonga join together in:

1. Objectively evaluating our methods for effectiveness in church planting at least once every year.

2. Turning our faces from static mission stations to the outside world where the conflict for the souls of men is most intense.

3. Breaking away from patterns of mission work which fail to plant churches, *no matter what the cost.*

4. Dedicating our lives to the planting of churches and bringing those being saved to the fullness of Christ.

5. Developing a sensitivity to areas of greatest growth potential for the Gospel and be willing to move into those areas as quickly as possible.

6. Learning the language well enough to share Christ meaningfully among responsive people *while they are receptive.*

7. Praying for *winnable units* instead of *isolated individuals.*

8. Allowing local churches to be truly independent in their expressions of worship and communication of the faith.

Throughout this book I have advocated change. For the Church to grow it will have to change its missionary methodology and policy in order to face and take advantage of the radical changes which are taking place among the peoples of Africa. Missions and missionaries must wake up. We no longer operate among a subservient colonial people. These are our people to love, to serve, to win to Christ, and to lead to a deeper experience with their God.

In keeping with the changes which have been suggested herein, I would like to conclude with the words of David M.

Paton:

> When a disaster has occurred, nothing is really wise, or even kind, save ruthless examination of the causes. If you have cancer, it is not in the long run a kindness on the part of your physician to fob you off with kind words and soda bicarbonate, when early recourse to the surgeon may save your life . . . the diagnosis that you have cancer does not preclude the possession also of excellent lungs and superb feet, nor does it mean that your constitution has always been weak and sickly and good for nothing, and that there is no hope for you. Criticism of missions then, is not denial of much faithful work now or in the past, nor of a great measure of success (1953:34).

We recognize that it is very easy to speak of reforms in terms of the first person plural as if *we*, the missionaries, were the sole actors in all these matters. To some extent this is inevitable in the pioneering stages of any Mission, but as soon as possible, the local church itself must be the actor, showing the initiative and taking the responsibility for church planting, for evangelistic progress, for adequate followup, and for dealing with the opportunities and problems of its own environment. *It needs to see itself as the Body of Christ in the local situation.* Only thus can the Church be truly indigenous.

Appendices

Appendix

- A Foreign and National Christians *170*
- B Churches and Missions Among the Tonga -1968 *172*
- C Protestant Christianity Among the Tonga *174*
- D Communicant Membership -1968 *175*
- E The Guatemalan Presbyterian Seminary *176*
- F Kabanga Lectureship *180*
- G Membership Roll Chart *181*

Appendix A

FOREIGN AND NATIONAL CHRISTIANS

The names of many church leaders who have contributed to the growth of the Church of Christ among the Tonga are listed below. They have been men and women of dedication, faith and sacrifice. In the case of missionaries, their tenures have been mentioned after each of their names.

A. Pre-World War II Missionaries:
    W. N. Short (1923-1930);(1945-1960)
    *Ray Lawyer   (1924-1927)
    J. D. Merritt   (1926-1968)
    *George M. Scott   (1927-1942)
    W. L. Brown   (1929-1936)
    A. B. Reese   (1929-1956)
    Alvin Hobby (1938-1961);(1969-   )
    Myrtle Rowe   (1938-1957)
    O. D. Brittell   (1938-1965)
    J. C. Shewmaker   (1939-1967)

B. Post-World War II Missionaries:
    R. B. Reese   (1941-1948)
    Eldred Echols   (1944-1951)
    J. A. Brittell   (1946-1966)
    L. Bailey   (1946-   )
    H. F. Short   (1947-1948)
    J. C. Reed   (1947-1948)
    K. E. Elder   (1949-   )
    H. E. Pierce   (1950-1951)
    Lester Brittell   (1953-1966)
    J. A. Bell (1953-1957);(1962-1964)
    Jesse Brown   (1955-1961)
    Jack Chrissop   (1955-1965)
    P. E. Rabick   (1960-1964)
    L. K. Pomeroy   (1961-1963)
    Stan Shewmaker   (1960-1965)
    Keith Besson   (1965-   )
    Dennis Mitchell   (1966-   )
    George Triplett   (1966-   )
    John Kledzik   (1966-   )
    James Pinegar   (1966-1968)
    S. D. Shewmaker   (1967-   )
    Roy Merritt   (1968-   )

*Deceased

Appendices

C. National Church Leaders:
   *Peter Masiya
   *Bulawayo Kukana
    Kambole Mpatamatenga
    Mafuta Simbeza
    Mooka
   *Jack Muzilwa
   *Mungambata
   *Matakala
   *Mubila
   *Siandubu
    Jim Muzumara
    Kabasikolo Sianjina
    Botiasi Kalulu
    King Mambeli
    Jakobo Sibbili
    Stephen Sinkwaya
    Phinlay Sibbili
    Samson Sekeleti
    Alfred Sebesi
    Geoffrey Kakoshi
    Maxwell Shukumbwe
    Leonard Malindi
    D. S. Mulamfu

*Deceased

Appendix B

CHURCHES AND MISSIONS AMONG THE TONGA - 1968

Church or Mission	Began Work	No. of Mission Stations	No of Local Cong.	Total No. of Communi-cants	Average Size of Churches	No. of Ministers For.	No. of Ministers Nat.	Composition of Churches	Main Emphases	Problems
Anglican (UCMA)	1911	1	26	1609	61.9	4	12	Largely children	Schools; hospitals.	Polygyny; migration; equation of "church" and "school."
Brethren in Christ (BC)	1906	3	48	1100	22.9	40	48	Largely children	Schools; hospitals; distribution of literature.	Foreign control; materialism; schools have priority over evangelism.
Church of Christ (CC)	1910	3	37	1200	32.4	9	47	Women and children	Schools; orphanage; some evangelism.	Mission-station centeredness; polygyny, drunkenness.
Pilgrim Holiness Church (PHC)	1934	4	55	2793	50.8	35	40	Young people	Schools; hospitals; evangelism.	Drunkenness; Economic pressure on national ministers.

Church	Year									
Seventh-Day Adventist (SDA)	1905	1	49[a]	5736	117.0	14	75	Mostly women	Schools until 1955; hospitals; evangelism since 1955.	Materialism; polygyny.
United Church of Zambia (UCZ)	1901	2	22	540[b]	24.5	4	39	Women and girls in rural churches.	Schools until 1965; recovering lost sheep since 1966.	Materialism; people not interested.
Salvation Army (SA)	--[c]	2	--	--	--	--	--	--	Secondary schools; hospitals.	--
New Apostolic Church	--[d]	-	--	--	--	--	--	--	Totally evangelistic.	--
TOTALS		16	237	1,2978	51.5 (average)	106	261			

[a] does not include "churchlets."
[b] includes figures for Choma D.C.C. only.
[c] statistics unavailable.
[d] statistics unavailable; informants uncooperative.

Appendix C

PROTESTANT CHRISTIANITY AMONG THE TONGA

Total Tonga Tribe
272,000

Total Community (est.)
54,000

Total Communicants* (est.)
17978

*Includes: Anglican, Brethren in Christ, Church of Christ, Pilgrim Holiness Church, Seventh-Day Adventist Church, United Church of Zambia, Salvation Army, New Apostolic Church

Appendix D

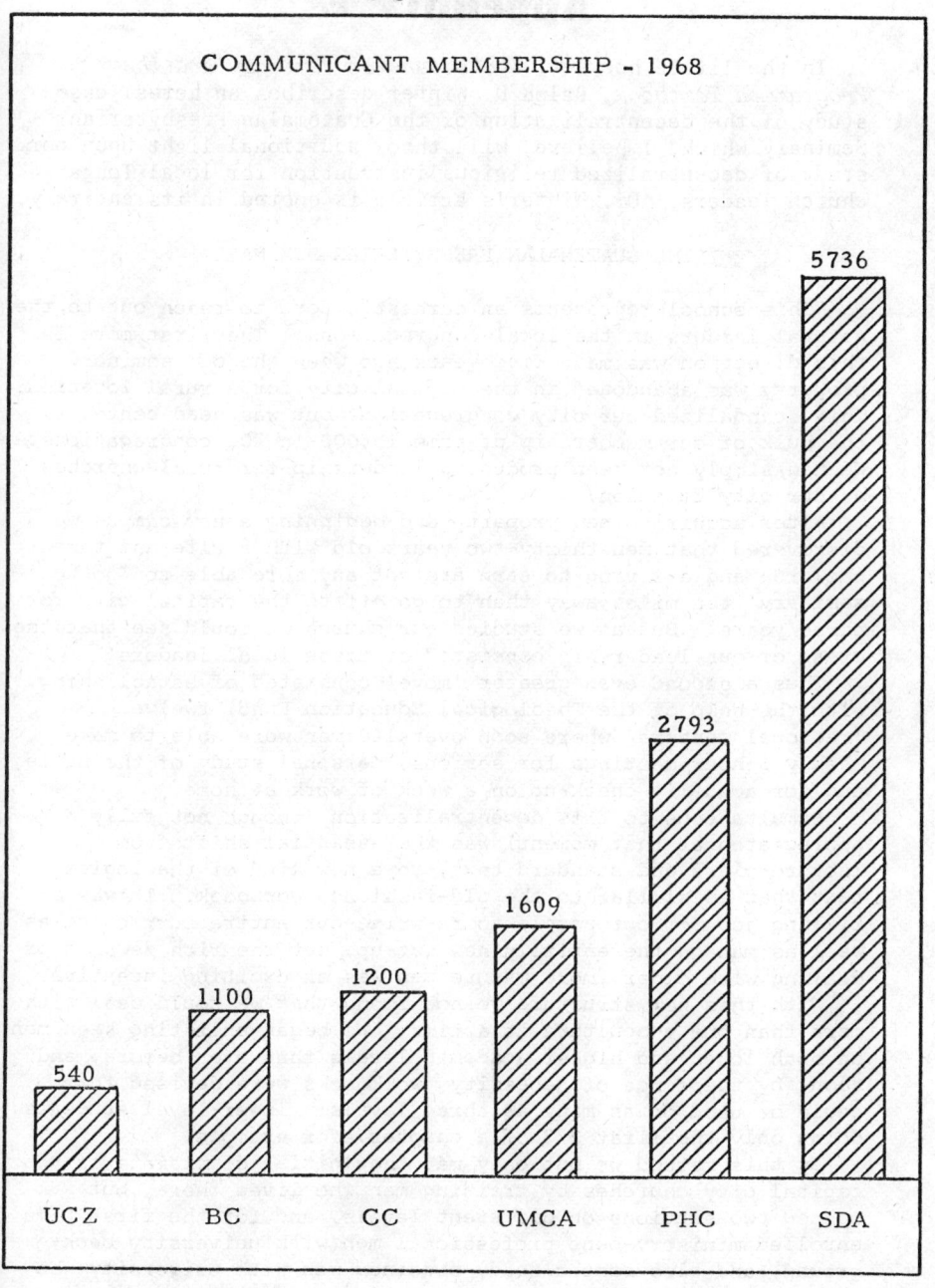

Appendix E

In the little booklet, *The Extension Seminary and the Programmed Textbook*, Ralph D. Winter describes an actual case study of the decentralization of the Guatemalan Presbyterian Seminary which, I believe, will throw additional light upon our study of decentralized religious instruction for local Tonga church leaders. Dr. Winter's article is quoted in its entirety.

THE GUATEMALAN PRESBYTERIAN SEMINARY

"This school represents an earnest effort to reach out to the natural leaders in the local congregations. The first move in this direction was made five years ago when the old seminary property was abandoned in the capital city for a rural location. This scandalized our city congregations but was dead center to the bulk of our membership of some 15,000 in 200 congregations. We had simply not been producing leadership for rural churches by our city location.

After acquiring new property and beginning a new campus we discovered that men thirty-two years old with a wife and three children and a living to earn are not any more able to 'go to seminary' ten miles away than to go off to the capital city for three years. But as we studied our church we could see that the cream of our leadership consisted of these local leaders!

Thus a second even greater 'move' consisted of establishing, with the help of the Theological Education Fund, twelve 'regional centers' where soon over 140 men were able to make weekly 3-hour meetings for serious, personal study of the Bible, and for academic check-up on a week of work at home.

Simultaneous to this decentralization (though not fully appreciated at that moment) was the essential shift from lecture-class and standard text, to a new kind of theological text that is similar to the old-fashioned workbook. It was a killing job for our people to re-write our entire curriculum as well as manage the entirely new set-up, but the rich rewards of dealing with older, more mature men was an exciting incentive.

With this new structure we now found that we could deal with more than one subculture at a time. We began enlisting keen men on both lower and higher academic levels than ever before, and soon, by the force of necessity, workbooks were devised that could be used on as many as three levels: lower-level students doing only the first 2/3 of a chapter, for example.

By this method we not only met the initial complaints of the capital city churches by training men who lived there, but opened two sections on different levels, and for the first time enrolled ministry-bent professional men with university background, and also some already-ordained men with university who wanted to continue on a higher level.

Appendices

"In addition to the weekly meetings on a decentralized basis, monthly 2-day "study-retreats" were set up. These allowed for 1) certain kinds of teaching not as easily managed in a smaller group, such as choral work, 2) courses like English and medicine requiring special teachers, 3) round table discussions on current topics that would augment course work, 4) examinations, and 5) general cross-cultural contact, sports, etc.

The chart . . . [on the following page] shows the relation between secular studies (vertical columns) and theological studies (horizontal bars), and it relates these levels to the five major subcultures making up our national church in Guatemala. The seminary offers a three-year course to a person on any of four academic levels. The resulting degree (names are those recognized by the ALET association) is in every case considered adequate for ordination by one or another of the regional "Presbyteries" of the church, which more or less correspond to the subcultures indicated.

Suppose a student has a sixth-grade diploma. He can take the "Diploma in Theology" series of courses. Later if he gets three years of secondary school somehow (say in night school), he does not now have to start over to get his "Bachiller A" degree, but can take a series of supplementary ("X") courses which will enable him to get a higher theological degree that corresponds to his higher secular training.

There are two levels that are dotted in because they are logically necessary but are not now offered by our seminary. These might be called "Doctorate" and "Certificate" although the ALET has not yet defined them. The higher level may eventually be offered in connection with the Evangelical University of Guatemala, but since this kind of a degree is almost by-definition an international education suitable more to a scholar than a pastor, it is probably desirable in the near future that such men take this kind of training in a U.S. or European school.

The lower level that could be called "certificate" is not now employed in Guatemala because an immense effort has been devoted in recent years to enable adults to get a 6th grade diploma. This has been an effort by a combination of churches, schools, and missions to write the necessary texts, and to organize the necessary extension network, and to gain government approval for a vast adult education program that now has over 1,000 students all over Guatemala in many churches. Prior to the development of this program our rural Presbyteries did train and ordain men who did not have six grades of school.

However, we feel that where it is not feasible to get proper government-backed elementary school credentials for adult leaders (and you ought not to give up easily on this--ALFALIT may come to our rescue at this point in Latin America), the effective *equivalent* of this training can and must be given, lest any "theological education" based on less than a general

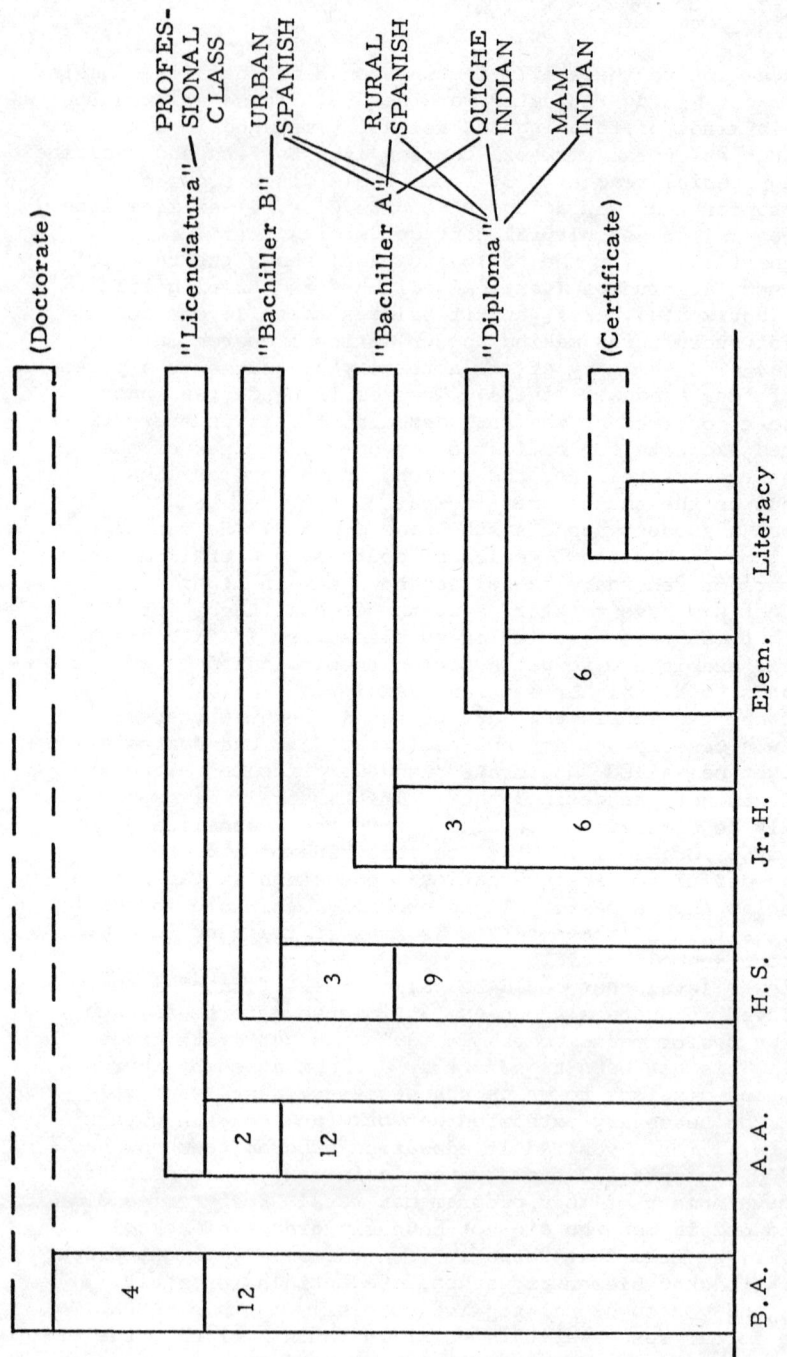

knowledge and a really solid familiarity with the printed page turn out to be a very great expense in teaching time and an inadequate result after all.

"The Christian leader simply cannot be trained into existence, as the Council of Trent supposed could be done by starting with twelve-year-old boys. The gifts qualifying a man to be a pastor show up as he grows in his marriage, in his relation to his children, in his concrete "secular" service in society, and in his role in the local church. No one can predict the result. The safest thing is apparently to bend the seminary to fit this situation rather than vice versa.

But in any case the Christian leader ought to be accredited in both civil and ecclesiastical worlds. We encourage our men to go as far in secular studies as they are able and desirous (in terms of the group they serve) and offer courses on that level that are what the church requires for ordination. Some schools "displace" secular training, and then are not even related properly to any church body that recognizes their theological training. One advantage in a single institution being multilevel is that there is no problem in later upgrading of a man's training. This way the seminary is able to stay with a mobile church in a rapidly changing society over the years.

When Dr. Ross Kinsler starts out on Wednesday for the capital, he stops at the 60 mile, half-way point and climbs down under the bridge over the Cocales River. There he meets three stalwart leaders from the coastal jungle area. Three hours later he heads on to the capital where he meets the professional section in the evening. The seminary is mobile socially as well as geographically."*

---

*Reprinted by permission of the Associacion Latino-americano de Escuelas Teologicas.

Appendix F

National brethren planned and directed a short lectureship at Kabanga Mission on July 9-11, 1968. The following is a schedule of that meeting:

KABANGA LECTURESHIP

Date	Time	Speaker	Subject	Song Leader
7- 9-68	8:30a.m.	Ngwira	"The Christian and His Attitude Toward Sin"	Muzumara
	10:30a.m.	Sibbili	"The Christian and Temptation"	Naini
	2:00p.m.	Ziba	"The Straight and Narrow Road"	Sinkwaya
	3:30p.m.		Classes as scheduled	
	7:30p.m.	Sichuundu	"Strife, Cursing and Swearing"	Sibbili
7-10-68	8:30a.m.	Kalulu	"What is Wrong with Drinking and Smoking?"	Muzumara
	10:30a.m.	Kachota	"Adultery and Uncleanness"	Naini
	2:00p.m.	Sekeleti	"Stealing and Lying"	Sinkwaya
	3:30p.m.		Classes as scheduled	
	7:30p.m.	Museta	"Envyings, Hatred, and Gossip"	Sibbili
7-11-68	8:30a.m.	King	"Funeral Meat, Blood, and Things Strangled"	Muzumara
	10:30a.m.	Banda	"Satan, Man's Adversary"	Naini
	2:00p.m.	Munkombwe	"Christ, Man's Savior"	Sinkwaya
	3:30p.m.		Panel discussion	
	7:30p.m.		Singing groups from different churches.	

NOTE: A series of lessons was taught throughout the lectureship by Kabasikolo Sianjina on "Mizimu-Kupiila-Kusonda," lessons having to do with the very relevant subject of spirits, ritual sacrifices, and divination.

Appendix G
Membership Roll

CHURCH _____ YEAR _____

NAME OF MEMBER	MAN, WOMAN, BOY OR GIRL				DATE BAPTIZED	BAPTIZED BY	CONVERTED FROM PAGANISM OR OTHER	LOST BY: EXCOMMUN. / REVERSION / TRANSFER / DEATH				DATE
	M	W	B	G								
TOTALS......												

Bibliography

Bibliography

ACHEBE, Chinua
    1967   *Things Fall Apart*. London, Heinemann Educational Books.

ALLEN, Roland
    n.d.   *Education in the Native Church*. London, World Dominion Press.

    1963   *The Spontaneous Expansion of the Church*. Grand Rapids, Wm. B. Eerdmans Publishing Company.

    1964a *Missionary Methods: St. Paul's or Ours?* Grand Rapids, Wm. B. Eerdmans Publishing Company.

    1964b *Missionary Principles*. London, World Dominion Press.

ALLEN, W., et al
    1948   "Land Holding and Land Usage Among the Plateau Tonga of Mazabuka District. A Reconnaissance Survey, 1945," *Rhodes-Livingstone Paper No. 14*.

ANDERSON, Gerald H., ed.
    1965   *The Theology of the Christian Mission*. New York, McGraw-Hill Book Company.

ANSTEY, Roger T.
    1963   "Christianity and Bantu Philosophy," *International Review of Missions*, Vol. 52.

APTHORPE, R. J., ed.
    1958   *Present Interrelations in Central African Rural and Urban Life*. Lusaka, Rhodes-Livingstone Institute.

APTHORPE, R. J.
    1961   *Social Research and Community Development*. Lusaka, Rhodes-Livingstone Institute.

    1966   *From Tribal Rule to Modern Government*. Lusaka, Rhodes-Livingstone Institute.

ARENSBERG, Conrad, and NIEHOFF, Arthur H.
    1964   *Introducing Social Change: A Manual for Americans Overseas*. Chicago, Aldine Publishing Company.

AYANDELE, E. A.
    1967   "Reviews, Christianity in Nigeria," *The Journal of African History*, Vol. VIII, No. 2.

BARBER, William J.
  1967 "Urbanization and Economic Growth: The Cases of Two White Settler Territories" in Horace Miner (ed.).

BARNETT, H. G.
  1953 *Innovation: The Basis of Cultural Change*. New York, McGraw-Hill Book Company.

BARRETT, David
  1968 *Schism and Renewal in Africa*. Nairobi, Kenya, Oxford University Press.

BASCOM, William R. and HERSKOVITS, Melville J., eds.
  1959 *Continuity and Change in African Cultures*. Chicago, University of Chicago Press.

BAVINCK, J. H.
  1964 *An Introduction to the Science of Missions*. Philadelphia, The Presbyterian and Reformed Publishing Company.

BEETHAM, T. A.
  1967 *Christianity and the New Africa*. London, Pall Mall Press.

BETTISON, David G.
  1962 "Numerical Data on African Dwellers in Lusaka, Northern Rhodesia," *Rhodes-Livingstone Communication*, No. 16.

BILLING, M. G.
  1959 "Tribal Rule and Modern Politics in Northern Rhodesia," *African Affairs*, Vol. 58.

BOER, Harry R.
  1964 *Pentecost and Missions*. Grand Rapids, Wm. B. Eerdmans Publishing Company.

BOOTH, Newell S.
  1945 *The Cross over Africa*. New York, Friendship Press.

BOUNDS, E. M.
  n.d. *Power Through Prayer*. Chicago, Moody Press.

BRELSFORD, W. V.
  1960 *Handbook to the Federation of Rhodesia and Nyasaland*. London, Cassell and Company.

  1965 *The Tribes of Zambia*. Lusaka, The Government Printer.

Bibliography

BREWER, Charles R., ed.
1966 *A Missionary Pictorial*. Nashville, Tennessee, World Vision Publishing Company.

BROWN, Ina Corinne
1963 *Understanding Other Cultures*. Englewood Cliffs, Prentice-Hall.

BRYAN, G. McLeod
1961 *Whither Africa?* Richmond, Virginia, John Knox Press.

BRYANT, A.T.
1965 *Bantu Origins: The People and Their Language*. Cape Town, C. Struik, Africana Specialist and Publisher.

BUSIA, D. A.
1959 "Ancestor Worship," *Practical Anthropology*, Vol. 6.

CAROTHERS, J. C.
1954 *The African Mind in Health and Disease*. Geneva, World Health Organization.

CLEMENTS, F.
1959 *Kariba: The Struggle with the River God*. London, Methuen.

CLEMMER, Myrtle and RYCROFT, W. Stanley
1962 *A Factual Study of Sub-Saharan Africa*. New York, Commission on Ecumenical Mission and Relations, The United Presbyterian Church in the U.S.A.

COLLINS, B.
1967 *Small English-Tonga Dictionary*. Lusaka, Jesuit Fathers in conjunction with Zambia Publications Bureau.

COLSON, Elizabeth
1949 "Life Among the Cattle-Owning Plateau Tonga," *The Occasional Papers of the Rhodes-Livingstone Museum*, No. 6.

1959 *Seven Tribes of British Central Africa*. Manchester, Manchester University Press.

1960a "Ancestral Spirits Among the Plateau Tonga," in Simon and Phoebe Ottenberg, (eds.).

1960b *Social Organization of the Gwembe Tonga*. Manchester, Manchester University Press.

COLSON, Elizabeth
   1962   *The Plateau Tonga of Northern Rhodesia*. Manchester, Manchester University Press.

   1965   "Ancestral Spirits and Social Structure Among the Plateau Tonga," in William A. Lessa and Evon Z. Vogt, (eds.).

   1967   *Marriage and the Family Among the Plateau Tonga of Northern Rhodesia*. Manchester, Manchester University Press.

COOK, Harold R.
   1966   *An Introduction to the Study of Christian Missions*. Chicago, Moody Press.

CUNNISON, Ian
   1959   *The Luapula Peoples of Northern Rhodesia*. Manchester, Manchester University Press.

DODGE, Ralph E.
   1964   *The Unpopular Missionary*. Westwood, New Jersey, Fleming H. Revell Company.

DOUGALL, J. W. C.
   1939   "The Case for and against Mission Schools," *Journal of the Royal African Society*, Vol. XXXVIII.

DUBB, A. A., ed.
   1962   *The Multitribal Society*. Lusaka, Rhodes-Livingstone Institute.

EKWENSI, Cyprian
   1965   *People of the City*. London, Heinemann Educational Books.

ELKINS, Phil
   1965   *Toward a More Effective Mission Work*. Dallas, Texas, Christian Publishing Company.

ENGLE, Anna R., CLIMENHAGA, John A., and BUCKWALTER, Leoda A.
   1950   *There Is No Difference*. Nappance, Indiana, E. V. Publishing House.

FIFE, Eric S. and GLASSER, Arthur F.
   1963   *Missions in Crisis*. London, Inter-Varsity Fellowship.

FITZGERALD, Walter
   1961   *Africa: A Social, Economic and Political Geography of Its Major Regions*. London, Methuen.

Bibliography

FORTUNE, G.
1959 "The Bantu Languages of the Federation: A Preliminary Survey," *Rhodes-Livingstone Communication*, No. 14.

FOSBROOKE, H. A., ed.
1960 "Plateau Tonga Entrepreneurs in Historical Inter-Regional Trade," *Rhodes-Livingstone Journal*, No. 26.

FOUNTAIN, O.
1966 "Religion and Economy in Mission Station-Village Relationships," *Practical Anthropology*, Vol. 13.

FRANCK, Thomas M.
1960 *Race and Nationalism: The Struggle for Power in Rhodesia and Nyasaland*. New York, Fordham University Press.

FRERICKS, A. C.
1957 *Anutu Conquers in New Guinea*. Columbus, Ohio, The Wartburg Press.

GANN, L. H.
1958 *The Birth of a Plural Society*. Manchester, Manchester University Press.

GELFAND, M.
1964a *Witch Doctor*. London, Harvill Press.

1965b *Medicine and Custom in Africa*. London, E. & S. Livingstone Ltd.

GIFFORD, Daniel L.
1897a "Polygamous Applicants-I, What Missionaries Think Should Be Done With Them," in *Missionary Review of the World*, Vol. X (New Series), February.

1897b "Polygamous Applicants-II, What Missionaries Think Should Be Done With Them," in *Missionary Review of the World*, Vol. X (New Series), March.

GLUCKMAN, Max, ed.
1963 *Order and Rebellion in Tribal Africa*. London, Cohen and West.

GOODENOUGH, Ward Hunt
1966 *Cooperation in Change*. New York, John Wiley and Sons.

GOODY, Jack
1962 *Death, Property and the Ancestors*. London, Tavistock Publications.

GRASSI, Joseph A.
   1965   *A World to Win.* New York, Maryknoll Publications.

GRAY, Richard
   1960   *The Two Nations.* London, Oxford University Press.

GRIMLEY, John B. and ROBINSON, Gordon E.
   1966   *Church Growth in Central and Southern Nigeria.* Grand Rapids, Wm. B. Eerdmans Publishing Company.

HAILEY, Lord
   1957   *An African Survey.* (Revised 1956), London, Oxford University Press.

HALL, Richard
   1965   *Zambia.* London, Pall Mall Press.

HARRELL, Pat E.
   1967   *Divorce and Remarriage in the Early Church.* Austin, Texas, R. B. Sweet Company.

HARRIS, W. T. and PARRINDER, E. G.
   1960   *The Christian Approach to the Animist.* London, Edinburgh House Press.

HASELBARTH, Hans
   1967   "The Place of the Ancestors in a Christian Theology for Africa," *Ministry,* Vol. 7, No. 4.

HOBBY, Alvin
   1945   "Miscellaneous Notes for Course of Lessons on African Missions." An unpublished manuscript.

   1946   *African Missions of the Church of Christ in Northern Rhodesia.* Searcy, Arkansas, Harding College Press.

HODGES, Melvin L.
   1953   *On the Mission Field: The Indigenous Church.* Chicago, Moody Press.

HOGG, W. Richey
   1963   "Pages from an African Journal," *The Hartford Quarterly,* Vol. III, No. 3.

HOPGOOD, Cecil R.
   1950   "Conceptions of God Amongst the Tonga of Northern Rhodesia," in Edwin W. Smith (ed.).

JAHN, Janheinz
1961   *Muntu: The New African Culture.* New York, Grove Press.

JASPAN, M. A.
1953   *The Ila-Tonga Peoples of North-Western Rhodesia.* London, International African Institute.

JENSEN, Gurli Vibe
1964   "Training During the First Furlough," *International Review of Missions,* Vol. 53.

KAUNDA, Kenneth
1966   *A Humanist in Africa.* London, Longmans.

1968   "Zambia Towards Economic Independence." Address (printed) before the National Council of the United National Independence Party, Mulungushi, Zambia.

KAY, George
1967   *A Social Geography of Zambia.* London, University of London Press.

KEIGHLEY, D. Alan
1960   *Review in Central Africa.* London, British Council of Churches.

KIMBLE, George H. T.
1961   *Tropical Africa,* Vols. I & II. New York, The Century Fund.

KRAEMER, Hendrik
1963   *The Christian Message in a Non-Christian World.* Grand Rapids, Kregel Publications.

KUPER, Hilda
1947   *The Uniform of Colour.* Johannesburg, Witwatersrand University Press.

LANTERNARI, Vittorio
1965   *The Religions of the Oppressed.* New York, The New American Library of World Literature.

LATOURETTE, K. S.
1953   *A History of Christianity.* New York, Harper and Row.

LESSA, William A. and VOGT, Evon Z., eds.
1965   *Reader in Comparative Religion.* (Second Edition), New York, Harper and Row.

LEWIS, Jack P.
    1966   "Shall I Speak Falsely for God." Lecture (printed) delivered at Summer Missions Seminar, Harding College, Searcy, Arkansas.

LINDSELL, Harold
    1955   *Missionary Principles and Practice.* Westwood, New Jersey, Fleming H. Revell Company.

LIVINGSTONE, David
    1857   *Missionary Travels and Researches in South Africa.* London, John Murray.

LIVINGSTONE, David and Charles
    1866   *Narrative of an Expedition to the Zambesi.* New York, Harper and Brothers.

LLOYD, P. C.
    1967   *Africa in Social Change.* Baltimore, Penguin Books.

LOEWEN, Jacob A.
    1965   "Self-Exposure: Bridge to Fellowship," *Practical Anthropology,* Vol. 12.

LUZBETAK, Louis J.
    1963   *The Church and Cultures.* Techny, Illinois, Divine Word Publications.

LYALL, Leslie T.
    1966   "Missionary Strategy in the Twentieth Century," *Evangelical Missions Quarterly,* Vol. 2, No. 2.

MACLAREN, P. I. R.
    1958   *The Fishing Devices of Central and South Africa.* London, Rhodes-Livingstone Museum.

MALINOWSKI, Bronislaw
    1949   *The Dynamics of Culture Change.* New Haven, Yale University Press.

    1954   *Magic, Science and Religion.* Garden City, N. Y., Doubleday and Company.

McCOLLOGH, M.
    1956   *A Social Survey of the African Population of Livingstone.* Manchester, Manchester University Press.

McGAVRAN, Donald
    1955   *The Bridges of God.* New York, Friendship Press.

Bibliography

McGAVRAN, Donald
   1963a   *Church Growth in Mexico.* Grand Rapids, Wm. B. Eerdmans Publishing Company.

   1963b   *How Churches Grow.* London, World Dominion Press.

   1967   "The Church Growth Point of View and Christian Mission," in *The Journal of the Christian Brethren Research Fellowship*, No. 13.

McGAVRAN, Donald, ed.
   1965   *Church Growth and Christian Mission.* New York, Harper and Row.

MINER, Horace, ed.
   1967   *The City in Modern Africa.* New York, Frederick A. Praeger.

MORRIS, Colin
   1963   *Nothing to Defend.* London, Cargate Press.

MORRIS, Colin and KAUNDA, Kenneth
   1960   *Black Government?* Lusaka, United Society for Christian Literature.

NCHENA, G. Henry
   1946   "A Visitor in the Printing Shop," in *Glimpses of Africa*, Vol. 2, No. 3.

NEVIUS, John L.
   1958   *The Planting and Development of Missionary Churches.* Philadelphia, The Reformed and Presbyterian Publishing House.

NIDA, Eugene A.
   1954   *Customs and Cultures.* New York, Harper and Row.

   1957   *Learning a Foreign Language.* New York, Friendship Press.

   1960   *Message and Mission.* New York, Harper and Row.

NIDA, Eugene A. and SMALLEY, William A.
   1959   *Introducing Animism.* New York, Friendship Press.

NORTHCOTT, Cecil
   1963   *Christianity in Africa.* Naperville, Illinois, SCM Book Club.

OLIVER, Roland
    1952   *The Missionary Factor in East Africa.* London, Longmans, Green and Company.

ORR, J. Edwin
    1965   *The Light of the Nations.* Grand Rapids, Wm. B. Eerdmans Publishing Company.

OTTENBERG, Simon and Phoebe, eds.
    1960   *Cultures and Societies of Africa.* New York, Random House.

PARRINDER, E. G.
    1953   *Religion in an African City.* London, Oxford University Press.

    1954   *African Traditional Religion.* London, Hutchinson House.

    1958   *The Bible and Polygamy.* London, SPCK.

    1961   *Worship in the World's Religions.* London, Faber and Faber.

    1963   *Witchcraft: European and African.* New York, Barnes and Noble Inc.

PATON, David M.
    1953   *Christian Missions and the Judgment of God.* London, SCM Press Limited.

PHILLIPS, Arthur, ed.
    1953   *Survey of African Marriage and Family Life.* London, Oxford University Press.

PICKETT, J. Waskom
    1960   *Christ's Way to India's Heart.* Lucknow, India, Lucknow Publishing House.

    1963   *The Dynamics of Church Growth.* Nashville, Abingdon Press.

PICKETT, J. W., WARNHUIS, A. L., SINGH, G. H., and McGAVRAN, D.
    1962   *Church Growth and Group Conversion.* Lucknow, India, Lucknow Publishing House.

POWDERMAKER, Hortense
    1962   *Cooper Town: Changing Africa.* New York, Harper and Row.

RADCLIFFE-BROWN, A. R. and FORDE, Daryll, eds.
1967   *African Systems of Kinship and Marriage.* London, Oxford University Press.

RADIN, Paul
1957   *Primitive Religion: Its Nature and Origin.* New York, Dover Publications.

RANDALL, Max Ward
1968   "New Proposals for Zambia Mission." An unpublished M.A. thesis, Fuller Theological Seminary, Pasadena, California.

READ, William R.
1965   *New Patterns of Church Growth in Brazil.* Grand Rapids, Wm. B. Eerdmans Publishing Company.

REESE, A. B.
1946   "Approach to the African," in *Glimpses of Africa,* Vol. 2, No. 5.

REYNOLDS, B.
1963a   *Magic, Divination and Witchcraft Among the Barotze of Northern Rhodesia.* London, Chatto and Windus.

1963b   *The African: His Place in a Changing Society.* Livingstone, Rhodes-Livingstone Museum.

RICHARDSON, Alan, ed.
1966   *A Theological Word Book of the Bible.* New York, The Macmillan Company.

ROSS, Emory and Myrta
1959   *Africa Disturbed.* New York, Friendship Press.

ROSSMAN, Vern
1963   "The Breaking In of the Future," *The International Review of Missions,* Vol. 52.

ROTBERG, Robert I.
1965a   *Christian Missionaries and the Creation of Northern Rhodesia. 1880-1924.* Princeton, New Jersey, Princeton.

1965b   *The Rise of Nationalism in Central Africa.* Cambridge, Mass., Harvard University Press.

ROWE, Myrtle
1967   *Silhouettes of Life.* Nashville, World Vision Publishing Company.

SCUDDER, T.
    1962   *The Ecology of the Gwembe Tonga.* Manchester, Manchester University Press.

SHEARER, Roy E.
    1966   *Wildfire: Church Growth in Korea.* Grand Rapids, Wm. B. Eerdmans Publishing Company.

SHEPPERSON, George and PRICE, Thomas
    1958   *Independent African.* Edinburgh, The University Press.

SHERLOCK, J.
    1963   *The Zambesi: A Bibliography.* Cape Town, University of Stellenbosch Library.

SMALLEY, William A.
    1960   "Making and Keeping Anthropological Field Notes," *Practical Anthropology,* Vol. 7.

SMALLEY, William A., ed.
    1967   *Readings in Missionary Anthropology.* Tarrytown, New York, Practical Anthropology.

SMITH, Edwin W.
    1923   *The Religion of Lower Races.* New York, Macmillan Company.

    1928a *The Way of the White Fields in Rhodesia.* London, World Dominion Press.

    1928b *The Golden Stool.* New York, Doubleday, Doran and Company.

    1936   *African Beliefs and Christian Faith.* London, United Society for Christian Literature.

    1946   *Knowing the African.* London, United Society for Christian Literature.

SMITH, Edwin W., ed.
    1950   *African Ideas of God.* London, Edinburgh House Press.

SMITH, Edwin W. and DALE, A. M.
    1920   *The Ila-Speaking Peoples of Northern Rhodesia.* London, Macmillan and Company.

SMITH, Gordon Hedderly
    1947   *The Missionary and Primitive Man.* Chicago, Van Kampen Press.

SMOKER, Dorothy Waterhouse
1961   *The Problem of Teaching the Law of Sorcery in Exodus to African Christians with an Animistic Background.* An unpublished master's thesis, Pasadena, California, Fuller Theological Seminary.

SOLTAU, T. Stanley
1965   *Facing the Field.* Grand Rapids, Baker Book House.

SOUTHALL, Aidan, ed.
1961   *Social Change in Modern Africa.* London, Oxford University Press.

SUNDKLER, Bengt
1960   "Bantu Messiah and White Christ," *Practical Anthropology,* Vol. 7.

1962   *The Christian Ministry in Africa.* London, SCM Press.

TAYLOR, John V.
1963   *The Primal Vision.* Philadelphia, Fortress Press.

TAYLOR, John V. and LEHMANN, Dorothea A.
1961   *Christians of the Copperbelt.* London, SCM Press.

TEMPELS, Placide
1959   *Bantu Philosophy.* Paris, Presence Africaine.

The Extension Seminary and the Programmed Textbook. The report of a workshop held in Armenia, Colombia, South America on the 4-9th September, 1967. Contributors of articles in the booklet are: Ralph D. Winter, Ross Kinsler, Louise Jeter Walker, and C. Peter Wagner.

TIPPETT, Alan R.
1966   "Church Growth or Else!" in *World Vision Magazine,* February 1966.

1967   "Religious, Group Conversion in non-Western Society," *Research-in-Progress Pamphlet Series,* No. 11.

1968a *Solomon Islands Christianity.* London, Lutterworth Press.

1968b "Church Growth and the Word of God." A manuscript awaiting publication from the library of Dr. Alan R. Tippett, Fuller Theological Seminary, Pasadena, California.

TROBISCH, Walter
   1967   "Omodo: My Wife Made Me a Polygamist," *Here is My Problem*. Booklet No. 1.

TROWELL, H. C.
   1956   *The Passing of Polygamy*. London, Oxford University Press.

TURNER, H. W.
   1967   "A Typology for African Religious Movements," *Journal of Religion in Africa*, Vol. 1.

TYLOR, Edward B.
   1965   "Animism" in William A. Lessa and Evon Z. Vogt (eds.).

VICEDOM, George F.
   1965   *The Mission of God*. St. Louis, Concordia Publishing House.

WARNECK, Joh.
   n.d.   *The Living Christ and Dying Heathenism*. London, Fleming H. Revell Company.

WELBOURN, F. B.
   1965   *East African Christian*. London, Oxford University Press.

WESTERMANN, Diedrich
   1949   *The African To-Day and To-Morrow*. London, Oxford University Press.

WESTLUND, Lester P.
   1968   "Avoiding the Dangers of Mission Institutions," *Evangelical Missions Quarterly*, (Summer) 227-236.

WHITE, C. M. N.
   1960   *An Outline of Luvale Social and Political Organization*. Manchester, Manchester University Press.

WILKINSON, F. O. Green
   1963   "Christianity in Central Africa," *Journal of the Royal African Society*, Vol. 62.

WILLIAMS, Stuart
   1962   "The Distribution of the African Population of Northern Rhodesia," *Rhodes-Livingstone Communication*, No. 24.

WILLOUGHBY, W. C.
  1928 *The Soul of the Bantu*. New York, Doubleday, Doran
        and Company.

WOLD, Joseph Conrad
  1968 *God's Impatience in Liberia*. Grand Rapids, Wm. B.
        Eerdmans Publishing Company.

ABOUT THE WILLIAM CAREY LIBRARY

William Carey is widely considered the "Father of Modern Missions" partly because many people think he was the first Protestant missionary. Even though there was a trickle of others before him, he deserves very special honor for many valiant accomplishments in his heroic career, but most particularly because of three things he did before he ever left England, things no one else in history before him had combined together:

    1) he had an authentic, personal, evangelical passion to serve God and acknowledged this as obligating him to fulfill God's interests in the redemption of all men on the face of the earth.

    2) he actually proposed a structure for the accomplishment of that aim - he did indeed, more than anyone else, set off the movement among Protestants for the creation of "voluntary societies" for foreign missions, and

    3) he added to all of this a strategic literary and research achievement: shaky those statistics may have been, but he put together the very best possible estimate of the number of unreached peoples in every part of the globe, and summarized previous, relatively ineffective attempts to reach them. His burning conclusion was that existing efforts were not proportional to the opportunities and the scope of Christian obligation in Mission.

Today, a little over 150 years later, the situation is not wholly different. In the past five years, for example, experienced missionaries from all corners of the earth (53 countries) have brought to the Fuller School of World Mission and Institute of Church Growth well over 800 years of missionary experience. Twenty-six scholarly books have resulted from the research of faculty and students. The best statistics available have at times been shaky -though far superior to Carey's - but vision has been clear and the mandate is as urgent as ever. The printing press is still the right arm of Christians active in the Christian world mission.

The William Carey Library is a new publishing house dedicated to books related to this mission. There are many publishers, both secular and religious, that occasionally publish books of this kind. We believe there is no other devoted exclusively to the production and distribution of books for career missionaries and their home churches.

William Carey Library
PUBLICATIONS

Africa

PEOPLES OF SOUTHWEST ETHIOPIA, by A. R. Tippett, Ph.D.
A recent, penetrating evaluation by a professional anthropologist of the cultural complexities faced by Peace Corps workers and missionaries in a rapidly changing intersection of African states.
1970: 320 pp, $3.95. ISBN 0-87808-103-8

PROFILE FOR VICTORY: NEW PROPOSALS FOR MISSIONS IN ZAMBIA, by Max Ward Randall.
"In a remarkably objective manner the author has analyzed contemporary political, social educational and religious trends, which demand a reexamination of traditional missionary methods and the creation of daring new strategies...his conclusions constitute a challenge for the future of Christian missions, not only in Zambia, but around the world."
1970: 224 pp, Cloth, $3.95. ISBN 0-87808-403-7

THE CHURCH OF THE UNITED BRETHREN OF CHRIST IN SIERRA LEONE, by Emmett D. Cox, Executive Secretary, United Brethren in Christ Board of Missions.
A readable account of the relevant historical, demographic and anthropological data as they relate to the development of the United Brethren in Christ Church in the Mende and Creole communities. Includes a reformation of objectives.
1970: 184 pp, $2.95. ISBN 0-87808-301-4

APPROACHING THE NUER OF AFRICA THROUGH THE OLD TESTAMENT, by Ernest A. McFall.
The author examines in detail the similarities between the Nuer and the Hebrews of the Old Testament and suggests a novel Christian approach that does not make initial use of the New Testament.
1970: 104 pp, 8 1/2 x 11, $1.95.
ISBN 0-87808-310-3

Asia

TAIWAN: MAINLINE VERSUS INDEPENDENT CHURCH GROWTH, A STUDY IN CONTRASTS, by Allen J. Swanson.

A provocative comparison between the older, historical Protestant churches in Taiwan and the new indigenous Chinese churches; suggests staggering implications for missions everywhere that intend to promote the development of truly indigenous expressions of Christianity.

1970: 216 pp, $2.95. ISBN 0-87808-404-5

NEW PATTERNS FOR DISCIPLING HINDUS: THE NEXT STEP IN ANDHRA PRADESH, INDIA, by B.V. Subbamma.

Proposes the development of a Christian movement that is as well adapted culturally to the Hindu tradition as the present movement is to the Harijan tradition. Nothing could be more crucial for the future of 400 million Hindus in India today.

1970: 212 pp, $3.45. ISBN 0-87808-306-5

GOD'S MIRACLES: INDONESIAN CHURCH GROWTH, by Ebbie C. Smith, Th.D.

The fascinating details of the penetration of Christianity into the Indonesian archipelago make for intensely interesting reading, as the anthropological context and the growth of the Christian movement are highlighted.

1970: 224 pp, $3.45. ISBN 0-87808-302-2

NOTES ON CHRISTIAN OUTREACH IN A PHILIPPINE COMMUNITY, by Marvin K. Mayers, Ph.D.

The fresh observations of an anthropologist coming from the outside provide a valuable, however preliminary, check list of social and historical factors in the context of missionary endeavors in a Tagalog province.

1970: 71 pp, 8 1/2 x 11, $1.45. ISBN 0-87808-104-6

Latin America

THE PROTESTANT MOVEMENT IN BOLIVIA, by C. Peter Wagner.

An excitingly-told account of the gradual build-up and present vitality of Protestantism. A cogent analysis of the various subcultures and the organizations working most effectively, including a striking evaluation of Bolivia's momentous Evangelism-in-Depth year and the possibilities of Evangelism-in-Depth for other parts of the world.

1970: 264 pp, $3.95. ISBN 0-87808-402-9

LA SERPIENTE Y LA PALOMA, by Manuel Gaxiola.
The impressive success story of the Apostolic Church of Mexico, (an indigenous denomination that never had the help of any foreign missionary), told by a professional scholar now the director of research for that church. (Spanish)
1970: 200 pp, $2.95. ISBN 0-87808-802-4

THE EMERGENCE OF A MEXICAN CHURCH: THE ASSOCIATE REFORMED PRESBYTERIAN CHURCH OF MEXICO, by James Erskine Mitchell.
Tells the ninety-year story of the Associate Reformed Presbyterian Mission in Mexico, the trials and hardships as well as the bright side of the work. Eminently practical and helpful regarding the changing relationship of mission and church in the next decade.
1970: 184 pp, $2.95. ISBN 0-87808-303-0

FRIENDS IN CENTRAL AMERICA, by Paul C. Enyart.
This book describes the results of faithful and effective labors of the California Friends Yearly Meeting, giving an analysis of the growth of one of the most virile, national evangelical churches in Central America, comparing its growth to other evangelical churches in Guatemala, Honduras, and El Salvador.
1970: 224 pp, $3.45. ISBN 0-87808-405-3

Europe

THE CHALLENGE FOR EVANGELICAL MISSIONS TO EUROPE: A SCANDINAVIAN CASE STUDY, by Hilkka Malaska.
Graphically presents the state of Christianity in Scandinavia with an evaluation of the pros and cons and possible contributions that existing or additional Evangelical missions can make in Europe today.
1970: 192 pp, $2.95. ISBN 0-87808-308-1

THE PROTESTANT MOVEMENT IN ITALY: ITS PROGRESS, PROBLEMS, AND PROSPECTS, by Roger Hedlund.
A carefully wrought summary of preliminary data; perceptively develops issues faced by Evangelical Protestants in all Roman Catholic areas of Europe. Excellent graphs.
1970: 266 pp, $3.95. ISBN 0-87808-307-3

U.S.A.

THE YOUNG LIFE CAMPAIGN AND THE CHURCH, by Warren Simandle.

If 70 per cent of young people drop out of the church between the ages of 12 and 20, is there room for a nationwide Christian organization working on high school campuses? After a quarter of a century, what is the record of Young Life and how has its work with teens affected the church? *"A careful analysis based on a statistical survey; full of insight and challenging proposals for both Young Life and the church."*

1970: 216 pp, $3.45. ISBN 0-87808-304-9

THE RELIGIOUS DIMENSION IN SPANISH LOS ANGELES: A PROTESTANT CASE STUDY, by Clifton L. Holland.

A through analysis of the origin, development and present extent of this vital, often unnoticed element in Southern California.

1970: 304 pp, $3.95. ISBN 0-87808-309-X

General

THEOLOGICAL EDUCATION BY EXTENSION, edited by Ralph D. Winter, Ph.D.

A husky handbook on a new approach to the education of pastoral leadership for the church. Gives both theory and practice and the exciting historical development in Latin America of the *"Largest non-governmental voluntary educational development project in the world today."* Ted Ward, Prof. of Education, Michigan State University.

1969: 648 pp, Library Buckram $7.95, Kivar $4.95. ISBN 0-87808-101-1

THE CHURCH GROWTH BULLETIN, VOL. I-V, edited by Donald A. McGavran, Ph.D.

The first five years of issues of a now-famous bulletin which probes past foibles and present opportunities facing the 100,000 Protestant and Catholic missionaries in the world today. No periodical edited for this audience has a larger readership.

1969: 408 pp, Library Buckram $6.95, Kivar $4.45. ISBN 0-87808-701-X

CHURCH GROWTH THROUGH EVANGELISM-IN-DEPTH, by Malcolm R. Bradshaw.

"*Examines the history of Evangelism-in-Depth and other total mobilization approaches to evangelism. Also presents concisely the 'Church Growth' approach to mission and proposes a wedding between the two...a great blessing to the church at work in the world.*" WORLD VISION MAGAZINE.

1969: 152 pp, $2.45. ISBN 0-87808-401-0

THE TWENTY FIVE UNBELIEVABLE YEARS, 1945-1969, by Ralph D. Winter, Ph.D.

A terse, exciting analysis of the most significant transition in human history in this millenium and its impact upon the Christian movement. "*Packed with insight and otherwise unobtainable statistical data...a brilliant piece of work.*" C. Peter Wagner.

1970: 120 pp, $1.95. ISBN 0-87808-102-X

EL SEMINARIO DE EXTENSION: UN MANUAL, by James H. Emery, F. Ross Kinsler, Louise J. Walker, Ralph D. Winter.

Gives the reasons for the extension approach to the training of ministers, as well as the concrete, practical details of establishing and operating such a program. A Spanish translation of the third section of *THEOLOGICAL EDUCATION BY EXTENSION*.

1969: 256 pp, $3.45. ISBN 0-87808-801-6

ABOUT THE AUTHOR: Stan Shewmaker was five years old when he first went to Central Africa in 1939. His parents were faith missionaries with Churches of Christ who had planned and saved for sixteen years before they could actually fulfill their dream of proclaiming the Gospel in Zambia (formerly Northern Rhodesia). During his first seven years in Africa, he became more fluent in Tonga than he was in his own mother language. He thus views the Tonga life-way almost as an "insider"--a factor which enhances his present book.

Shewmaker, who holds the B.A. (Harding College) and M.A. (Fuller School of World Mission) degrees, is a member of a five-family missionary team which is planting churches among the Toka (Tonga) people of Zambia.